SURVIVORS OF NAZI PERSECUTI(
AFTER THE SECOND WORI

Survivors of Nazi Persecution in Europe after the Second World War

Landscapes after Battle Volume 1

Edited by
DAVID CESARANI, SUZANNE BARDGETT,
JESSICA REINISCH AND
JOHANNES-DIETER STEINERT

VALLENTINE MITCHELL
LONDON • CHICAGO, IL

First published in cloth in 2010 by Vallentine Mitchell
Paper edition in 2021

Catalyst House
720 Centennial Court, Centennial Park
Elstree, WD6 3SY, UK

814 N. Franklin Street
Chicago, Illinois
60610, USA

www.vmbooks.com

British Library Cataloguing in Publication Data

Survivors of Nazi persecution in Europe after the Second World War. -- (Landscapes after battle ; v. 1)
1. Holocaust survivors. 2. Holocaust survivors--Rehabilitation. 3. World War, 1939-1945--Refugees.
4. World War, 1939-1945--Forced repatriation. 5. Jewish refugees--Europe--Social conditions--20th century.
I. Series II. Cesarani, David.
940.5'31814-dc22

ISBN 978 0 85303 902 0 (cloth)
ISBN 978 1 912676 62 0 (paper)

Library of Congress Cataloging in Publication Data
an entry can be found on request

Contents

Illustrations

Contributors

Suzanne Bardgett is head of holocaust and genocide history at the Imperial War Museum in London. She led the teams that created the *Holocaust Exhibition* (2000) and *Crimes against Humanity*, an exploration of genocide and ethnic violence (2002) at the IWM, and was subsequently consultant project director on the Srebrenica Memorial Room in Bosnia Hercegovina (2007). She co-edited with David Cesarani *Belsen 1945: New Historical Perspectives* (London: Vallentine Mitchell, 2006) and has published articles in newspapers, magazines and journals – the most recent on the collecting of Holocaust-related artefacts.

David Cesarani is research professor in history at Royal Holloway, University of London. His research interests include the Holocaust and modern Jewish history. His most recent book is *Major Farran's Hat: Murder, Scandal, and Britain's War against Jewish Terrorism, 1945–1948* (London: Heinemann, 2009).

Kurt Düwell is emeritus professor of contemporary and regional history at Heinrich-Heine-University, Düsseldorf. His research fields are nineteenth- and twentieth-century history, including the Weimar Republic, National Socialism, and contemporary German and European history. He is the editor of *Geschichte im Westen* (1994–2004), and co-editor of *Archiv für Kulturgeschichte*. His publications include: *Vertreibung jüdischer Künstler und Wissenschaftler aus Düsseldorf 1933–1945* (Düsseldorf: Droste, 1998); *Anfänge und Auswirkungen der Montanunion auf Europa* (Essen: Klartext, 2007); *Heimat Nordrhein-Westfalen. Identitäten und Regionalität im Wandel* (Essen: Klartext, 2010).

Michael Fleming lectures in politics and history at the Academy of Humanities and Economics in Łódz, Poland. He has previously taught human geography at Jesus College and Pembroke College, Oxford University and has been a visiting researcher at the Pułtusk

School of Humanities and at the Institute of History, Polish Academy of Sciences, in Warsaw. His research focuses on post-Second World War Polish history and politics. His latest book is *Communism, Nationalism and Ethnicity in Poland, 1944–1950* (London: Routledge, 2010).

Aleksandra Loewenau is a PhD candidate in history of medicine at the Centre for Health, Medicine and Society at Oxford Brookes University. She holds the Arts and Humanities Research Council doctoral scholarship attached to a research project, 'Victims of Human Experiments under National Socialism', lead by Professor Paul Weindling. In the past two years she was a holder of AHRC/Library of Congress American Scheme, Grand-in-Aid from the Immigration History Research Center at the University of Minnesota, and the International Fellowship from Middle Tennessee State University. Her research interests are the history of medicine, the Holocaust, the Second World War and medical crimes.

Jessica Reinisch is a Lecturer in Contemporary History at Birkbeck College, University of London. Previously she has held a Leverhulme Early Career Fellowship and a research fellowship on the Balzan Project on Post-War Reconstruction. Her research interests lie in European and international social, political and intellectual history, and she has published on Europe's post-war reconstruction, population movements and migration, and internationalism and international organizations. Her monograph, *Public Health in Germany under Allied Occupation*, will be published by Rochester University Press.

Silvia Salvatici teaches modern history at the University of Teramo, Italy. She has been associate research fellow at the Italian Academy of Columbia University and visiting fellow at the European University Institute; she is honorary research fellow at the School of History, Classics and Archaeology of Birkbeck College, London. Among her most recent publications are: *Senza casa e senza paese: Profughi europei nel secondo dopoguerra*, (Bologna: Il Mulino, 2008) and 'From Displaced Persons to Labourers: Allied Employment Policies towards DPs in Post-war West Germany', in J. Reinisch and E. White (eds), *The Disentanglement of Populations: Migration, Expulsion and Displacement in Post-War Europe, 1944–1949* (London: Palgrave, 2010).

Stefan Schröder is head of the city archives of Greven, Germany. He has a PhD from Münster University, 2000; his thesis on Displaced Persons in the Münster was published in 2005. His research interests are Displaced Persons in the British Zone of Germany and the regional history of Westphalia. His recent major publications are: 'Nachbarschaft und Konflikt: Die DPs und die Deutschen', in Christian and Marianne Pletzing (eds), *Displaced Persons, Flüchtlinge aus den baltischen Staaten in Deutschland* (Munich, 2007), pp.63–83, and 'Zwangsarbeiter und Displaced Persons', *Westfälische Forschungen* 58 (2008), pp.471–87.

Svetlana Shklarov teaches at the University of Calgary, Faculty of Medicine, Community Rehabilitation and Disability Studies. She has practised medicine in Russia and Israel, and holds a PhD degree from the University of Calgary. Svetlana is a daughter of Holocaust survivors, born and raised in the Soviet Union. Her research interests are resilience and trauma in later life, mental health and cross-cultural research. Her recent publications are 'Aging Holocaust Survivors – Recent Soviet Émigrés: From Alienation to Inclusion', *Journal on Jewish Aging*, 2 (1), 2008, pp.23–32, and 'Grounding the translation: Intertwining Analysis and Translation in Cross-Language Grounded Theory Research', *The Grounded Theory Review*, 8 (1), 2009, pp.53–74.

Raphaël Spina has studied at the Ecole Normale Supérieure, Paris (2000–2005). Agrégé, then history assistant at ENS Cachan, then faculté d'histoire-géographie, Université Jules-Verne, Amiens. Laboratory: Institutions et Dynamiques Historiques de l'Economie, ENS Cachan. His thesis in progress since 2004 (supervisor: Olivier Wieviorka) is 'La France et les Français devant le Service du Travail Obligatoire' (a study on the compulsory labour scheme in France, including repatriation and questions of memory and remembrance).

Johannes-Dieter Steinert is professor of modern European history and migration studies at the University of Wolverhampton. His research interests focus on German, British and European social and political history, with special emphasis on international migration and minorities, forced migration, forced labour, survivors of Nazi persecution, and international humanitarian assistance. His most recent publications are *Nach Holocaust und Zwangsarbeit: Britische humanitäre Hilfe in Deutschland: Die Helfer, die Befreiten und die Deutschen* (Osnabrück: Secolo, 2007; *Beyond Camps* *and Forced Labour: Current International Research on Survivors of Nazi Persecution: Proceedings of the International Conference, London, 11–13 January 2006*, edited with Inge Weber-Newth (Osnabrück: Secolo, 2008).

Lynne Taylor, PhD, is an associate professor in the Department of History at the University of Waterloo, Canada. She studies state–society relations in the context of war, focusing on the impact of the Second World War on European society. She is currently engaged in a study of the Displaced Persons crisis in Germany after 1945, using 'unaccompanied children' as a window onto the challenges posed by this population for the governments and international agencies responsible for caring for them. Her most recent major publication is *The Polish Orphans of Tengeru* (Toronto: Dundurn Press, 2009).

Anika Walke is a PhD candidate at UC-Santa Cruz and the University of Oldenburg, Germany, and currently a fellow in residence at the US Holocaust Memorial Museum. Her dissertation focuses on personal and cultural commemorations of the Nazi genocide and Jewish resistance in the USSR. Her recent publications include 'Remembering and Recuperation: Memory Work in the Post-Soviet Context', *Zeitgeschichte*, 36, 2 (2009); 'Reconsidering the Past: Interviews with Jewish Survivors of the Nazi Genocide in the Post-Soviet Context'; *Sociology of Memory: Papers from the Spectrum* (Cambridge: Cambridge Scholars Publishing, 2009), and her first book, *Jüdische Partisaninnen: Der verschwiegene Widerstand in der Sowjetunion* (Berlin: Dietz, 2007).

David Weinberg is professor of history and director of the Cohn-Haddow Center for Judaic Studies at Wayne State University, Detroit, MI, USA. He is presently engaged in preparing a book on West European Jewry after the Holocaust, which will be published in the Littman History of Jewish Civilization series. His general research interests focus on modern European Jewish history.

Preface

This collection of original essays brings together the work of established researchers and young scholars in an area that is increasingly recognized as the crucible of post-war Europe. After exhaustive research on the war years, attention is now finally turning to 'aftermath issues' and the crucial, longer-term implications for European politics, society and culture. This new work is characterized by awareness of how national and international policies framed justice and shaped memory. Applying multidisciplinary insights and techniques, the essays in this volume show how the outcomes of judicial decisions were never inevitable; choices and decisions made between 1945 and 1950 had profound consequences for nations, groups and individuals. Yet it took decades for these processes to become apparent. It was only with the end of the Cold War that researchers in the east and the west began to collaborate, explore archives that were once closed and excavate memories that had been silenced. This innovative and often moving body of work, originating in a dozen countries and drawing on the results of several major European-funded research projects, maps the landscape after the Second World War on which a divided Europe was subsequently constructed. Crucially, essays consider experiences from both eastern and western Europe. Together, they represent the best, broadest and newest research in a transnational and international enterprise to recover a submerged past that, while obscure and half-forgotten, shaped the lives of millions of people.

Suzanne Bardgett
David Cesarani
Jessica Reinisch
Johannes-Dieter Steinert

Acknowledgements

The editors would like to thank Stewart Cass at Vallentine Mitchell for his personal interest in this project and Heather Marchant for her editorial assistance.

The chapters in this volume are based on papers that were first presented at the third international multi-disciplinary conference in the series Beyond Camps and Forced Labour held at the Imperial War Museum, London, 7–9 January 2009. The conference could not have taken place without the generosity and encouragement of the German Embassy, London; the Austrian Cultural Forum, London; the Embassy of the Republic of Poland in London; the German Historical Institute, London; Renovabis, Freising; and the Imperial War Museum.

For their continuing commitment to research the editors would also like to thank the History and Governance Research Institute, University of Wolverhampton; Birkbeck, University of London; and the Holocaust Research Centre and History Department, Royal Holloway, University of London.

Suzanne Bardgett
David Cesarani
Jessica Reinisch
Johannes-Dieter Steinert

Introduction

DAVID CESARANI

It is a truism to say that war, especially civil war, shatters society and destroys the frameworks that give individuals a sense of belonging. Yet the extent of this disruption, and its terrible effect on the plane of lived human experience, is often most starkly revealed in the aftermath of conflict. Until then, combatants and civilians alike are so involved in the everyday minutiae of fighting and surviving that other existential questions are put on hold. In any case, the outcome of the struggle may be uncertain. Peace, by a cruel paradox, frequently leaves victors and vanquished facing a bewildering new constellation of problems. Battered, exhausted, longing for recuperation, they are faced with unprecedented and unforeseen challenges.

In the history books that traditionally end with the cessation of hostilities and the declaration of 'peace' this phase has usually been overlooked. Historians have only recently become interested in the aftermath. In part, this has been the result of new trends in the history of war that accentuate the social dimension of conflict, paying attention to the dynamics within military formations as well as the relations between the civil and the military fronts.[1] Such approaches have become ever more necessary with the appreciation that the Second World War was unlike any that preceded it, even in the already blood-soaked first half of the twentieth century. It was a total war. It involved totalitarian regimes that had already collapsed the political and the private, integrating entire populations into a war-fighting machine. Nazi Germany, above all, sought to militarize as well as racialize every aspect of life. Once the war began even liberal and pluralistic societies were forced to regiment society and completely integrate the home front into the war effort. Thus, for the Third Reich, the territories it occupied, its allies and opponents, racial war and total war had a kaleidoscopic effect on pre-existing social formations. By the time the war was over everything had changed. National boundaries, notions of citizenship, social structures, family ties and individual identities – all were in flux. With 'peace' came the war after the war, the subject for this volume of essays.[2]

However, because one half of Europe tended to celebrate 'liberation' uncritically while the other half was locked away behind the Iron Curtain for forty years, it was not easy for historians to question what really happened in the months and years after the guns fell silent. The end of the Cold War eventually freed western historians from inhibitions about exposing the iniquities of the Anglo-American allies, while the opening of archives in the former Soviet bloc made it possible for local historians and outside researchers to fill in the blanks for eastern and central Europe. As always, journalists and popular historians were often the first to see the potential for new and sensational accounts based on the first wave of archive-based research.[3]

The essays collected in this volume represent a small fraction of the work of historians across Europe who are excavating the experiences of everyday life in the wake of war and genocide. The research presented here concentrates on individual experiences and stories or themes of such particularity that they tend to get lost in a wider panorama. However, the fate of one person or a small group can shed light on larger forces at play across the battered landscape. While we know the major decisions from the familiar narratives, we know much less about how they were implemented or experienced at ground level. Indeed, it is only by sifting through the joys and agonies of individuals amongst the myriad, and looking at how grand strategy or high politics had an impact on ordinary men and women, that it is possible to appreciate the ramifications of decisions taken by generals and statesmen.

The military were the first to encounter liberated or conquered civilians, but in their wake came hundreds of relief workers. The policies they put into effect reflected decisions made at the highest level, embodying crucial distinctions between the vanquished and their former victims. Johannes-Dieter Steinert draws on letters, diaries and memories of relief workers following the British Army into north Germany to reveal how Germans, Displaced Persons

(DPs) and Jews were perceived in the first weeks of 'liberation'. Through their words he exposes their ignorance and lack of preparation for the tasks awaiting them. Consequently, many expressed disparaging opinions about the inmates of the concentration camps who appeared ungrateful towards the liberators and even animalistic in their conduct towards each other. These contemporary voices contrast jarringly with the idealized notion we have today of 'liberators' and 'victims'. The DPs soon became a source of irritation to the troops and the relief workers, while the Germans appeared respectable even though they seemed utterly unwilling to take responsibility for what had been done in their name, with their cognizance and often their complicity.

Responsibility for the DPs was quickly handed over from the military to the United Nations Relief and Rehabilitation Administration (UNRRA). But there was nothing simple about their task, either. Field operatives soon discovered that seemingly elementary decisions made at UNRRA HQ about who was qualified for assistance proved anything but straightforward when it came to implementation.[4] Lynne Taylor explains that initially UNRRA believed that once on German territory its agents would only need to distinguish between enemy and non-enemy civilians. However, due to protests against their treatment by the US Army, Jews were soon placed in a category (essentially a nationality) of their own. There was another exception. Following agreements made at the Yalta conference, Soviet citizens were supposed to be repatriated at the earliest opportunity. But who was a Soviet citizen? Many refugees from areas annexed to the USSR in 1939/40 clung to their prior nationality as Poles, Lithuanians, Latvians or Estonians. As a result of shifting borders and the reluctance of many DPs to return to areas now under Soviet control, the list of national and ethnic identities of those who qualified for assistance and not for repatriation grew. By late 1946, UNRRA field officers were using eighty-eight categories of identity; there were eleven types of Ukrainian alone. In their naivety, UNRRA policymakers had not anticipated that the definition of eligibility would also confer legitimacy and a degree of security on certain identities. Relief policy became a prism through which identity, ethnicity, nationality and citizenship were refracted with baffling effect.

At the same time as trying to sort out this mess, UNRRA public relations officers were supplying the press and media with photographs of their clients. Needless to say, they were framed in such a way as to give a benign impression of UNRRA's work rather than hint at the chaos on the ground. Stefan Schröder uses photograph collections to illustrate the way in which the liberators, and the journalists who accompanied them, wanted to see the liberated and to celebrate their own achievements. His exploration of neglected picture archives of military units and relief organizations shows how photographs mediated the experiences of the DPs and asks why it took so long for this resource to be critically appreciated and exploited by historians.[5]

Far away from the cameras of western journalists, in the rural areas of Poland, entire national and ethnic groups were being relocated. Here, too, classification had profound consequences. It is well known that ethnic Germans were systematically driven out of Poland while Jews were the target for sporadic anti-Semitic attacks.[6] Yet the violence in Poland was even more widespread, affecting thousands of Ukrainians and Belorussians. Michael Fleming maintains that this violence was not simply the release of wartime tensions, the continuation of old hatreds, or even a consequence of the drive towards an ethnically homogenous Poland. He argues that the Polish Workers Party (PWP), with Moscow's sanction, deliberately unleashed inter-communal violence in order to draw it closer to a Polish population that otherwise viewed the PWP as a foreign imposition. The party cynically used violence against minorities to win legitimacy as the protector of Polish ethnic interests. Shockingly, the Roman Catholic Church colluded in this policy. Far from evincing antagonism towards each other, the Church and the communists found 'a unifying logic' in the merciless targeting of 'alien' elements.

The construction of national unity was no less cynical, although it was generally less violent, in western Europe. With alacrity the liberated nations fabricated histories of universal resistance to German occupation. These mythical versions required that, on the one hand, collaborators should be subjected to exemplary punishment. On the other, the resistance demanded that its sacrifices should be recognized in law, and that captured fighters returning from the concentration camps should be received home as heroes and given privileges.[7]

In France, the 600,000 men and women who had been sent to Germany under the *Service du Travail Obligatoire* (STO), and even more so the 200,000 who volunteered to work in the Third Reich, aroused intense ambivalence.[8] The returning workers quickly formed a representative body that stressed how they had been sent as a 'sacrifice' to ensure the nation's well-being and played up their suffering in Germany. Raphaël Spina notes that although the Fédération National des Déportés du Travail exaggerated the numbers that had perished in Germany and the reasons why, he points out that they had suffered from the relentless allied bombing campaign and spent the winter of 1944/45 in miserable conditions, cut off from their liberated homeland. At least 35,000 died and some 50,000 returned to France with various illnesses. Yet their efforts to assume the mantle of '*déportés*' ultimately failed. They could make little headway against the far superior claims of the survivors of the concentration camps. Those who had been deported as a consequence of Resistance activity or the misfortune of being Jewish established sole right to the title and the benefits that flowed from it. Despite their uncomfortable experiences the men and women of the STO found themselves marginalized in national narratives of the war, victims of the need for a heroic myth of defiance.

Even survivors of the camps could find themselves marginalized if they ended up in the wrong place at the wrong time. Aleksandra Loewenau draws attention to a small cohort of Polish political prisoners who found their way to England after the war. They were mainly men who had become DPs in Italy and joined the Polish 2nd Corps of the British Army at the war's end. They came to the UK with the Polish Resettlement Corps, which was the vehicle by which the British honoured their obligation to Poles who had fought in British uniforms and refused to return to a communist Poland. Others reached England via schemes that brought DPs from Europe as volunteer workers.[9] Once in the country they faced severe problems finding employment. Many suffered from poor health. They frequently encountered rank prejudice. Yet they were deemed ineligible for reparations and received almost no assistance in recognition of their wartime suffering. The Polish Association of Ex-Political Prisoners of German Prisons and Concentration Camps in Great Britain lobbied the West German government repeatedly but achieved only partial success in 1965. Unlike the STO the Polish camp survivors were unequivocally on the right side of the political line, but fate had cast them up in the wrong place to derive any benefit from their wartime plight.

Ironically, they would probably have fared better if they had stayed in Germany. The West German state moved relatively quickly to recognize the victims of Nazi persecution and offer them compensation, although not without intense political debate and popular controversy over the definition of who was a deserving case.[10] For obvious reasons, German Jews who opted to stay in the country or returned there were the earliest and least contested beneficiaries. In his vignette examining the lives of Stephan Prager and Philipp Rappaport, Kurt Düwell illuminates the fate of German Jews between 1933 and the post-war era. Although Prager and Rappaport both converted to Christianity and served with distinction in the German Army during the First World War, they were both dismissed from their jobs as architects and urban planners and eventually sent to Nazi camps. Following liberation, however, they returned to Germany and carved out successful careers. They were recognized as victims of Nazi persecution and eventually honoured.

Their experiences contrast sharply with the sad story of German women who had been persecuted for committing 'race shame' crimes in the Third Reich. They found little sympathy even after the Nazi regime was a thing of the past. Alois Nussbaumer presents a study of several women from villages in the Salzburg district who were sent to prisons and camps after being denounced and convicted in Nazi courts for having sexual relations with foreign workers. The denunciations and the trials reveal a great deal about the pervasive Nazification and racialization of Austrian society after the Anschluß, as well as the prurience of small town life.[11] The aftermath reveals equally as much about the dismal state of 'liberated' Austria. When these women appealed for compensation they were told that they did not qualify as 'victims in the struggle for a free and democratic Austria'. The humiliation they suffered due to Nazi race laws was perpetuated long after the wár, in the form of social ostracism. Here gender was a decisive factor, cutting across the category of victim.

As in the previous cases we have briefly examined, the definition of victimhood and aid or reparation was highly politicized and sometimes owed little to actual wartime suffering. Time and again, those who suffered very specifically from Nazi persecution found that after the war they were subjected to arbitrary and fickle decisions by the newly-installed authorities. Contrary to the simplistic black-and-white perception that we tend to have today of the Nazis and their victims, in the immediate aftermath of the war victimhood was never a straightforward ascription – either in ethno-national terms or as a juridical category.[12]

Gender and age were as crucial in determining an individual's fate as political allegiances, religion, ethnicity or nationality. Through the miserable experiences of a DP couple from the eastern Ukraine Silvia Salvatici illustrates the iniquities of such classification. They hid their Soviet nationality to avoid repatriation and pretended to be married in the hope of qualifying as DPs and emigrating to the USA. Ultimately their efforts were frustrated by illness and pregnancy. For them, marriage and family turned out to be a trap. Salvatici uses this case history to question the celebratory way in which accounts of DP life usually treat family constitution. She shows that national communities in the camps, the religious authorities and the refugee agencies all pushed couples towards legal – that is to say civil – marriage. But the DPs viewed wedlock in far more pragmatic terms, as a way to gain certain benefits. At other times it became a burden to be shuffled off with barely a second thought for the 'sacred' institution. Contrary to the romantic myth of love matches and eternal devotion, 'unions among DPs were flexible and unstable' and were constantly being adjusted to 'changing trajectories of displacement'.

Marriage was no longer sacred, nor was childhood any longer a matter of purity or innocence. Instead, communities squabbled over the fate of youngsters, notably orphans, with more concern about the future of their respective collectivities than the feelings of individual children. As David Weinberg explains, one of the most pressing issues facing the surviving Jews of France, Belgium and the Netherlands was the recovery of Jewish children, now orphaned, who had been placed with Christian families by parents desperate to save them from deportation. Many had been converted and their adoptive families refused to surrender them. Others had grown genuinely fond of their new families and become estranged from their biological parents, even if they returned alive. It took huge and costly efforts to retrieve these youths for the Jewish community. Meanwhile, youngsters who had endured years in the ghettos and camps presented a different sort of challenge. They had lost schooling and become almost feral in their behaviour. Older youths found it hard to get jobs and drifted into delinquency. Communal leaders feared that, if this situation continued, an entire generation would be lost, and possibly with it the regeneration of Jewish life. To prevent this, they imported from the USA the idea of the Jewish community centre and set about attracting Jewish youth into the fold. Weinberg analyses the success of this and other strategies adopted in order to rehabilitate survivors and contribute to the reintegration of Jewry, as a whole, into the wider society.[13]

While there was at least partial recognition of the persecution of the Jews in France, Belgium and the Netherlands, an almost complete silence descended over their experiences in the Soviet bloc.[14] Anika Walke analyses the reasons for the reluctance to acknowledge that Jews had been the targets of specific German policies and had endured a disproportionate degree of misery. Russian society as a whole had been subjected to dreadful depredations at the hands of the invader, and no one expected to get any relief amidst the general impoverishment and destruction. The authorities were also loathe to allow attention to linger on the Jews because this risked exposing evidence about local collaboration with the invaders. Furthermore, they feared it would spur a Jewish sense of separateness, leading towards sympathy for Zionism. Yet Jews were in a worse situation than other groups. Many survivors of communities in the western USSR had lost their families and lacked any kind of support network. They were destitute. Few who had survived in the forests had managed to preserve the papers essential for dealing with the authorities. They emerged to find a society that was rife with prejudice. Even those who had fought with the partisans were denied recognition as Jews. As a final indignity, they were forced to watch as the sites of ghettos, camps or massacres were reused without any thought for commemorating the tragedies that had unfolded in those places.

For Jewish child survivors in the USSR the silence was more acute.[15] They grew up in an environment that seemed to deny their experiences. Indeed, the heroic narrative of 'The Great Patriotic War' allowed little room for the anguish of ordinary citizens or the commemoration of loss, as against the celebration of victory.[16] However, Svetlana Shklarov uses oral history to tease out the mechanisms by which they nevertheless managed to develop a collective memory and a subculture of commemoration. Family and community became the vehicle for expressing and perpetuating the memory of genocide, compensating in some measure for the apparent indifference of society at large.

What all these essays show is that the Second World War in Europe did not end neatly on 8 May 1945 and that 'liberation' did not release the victims of Nazi persecution or the survivors of genocide from brutality, fear or injustice. Some victims went unrecognized, while certain groups continued to suffer ill-treatment. Perpetrators could turn into victims and more than a few victims quickly became murderers. Violence continued to erupt across the Continent. It took months, in some places years, to restore order and to mete out justice. Frequently it came too late to avoid lynch law or to catch the more elusive amongst the guilty. It took even longer for mechanisms to be set up to deliver reparations, and the results were still uneven. In the meantime, as during the war years, age and gender as well as ethnicity, religion and nationality could be decisive in fixing the destiny of individuals. Behind the rhetoric of 'liberation' and grandiose plans for 'reconstruction' it often seemed as if ordinary men and women were the playthings of fate. For all too many survival came down to nothing more than taking your chances under a new flag, dealing with people in a different uniform, always having to find your way towards an uncertain future.

REFERENCES

Barnouw, Dagmar, *Germany 1945* (Bloomington, IN: Indiana University Press, 1996).

Beevor, Anthony, *Berlin: The Downfall, 1945* (London: Viking, 2002).

Beevor, Anthony, *D-Day* (London: Viking, 2008).

Bogner, Nahum, *At The Mercy of Strangers. The Rescue of Jewish Children with Assumed Identities in Poland* (Jerusalem: Yad Vashem, 2009).

Deak, Istvan, Gross, Jan T. and Judt, Tony (eds), *The Politics of Retribution in Europe: World War II and Its Aftermath* (Princeton, NJ: Princeton University Press, 2000).

Diehl, James M., *The Thanks of the Fatherland: German Veterans After the Second World War* (Chapel Hill, NC: University of North Carolina Press, 1993).

Evans, Richard J., *The Third Reich At War* (London: Allen Lane, 2008).

Gafny, Emunah Nachmany, *Dividing Hearts. The Removal of Jewish Children from Gentile Families in Poland in the Immediate Post Holocaust Years* (Jerusalem: Yad Vashem, 2009).

Gitelman, Zvi (ed.), *Bitter Legacy: Confronting the Holocaust in the USSR* (Bloomington, IN: Indiana University Press, 1997).

Gross, Jan T., *Fear: Anti-Semitism in Poland After Auschwitz* (Princeton, NJ: Princeton University Press, 2006).

Hastings, Max, *Armageddon: The Battle for Germany 1944–45* (London: Macmillan, 2004).

Hitchcock, William I., *Liberation: Europe 1945* (London: Faber & Faber, 2008).

Hughes, Michael, *Shouldering the Burdens of Defeat: West Germany and the Reconstruction of Social Justice* (Chapel Hill, NC: University of North Carolina Press, 1999).

Judt, Tony, *Postwar: A History of Europe Since 1945* (London: Heinemann, 2005).

Lagrou, Pieter, 'Victims of Genocide and National Memory: Belgium, France and the Netherlands 1945–1965', *Past and Present*, 154 (1997), pp.181–222.

Lagrou, Pieter, *The Legacy of Nazi Occupation: Patriotic Memory and National Recovery in Western Europe, 1945–1965* (Cambridge: Cambridge University Press, 2000).

Lebow, Richard Ned, Kansteiner, Wulf and Fogu, Claudio (eds), *The Politics of Memory in Postwar Europe* (Durham, NC: Duke University Press, 2006).

Merridale, Catherine, *Ivan's War: The Red Army 1939–1945* (London: Faber & Faber, 2000). .

Merridale, Catherine, *Night of Stone: Death and Memory in Russia* (London: Granta, 2000).

Naimark, Norman, *Fires of Hatred: Ethnic Cleansing in Twentieth Century Europe* (Cambridge, MA: Harvard University Press, 2001).

Pross, Christian, *Paying for the Past: The Struggle Over Reparations For Surviving Victims Of The Nazi Terror* (Baltimore, MD: Johns Hopkins University Press, 1998).

Reiter, Andrea (ed.), *Children of the Holocaust* (London: Vallentine Mitchell, 2005).

Shephard, Ben, *The Long Road Home. The Aftermath of the Second World War* (London: Bodley Head, 2010).

Stafford, David, *Endgame 1945: Victory, Retribution, Liberation* (London: Little, Brown, 2007).
Sword, K., Davies, N. and Ciechanowski, J., *The Formation of the Polish Community in Great Britain 1939–1950: The M.B. Grabowski Polish Migration Project Report* (London: School of Slavonic and East European Studies, University of London, 1989).
Timm, Annette, 'The Ambivalent Outsider: Prostitution, Promiscuity, and VD Control in Nazi Berlin', in Robert Gellately and Nathan Stoltzfus (eds), *Social Outsiders in Nazi Germany* (Princeton, NJ: Princeton University Press, 2001), pp.192–211.
Vinen, Richard, *The Unfree French: Life Under Occupation* (London: Allen Lane, 2006).
Wyman, Mark, *DP: Europe's Displaced Persons, 1945–1951* (Philadelphia, PA: Associated University Presses, 1989).

NOTES

1. Examples of the new trend are: Ben Shephard, *The Long Road Home. The Aftermath of the Second World War* (London: Bodley Head, 2010); William I. Hitchcock, *Liberation: Europe 1945* (London: Faber & Faber, 2008) and David Stafford, *Endgame 1945: Victory, Retribution, Liberation* (London: Little, Brown, 2007).
2. For the best overview of the war's multifaceted impact on Europe, see Tony Judt, *Postwar: A History of Europe Since 1945* (London: Heinemann, 2005), especially pp.1–237, 803–31.
3. The work of Anthony Beevor conveniently illustrates both trends. His *Berlin: The Downfall, 1945* (London: Viking, 2002) exposed the brutality of the Red Army, while *D-Day* (London: Viking, 2008) did not spare the Americans, the British and the Canadians from criticism for the callous disregard of civilian life. See also Max Hastings, *Armageddon: The Battle for Germany 1944–45* (London: Macmillan, 2004).
4. The standard account of the DPs remains Mark Wyman, *DP: Europe's Displaced Persons, 1945–1951* (Philadelphia, PA: Associated University Presses, 1989).
5. Cf. Dagmar Barnouw, *Germany 1945* (Bloomington, IN: Indiana University Press, 1996), pp.2–22, who looks searchingly at photographs of German civilians.
6. A good overview of post-1945 ethnic cleansing is Norman Naimark, *Fires of Hatred: Ethnic Cleansing in Twentieth Century Europe* (Cambridge, MA: Harvard University Press, 2001), chapter 4; on the fate of Jews in post-war Poland, see Jan T. Gross, *Fear: Anti-Semitism in Poland After Auschwitz* (Princeton, NJ: Princeton University Press, 2006).
7. Istvan Deak, Jan T. Gross and Tony Judt (eds), *The Politics of Retribution in Europe: World War II and Its Aftermath* (Princeton, NJ: Princeton University Press, 2000); Pieter Lagrou, *The Legacy of Nazi Occupation: Patriotic Memory and National Recovery in Western Europe, 1945–1965* (Cambridge: Cambridge University Press, 2000).
8. On the STO, see Richard Vinen, *The Unfree French: Life Under Occupation* (London: Allen Lane, 2006), pp.247–312.
9. See K. Sword, N. Davies and J. Ciechanowski, *The Formation of the Polish Community in Great Britain 1939–1950: The M.B. Grabowski Polish Migration Project Report* (London: School of Slavonic and East European Studies, University of London, 1989).
10. For the complexities of the compensation laws and the controversies that raged around them, see James M. Diehl, *The Thanks of the Fatherland: German Veterans After the Second World War* (Chapel Hill, NC: University of North Carolina Press, 1993); Michael Hughes, *Shouldering the Burdens of Defeat: West Germany and the Reconstruction of Social Justice* (Chapel Hill, NC: University of North Carolina Press, 1999); Christian Pross, *Paying for the Past: The Struggle Over Reparations For Surviving Victims Of The Nazi Terror* (Baltimore, MD: Johns Hopkins University Press, 1998).
11. For an introduction to sexual politics in Nazi Germany in wartime, see Richard J. Evans, *The Third Reich At War* (London: Allen Lane, 2008), pp.541–5. For other victims of the peculiar Nazi blend of racial and sexual prejudice, see Annette Timm, 'The Ambivalent Outsider: Prostitution, Promiscuity, and VD Control in Nazi Berlin', in Robert Gellately and Nathan Stoltzfus (eds), *Social Outsiders in Nazi Germany* (Princeton, NJ: Princeton University Press, 2001), pp.192–211.
12. See Richard Ned Lebow, Wulf Kansteiner and Claudio Fogu (eds), *The Politics of Memory in Postwar Europe* (Durham, NC: Duke University Press, 2006), for the shifting perception of victimhood in several national contexts.

13. For new work on the post-war fate of Jewish children in eastern Europe see Nahum Bogner, *At The Mercy of Strangers. The Rescue of Jewish Children with Assumed Identities in Poland* (Jerusalem: Yad Vashem, 2009) and Emunah Nachmany Gafny, *Dividing Hearts. The Removal of Jewish Children from Gentile Families in Poland in the Immediate Post Holocaust Years Poland* (Jerusalem: Yad Vashem, 2009).
14. Pieter Lagrou, 'Victims of Genocide and National Memory: Belgium, France and the Netherlands 1945–1965', *Past and Present*, 154 (1997), pp.181–222; Zvi Gitelman (ed.), *Bitter Legacy: Confronting the Holocaust in the USSR* (Bloomington, IN: Indiana University Press, 1997).
15. On child survivors in general, see Andrea Reiter (ed.), *Children of the Holocaust* (London: Vallentine Mitchell, 2005).
16. Catherine Merridale, *Night of Stone: Death and Memory in Russia* (London: Granta, 2000); and Catherine Merridale, *Ivan's War: The Red Army 1939–1945* (London: Faber & Faber, 2000), pp.321–35.

PART 1
IDENTIFYING THE SURVIVORS

1

Jewish Survivors, Displaced Persons and Germans in British Eyes

JOHANNES-DIETER STEINERT

From mid-1944, allied troops came across sites and remains of former German concentration, labour and death camps during their military offensives. Among those liberated from the camps were an estimated 100,000 Jews from countries throughout Europe who had survived the German mass murder – and also political prisoners, Gypsies, homosexuals, Jehovah's Witnesses and civilian internees, to name just a few.[1] The (non-German) survivors of these camps made up only a small part of the group known as Displaced Persons (DPs), which consisted of more than ten million United Nations nationals, the majority of them forced labourers. According to allied plans, care for the DPs was to be provided by the United Nations Relief and Rehabilitation Administration (UNRRA), which had been created in November 1943. However, delays in the full establishment of this organization resulted in the military taking over this responsibility, with the assistance of relief teams provided by several British voluntary organizations under the umbrella of the British Red Cross.[2]

In April 1945, there were 455 humanitarian relief workers deployed in north-western Europe; a further 115 were active in Italy, 300 in Greece, and thirty-seven in Yugoslavia.[3] Once hostilities ended, most of the teams already in north-western Europe were transferred to British-controlled Germany. New teams also came directly from Britain to take up postings in Germany. The number of teams increased sharply after the war and continued to rise. Numbers peaked in the summer of 1946, at which stage there were some sixty groups and 600 relief workers.[4] This was in large part due to an expansion of field activity carried out under the banners of 'German welfare' and 'Battle of the winter' in late 1945. While initially British humanitarian assistance focused on UN nationals only, it was now extended to certain groups of Germans, among them children and refugees. British relief teams also became involved in rebuilding German charitable organizations, and they took on a semi-liaison role between these organizations and the military government. By 1946, German welfare work dominated relief efforts, and by 1947, with around thirty-eight teams focusing solely in this area compared to the sixteen teams working with DPs, it had almost completely taken over.[5]

Relief workers were excellent observers. Their official reports and private papers do not only describe how British voluntary organizations operated in Germany, they also contain information about how those organizations perceived those they helped. Other documents give detailed descriptions of post-war Germany and the German population, their attitudes and behaviour.

This chapter will focus on survivors of the Holocaust and the German forced labour system, as well as on the German population as perceived by British relief workers. It will argue that the perception of the survivors of Nazi persecution was influenced by a lack of background knowledge and psychological training, but also by building bridges to the Germans, many of whom perceived themselves as victims of National Socialism and war.

BELSEN: EMERGENCY RELIEF WORK AND THE PERCEPTION OF JEWISH SURVIVORS

The initial period following the liberation of Bergen-Belsen concentration camp on 15 April 1945 was marked by ad hoc measures, improvisation, attempts to get an idea of the situation, and some emergency relief activities. All of this followed two aims: firstly, to provide help for the 60,000 victims as soon as possible, and secondly, to prevent a further spread of typhus.

However, on 17 April 1945 the period of waiting, taking stock and planning was over; on this day some of the prisoners got to see their liberators for the very first time, as the 224th Military Government Detachment rolled in followed by the 11th Field Ambulance, the 32nd Casualty Clearing Station, the 30th Field Hygiene Section and the 7th Mobile Bacteriological Laboratory. Further military units followed in the next days and weeks.[6] They were accompanied by a group of almost a hundred British medical students, who had actually intended to provide assistance in areas ravaged by hunger in the Netherlands. They remained at the camp for a month, before being replaced by a group of 150 Belgian students[7] and a group of six doctors and twelve nurses from Switzerland, who had also initially planned to go to the Netherlands.[8]

There were also six British relief teams involved in the provision of humanitarian assistance: five from the British Red Cross and a team from the Friends Relief Service. They arrived almost a week after the camps had been liberated, and none of them had been especially equipped or trained for work in a former concentration camp. It was much more a case of these teams having already been in operation on the Continent; at least two of them, the Quaker team and a team from the Red Cross, were redirected to Belsen from Antwerp.[9] Each team consisted of twelve male and female members, each one of whom was qualified to undertake a different task, including four trained nurses and some nursing auxiliaries. Among the other members of the team there was, for example, a driver, a cook, a quartermaster, a secretary and general welfare workers.[10] They were given standard equipment to allow a degree of self-sufficiency, including cooking and washing facilities. According to *The Times*, each team consisted of two ambulances, two lorries and a three-ton truck.[11] Their arrival coincided with the first phase of humanitarian aid, in which survivors were given emergency care, a hospital area was established and initial evacuations were begun. Improvisation was still the order of the day; routine was slow to emerge.

The members of the relief teams were allocated their duties by the military. Only very few were actually deployed in areas for which they had been specifically trained, or in which they had gained experience through their prior career. The decisive factor was far more likely to be their gender. Women, for instance, were only allowed to enter the former concentration camp with special permission, and forbidden from working there. They were, more often than not, allocated work in the hospital area, whereas their male colleagues could work in both areas. Apparently, the women were to be spared the most horrific sights.

Sylvia Jones and M.F. Beardwell were among those few British women to be allowed entry into the concentration camp during the first few days. Both were qualified nurses, belonging to the

British Red Cross teams. They were taken inside the camp the day after their arrival, by Colonel Johnston of the 32nd Casualty Clearing Station:

> The smell was terrible – the sickly smell of death mingled with the stench of excreta and burning boots, shoes, and rags of clothing ... The few broken-down arid derelict looking wooden huts were full of people – the dead lying on the living and the living on the dead; corpses were hanging out of the windows – heaps of dead thrown in grotesque masses – skeleton arms intertwined with skeleton legs and great vacant eyes staring up through the morass of sprawling dead. The majority of the living inmates looked more like animals than human beings. They were clad in filthy rags – and were crawling and grovelling in the earth for bits of food. They took no notice of us or anyone – they vomited and stooled where they stood or sat – lavatories just did not exist – large square holes about ten feet square had been dug with a crude pole around, but most of the inmates were beyond getting to that pole.[12]

It appears that a week after the liberation, conditions in the camp had hardly changed. The improvements that had already been made remained unnoticed by the women; the horror and incomprehensibility dominated everything.

On the other side, the relief teams' accommodation appeared to be sheer luxury. They had been allocated 'well built houses among the trees' on the grounds of a former military training area where, as a team member assumed, married Wehrmacht officers had previously been quartered. A boiler that they had brought with them provided continuous hot water, which could be used to fill thermos flasks or carried into their rooms in buckets, thus sparing them from having to wash in a basin full of cold water. In addition, there was a bathhouse with twenty-four bathtubs and hot running water, 'that just makes all the difference to comfort at the end of a long and gruelling day in those grim surroundings'.[13] The quarters had only just been vacated by the Wehrmacht a few days earlier, and they were quickly cleaned, tidied and made comfortable, once all the Hitler portraits had been taken down.[14]

In the course of their work, the female members of the relief teams came particularly close to the survivors of Belsen. In the few written sources available, one sees a mixture of disgust at the German crimes, an open curiosity and an absolute willingness to help. Jane Leverson, the first Jewess relief worker and member of the first Quaker team to arrive in Belsen, praised in her report (dated 5 May) the British helpers' spirit, but warned of a possible change:

> In the early days of the liberation of the camp, the British workers were amazed at the horrors which they saw, and could not do enough to help the internees; they lived on half-rations for a fortnight, to feed the camp. They gave enormous presents of cigarettes and sweets. English sergeants blew the noses of invalid children, and 'potted' them. No job was too much, no hours were too long. The situation was more stimulating than the worst of London's blitzes. However, many of the British workers are tired now; as the internees gain strength, and as it dawns upon them that 'liberation' will not prevent them from catching typhus, nor give them immediate happiness and freedom, they become more difficult and less grateful, and this reacts most unfavourably on the British workers. So far I have not heard anti-Semitic remarks on this account ... I await them, however.[15]

These remarks reflect not only the dilemma facing British helpers in Belsen, but the whole allied liberation of concentration camps in general. Not only were there deficiencies in the advance material planning, but it was also clear, even within the first few days, that the psychological training of team members had not been intensive enough. In view of their inadequate psychological training, many liberators greeted the attitudes of those liberated with shock, bewilderment and a lack of understanding; often, they interpreted it as ingratitude. In addition to this there were also massive difficulties with language and communication, despite the fact that these had been predicted and discussed prior to this. In one of her first letters from Belsen, Jane Leverson described the attitude of the liberated prisoners in very positive terms: 'We can do practically nothing, but they are so glad to have us here.' She even asked for 20,000 Magen Davids and *Mesusoth* to be sent across from London:

> A large number of them are Jews, and you can't imagine how thrilled they are (nurses and patients) at seeing my Magen David, they can hardly believe that I am a Jewess from London. I feel horribly inadequate, but they don't seem to mind at all

> that I can't speak Yiddish! When they ask me, I just say 'Nein, ich bin Meshugener' and they love it.[16]

A short while later, however, there was already a degree of misunderstanding and criticism evident in her observations, when she wrote: 'Everyone steals some things; some steal everything. It makes life a little bit difficult.' In a different context, she also wrote that it appeared as though the people were waking up from a bad dream and now remembering their earlier lives:

> They are very often not grateful for that which is done for them. They are extremely fussy about the clothes with which they are issued. They grumble about their food; they complain if they are asked to eat their meat and vegetable course from their soup plates. They will not take 'no' for an answer, and will beg in an irritatingly 'whiney' voice, for preferential treatment; they will bribe one in a most pathetic way ... If they are like this now, so soon after liberation, one wonders how they will react when once again they are really free.

Furthermore, according to Jane Leverson, many of the former prisoners criticized the British intensively, and rarely offered any praise, despite the fact that they 'have brought a remarkable amount of order into this area of chaos'.[17]

Such observations were, by no means, the exception. One clearly senses the irritation and lack of understanding felt when the liberated failed to respond as the liberators had wished or expected. Many had survived months or even years in the most extreme conditions, and had adopted modes of behaviour and survival strategies that could not be simply shaken off within a matter of days. Primo Levi managed to capture this phenomenon in a simple sentence: 'However, it took several months, before I lost the habit of fixing my gaze to the ground whilst I went about, as though I was continually searching for something edible or something I could swiftly put in my pocket and swap for bread.'[18]

Before liberation, possession of a piece of bread or other foodstuff marked the difference between life and death. Eating not only satisfied a moment of hunger, it also prevented starvation, for a certain length of time at least. That was why patients lying in bed, sometimes weeks later, would still loudly draw attention to themselves when the food was being distributed: 'When they began to carry round the bowls of soup a horrible animal-like clamour broke out', reported a British journalist. 'Skinny arms were held out, blankets fell back, and naked, scarecrow figures flung themselves forward in their beds. They were not really hungry, but craved food.'[19] Those who did not need to be served food in bed often refused to eat in the hastily furnished dining rooms set up directly next to the kitchens in the hospital area. They preferred to take their food back to their rooms, where they could eat half of it and hide the rest. Much to the annoyance and bafflement of the helpers, a lot of this food then rotted under mattresses or pillows and behind lockers: 'Camp commanders and care workers fought a hopeless battle to stop this practice and to persuade their charges that food was no longer in short supply and that keeping it in bedrooms constituted a health hazard.'[20]

Written sources frequently contain comparisons with 'animal' or 'inhuman' behaviour: children attack their food like wolves,[21] the liberated prisoners 'are hardly reminiscent of human beings', 'people who were ill gained super-human powers as soon as any food appeared'.[22] But occasionally there are also indications of more extreme behaviour; such instances were presented as early as in the summer of 1945 at a medical conference and were interpreted within the context of the level of prior suffering: 'Loss of normal moral standards and sense of responsibility for the welfare of others was widespread; in severe cases interest in others did not extend beyond child or parent; eventually the instinct to survive alone remained even to the extent of eating human flesh. These psychological changes were proportional to the degree of starvation.'[23]

As in the case of food, there was also a great demand for clothing and this too involved safety issues. Many of the prisoners had been found naked, whilst others wore clothes that offered no protection against the weather. The living had taken the shoes and clothes from the dead, in order to survive. Appropriate or not, the clothing department that the relief teams ran at Belsen was nicknamed 'Harrods'. To begin with, it had been necessary for the team members to check the freshly dressed former internees before they left the department; however, just a short while later it proved difficult to satisfy the camp residents with these mainly donated or requisitioned garments.[24] There were others, on the other hand, who insisted on wearing their old prison uniforms even after they had received the fresh clothing, and some who continued to go about the camp naked.[25]

The behaviour of some of the patients was equally as striking.

In some cases, ill patients continued to be up and about, even though it would have been 'better' for them to lie down in bed; but it had been their past experience that those who lay around in bed were soon taken to the gas chamber.[26] Even months later, patients refused to be treated by German doctors out of sheer terror, and because of this the Jewish Committee for Relief Abroad decided to send a mobile medical team through the German towns and cities.[27] Patients also refused to wear British Red Cross pyjamas out of fear that it was just another German deception, using the red emblem to reassure the patients before sending them to the gas chambers after all.[28] Fearing this to be the case, patients also refused to get into the Red Cross Ambulances that were due to take them to a ship bound for Sweden.[29]

There are many examples of this type of behaviour, and they are all expressions and consequences of German crimes, deathly fear, and other serious and extreme experiences. There were few indeed, among the military or civilian helpers, who were adequately prepared for what they found. According to Michael Marrus, the military kept the liberated prisoners at a distance, were annoyed by their needs, and misunderstood their curses.[30]

Criticism of the British, as already recorded by Jane Leverson, could easily lead to aggression, until the former prisoners themselves, and especially the Jews among them, were viewed solely as a nuisance.[31] Frank Stern quoted a British officer, who had become involved in an argument with a Jewish survivor: 'There was a great barrier between us.' During a tour of one of the camps the survivor had stood on a mound of white ashes and asked the officer if he knew what it was he was standing on. Before the former prisoner could even finish the sentence, 'I am standing on the bodies of ...', the officer screamed at him to get down off the mound. According to Frank Stern, 'This great barrier between the liberators and the liberated ... who had differing experiences and perceptions of the horror of everyday death' only intensified the problems between the two groups in the time that followed.[32] 'You must realise that we and our liberators saw the camp with different eyes', Anita Lasker-Wallfisch later wrote:

> We had lived surrounded by filth and death for so long that we scarcely noticed it. The mountains of corpses in their varying degrees of decay were part of the landscape and we had even got used to the dreadful stench. It would be wrong

> to assume that everything was instantly transformed the moment the first tank entered Belsen. What the British Army found was far removed from anything it had ever had to deal with, even in wartime.[33]

The tense relationship continued. Survivors such as Josef Rosensaft complained that during the early months the liberators had viewed them as nothing more than pitiful objects. This attitude was invariably accompanied by the question of whether psychiatrists should be called in; sometimes psychiatrists were even sent to see the survivors without having been requested: 'They had forgotten that we were not brought up in Belsen, Auschwitz and other concentration camps, but had, once upon a time, a home, and a background and motherly love and kindness; that before the calamity we, too, had our schools and universities and Yeshivot.'[34] With this, Josef Rosensaft raised important questions concerning human dignity and self-determination even under the most pitiful conditions. It was in connection to this that Henri Stern spoke about the dependence of an 'outcast and frustrated population ... on the paternal benevolence of the relief bodies'.[35]

Only a few were capable of providing mental support and psychological help, and when this did happen it was usually a female relief worker that provided it. Helen Bamber was just such a person, and she reported:

> there was a need to tell you *everything*, over and over and over again. And this was the most significant thing for me, realizing that you had to take it all. They would need to hold onto you, and many of them still had very thin arms, especially the ones who had come from or gone back to the East and then dragged themselves to Belsen, hands almost like claws, and they would hold you, and it was important that you held them, and often you had to rock, there was a rocking, bowing movement, as you sat on the floor – there was very little to sit on – and you would hold onto them and they would tell you their story. Sometimes it was Yiddish, and although I had learned some, it was as though you didn't really need a language. It took me a long time to realize that you couldn't really do anything but that you just had to hang onto them and that you had to listen and to *receive* this, as if it belonged partly to you, and in that act of taking and showing that you were available you were playing some useful role. There wasn't

> much crying at that time, it was much later that they began really to grieve; some people had got far beyond that and they might never again have been able to weep; it wasn't so much grief as a pouring out of some ghastly vomit like a kind of horror, it just came out in all directions.[36]

One survivor gave Eva Kahn-Minden a lock of hair, and in so doing, the survivor 'unburdened [herself] for the first time about the worst period of [her] life'. Senta Hirtz wrote about 'hungry people ... not only hungry for physical food but also hungry for love, hungry for life'.[37] Others, however, with the best of intentions, avoided all confrontations with the past. In her 1945 essay, 'Children of Belsen', Ruth Abrahams wrote:

> It is difficult to say how far these children will be permanently affected by their experiences in the concentration camps. We obviously did not discuss horrors with them and all our efforts were concentrated on driving out of their minds the memories of these terrible things. They certainly look happy, are not shy or nervous when you speak to them and one can only hope that kind treatment, good food and decent living conditions may have succeeded in clearing these terrors from their thoughts.[38]

With this approach, Ruth Abrahams came very close to the contemporary view, that was later mockingly referred to as 'Wiener Wald- und Wiesenpsychoanalyse' by Ruth Klüger, whereby it was considered that the concentration camps would be of 'no lasting significance' for those under 6 years old.[39]

Indeed, nobody was thinking about the lifelong consequences of the traumatic events and experiences. To begin with, it was just a matter of providing 'relief', although it was also clear that 'rehabilitation' would have to follow. But this again was geared far more towards material needs, to improving the chances for a new start in life, which despite being hugely important made little allowances for the emotional needs. Colonel F.M. Lipscomb, who was temporarily assigned to the 32nd Casualty Clearing Station, as medical advisor to the senior medical officer, advised that as the liberated prisoners' physical recovery progressed, 'normal behaviour' would also resume accordingly; 'leaving only a feeling akin to that of having had a bad dream'.[40]

THE DISPLACED PERSONS

Looking at contemporary reports, letters and memoirs the perception of post-war DPs spread from gangs who looted, stole and killed on the one side, and pitiful victims of war and Nazi persecution on the other. Based on the city of Bremen's post-war crime statistics, Wolfgang Jacobmeyer's 1985 study already opposed the idea that DP criminality was significantly higher than German criminality.[41] German collective memory, however, preserves a different story. Mental predispositions, the limits of personal experience and individual expectations affected strongly the development of perceptions on both sides. 'The former forced labourers saw themselves surrounded by people, who still lived a comfortable life, while their accommodation was still very poor', Margaret McNeill (Friends Relief Service) noted in 1949, and 'many DPs realize with painful astonishment that the Quakers are not willing to confiscate on a large scale from the Germans what is urgently needed by the DPs.'[42]

Writing about their perceptions of the DPs, relief workers often compared them with the German population. Margaret Wyndham, for example, who worked with a British Red Cross team in Belsen, reported on 15 May 1945, to her mother in England, that she had visited the local German mayor to request two German female workers to clean the quarters and take care of the washing. Both of them, however, immediately offered more than that:

> They also tell us that they will prevent the Russians from pinching our things. Altogether this is such an amazing place that I have forgotten who are allies and who are enemies. The Russians are the terror of the countryside and the sooner they are sent home the better for everybody![43]

It seems that only a month after liberation, the perception of those liberated already started to change, when the Russian/Soviet non-Jewish DPs were described in such a negative way. Remarkably, the German women also offered to protect the relief workers' possessions, which created a common interest of Germans and British against the DPs.

Jane Leverson reported that 'self-righteous Germans' poured into the offices of the military to complain about looting 'Russians'.[44] Similar remarks can be found in Julius Posener's report about German 'half honest, half exaggerated propaganda' against 'the Russians'.[45] The pattern is always the same: Germans complain about looting to ensure British protection, and it seems that the real or alleged threat caused by the DPs built a bridge between the German and the British side. The British Foreign Office had foreseen this development in advance and had warned against it.[46]

According to William Strang, during the early weeks of occupation members of the Control Commission already sympathized more with the Germans than with the DPs, while British combat soldiers were more on the side of the DPs.[47] However, such observations were by no means limited to the British zone of occupation. Following Frank Stern, in 1945 many American soldiers preferred the company of 'well educated, modest, compliant, nice, clean and neat Germans' to DPs, who were regarded as 'dowdy, dirty and depressive'.[48]

The growing negative image was certainly reinforced by the unwillingness of many DPs to be repatriated, while the image of the Germans became increasingly positive. It took only months before the victims of Nazi persecution became a problem for the allies, a problem that in 1947 had to be solved urgently with the disintegration of the anti-Hitler coalition and the onset of the Cold War.[49] However, both Jewish and non-Jewish DPs equally experienced 'a lack of understanding and annoyance'.[50] Zionist activities, for example, were negatively perceived, while Jewish DPs who declared openly that Palestine was not their first choice for emigration could expect sympathy.[51]

Finally, in 1947, the British perception of DPs changed again after the British government decided to fill the gap on the British labour market with the help of migrants and to recruit DPs in Europe. Jewish DPs, however, were explicitly excluded.[52]

GERMANY AND THE GERMANS

The first impression of Germany and the Germans for British troops and relief workers was the enormous destruction of the towns and cities as well as the good physical condition of the German civil population. 'People were well fed and well dressed: the cellars of the undestroyed houses were well stocked with food', a Salvation Army officer noted.[53] Other relief workers referred to exhausted, war-weary and apathetic people with often unpredictable behaviour, and noted that it was 'especially hard ... to get no friendly response from the children in those early days'.

Pip Turner, a member of a Friends Ambulance Unit, recognized that her 'Guten Morgen' was not answered at the beginning, because 'they felt hostility to us'.[54] On the other hand, we find remarks about refusal on both sides: 'People turned away from us – somehow we did not want to look at them and they did not want to look at us.'[55]

In mid-June 1945, all British Relief Teams operating in Germany were once again warned not to fraternize with the Germans.[56] Only a little later, however, when the British military government in Germany started preparations for the 'Battle of the winter', positive remarks about the Germans and comments on their miserable situation increased. Now a member of a Friends Ambulance Unit stressed the 'friendliness of the ordinary people',[57] and in November 1945 another report stated:

> In the midst of such fearful destruction caused by British bombs, it would be expected that the German mind would be filled with hatred, but even in Hamburg and down in the Ruhr there is a remarkable absence of resentment. The people seem to feel that they have been saved from something rather terrible; and to be thankful that they live in the British rather than any other zone.[58]

During the winter of 1945/1946, the perception of the physical condition of the German population changed as well. From now on, remarks no longer appear about 'well fed and well dressed' people. Instead, there are descriptions of the effects the supply bottleneck had on people: hunger was visible in the 'yellow lined faces' of the elderly, the 'pinched, grey faces' of the workers, and the 'pasty, dull faces' of the children.[59]

Not surprisingly, when the food supply worsened at the end of 1945, the self-pity of the German population increased. Relief workers described German people as 'poisoned by self-pity',[60] 'full of misery' and 'bitterness'.[61] Trapped in 'coma and apathy',[62] nobody had any interest in what was going on outside the tiny area of personal life. 'All the teams are troubled by the indifference of the German population to the misery of Europe', Roger Wilson (Friends Relief Service) noted during his visit in Germany in October and November 1945.[63]

Barbara Walker, a member of a relief team in Oberhausen, wrote in March 1947:

> We should try to make the Germans understand why they are hated by telling them what has been done in the name of Germany. Since arriving here it seems to me that the people of Oberhausen do not know these facts and if they do that they do not believe them. They are, as we had been told before we came, very preoccupied with their own suffering, which is quite understandable of course. But I do feel that it can be one of our functions to tell them the facts and try to make them understand that they did happen.[64]

Reports compiled by British relief workers stressed the point that most Germans ignored or rejected any responsibility for the misery in European countries occupied by Germany during the war. At the same time, however, they strongly demanded British food supplies.[65] Britain was regarded as a land of milk and honey that could easily solve all German problems,[66] and when it became obvious that this would not be the case, the British reputation in Germany fell dramatically. Additionally, more and more Germans regarded themselves as victims of the war[67] and Germany as the most needy country in Europe.[68]

It is difficult to draw a line between the denial of reality and the inability to accept it. Relief workers often described their German contacts as unwilling to listen when they talked about forced labour, war crimes and mass murder. Many of them treated the survivors of Nazi persecution with 'suspicion' and 'open hostility'.[69] It is one of the myths of German history that nobody knew anything about the Holocaust. But it is simply incomprehensible that, for example, hundred of thousands of German soldiers and members of the SS had never, ever talked about what they had committed or witnessed in eastern Europe when on home leave during the war. Recent research demonstrates that the German population had a high degree of, or at least a general knowledge about, the Holocaust – and whoever really wanted to know about the Holocaust could have done so easily.[70] Or, in the words of a British soldier: 'I'm quite willing to believe they didn't really know what was going on but in this particular case ignorance must be regarded as a crime.'[71]

When relief workers and Germans talked about the past, nearly all stated that they had never even been a Nazi. And even those Germans whose involvement was obvious 'produced one excuse or another to explain away their former association with the Nazi activities', according to Moses Moskowitz in his 1946 article, 'The Germans and the Jews'.[72] Moskowitz's article was published only a year after the end of the war, but he described very clearly the mechanism of how the German population regarded themselves not only as victims of National Socialism but as the greatest victims of all.

There was a close link between trauma, silence, apathy and indifference. In this context we should mention Margarete and Alexander Mitscherlich's book, *The Inability to Mourn*, as well as Hannah Arendt's publication, *Besuch in Deutschland*, first published in 1950.

> Nowhere can you feel the nightmare of destruction and horror less than in Germany, and nowhere do people talk less about it. Everywhere you are struck by the lack of reaction to what has happened, but it is difficult to say whether this is somehow a deliberate refusal to mourn or an expression of a real lack of feeling. In the midst of ruins the Germans write picture postcards of churches, market squares, public buildings and bridges that no longer exist. And the indifference they show when moving through the ruins corresponds to the fact that nobody grieves for the dead; it mirrors the apathy of how they react or rather do not react to the refugees in their midst. This lack of emotion, however, this heartlessness, which is sometimes concealed by tacky sentimentality, is nothing other than an obvious external symptom of a deep rooted, persistent and sometimes even cruel refusal, to face what has happened and to accept it.[73]

CONCLUSION

Looking back, we can see that the contemporary pattern of humanitarian assistance is the result of a long learning process, in which the two world wars acted as important catalysts. Based on experiences gained from the First World War, Britain pursued a far-sighted policy of advance planning during the Second World War, which was successfully translated into practice immediately after D-Day, when the first relief teams of British voluntary organizations were deployed in north-western Europe. To begin with, all activities were confined to helping UN nationals, among them the survivors of the Holocaust and of forced labour.

Only a few days after the liberation, relief teams of the British Red Cross and the Society of Friends arrived at Belsen concentration camp, and they played a crucial role in the emergency relief efforts for the 60,000 prisoners, many of them too weak and ill to survive. Letters and reports written by British military and relief workers immediately after liberation present unique sources, not only for the history of liberation, relief and rehabilitation; they also shed light on the question of how liberators and relief workers perceived their own work and how they perceived the survivors of Nazi persecution as well as the German population. Their sources clearly demonstrate that the German self-perception as victims of war began as early as 1945.

REFERENCES

Archives

British Red Cross Archive (BRC).
Friends Library, London (FL).
Modern Record Centre, University of Warwick (MRC).
Public Records Office (PRO), Kew.
Salvation Army International Heritage Centre, London (SA).
Wiener Library, London (WL).

Published Sources

Abrahams, R., 'Children of Belsen', *The World's Children*, November 1945, pp.175–6.

Arendt, H., *Besuch in Deutschland* (Berlin: Rotbuch, 1993).

Barer, R., *One Young Man and Total War (From Normandy to Concentration Camp: A Doctor's Letters Home* (Edinburgh: Pentland Press, 1998).

Bark, E., *No Time to Kill* (London: R. Hale, 1960).

Beardwell, M. F., *Aftermath* (Devon: Ilfracombe, 1953).

Belton, N., *The Good Listener: Helen Bamber: A Life against Cruelty* (London: Phoenix, 1999).

Carey, M.C., 'Progress at Belsen camp', *British Red Cross Quarterly Review*, July 1945, pp.103–7.

Collis, R. and Hogerzeil, H., *Straight On* (London: Methuen, 1947).

Donnison, F.S.V., *Civil Affairs and Military Government North-West Europe 1944–1946* (London: HMSO, 1961).

Gershon, K. (ed.), *Postscript: A Collective Account of the Lives of Jews in West Germany Since the Second World War* (London: Gollancz, 1969).

Jacobmeyer, W., *Vom Zwangsarbeiter zum Heimatlosen Ausländer: Die Displaced Persons in Westdeutschland* (Göttingen: Vandenhoeck & Ruprecht, 1985).

Johnson, E. and Reuband, K.-H., *What We Knew: Terror, Mass Murder and Everyday Life in Nazi Germany* (London: John Murray, 2005).

Kelber, M., *Quäkerhilfswerk, Britische Zone 1945–1948* (Bad Pyrmont: Friedrich, 1949).

Klüger, R., *Weiter leben: Eine Jugend*, 10th edn (Munich: DTV, 2001).

Kolinsky, E., 'Jewish Holocaust Survivors between Liberation and Resettlement', in J.-D. Steinert and I. Weber-Newth (eds), *European Immigrants in Britain 1933–1950* (Munich: Saur, 2003), pp.121–35.

Königseder, A. and Wetzel, J., *Lebensmut im Wartesaal: Die jüdischen DPs (Displaced Persons) im Nachkriegsdeutschland* (Frankfurt a. M: Fischer, 1994).

Lasker-Wallfisch, A., *Inherit the Truth, 1939–1945: The Documented Experiences of a Survivor of Auschwitz and Belsen* (London: Giles de la Mare, 1996).

Lavsky, H., 'The Day After: Bergen-Belsen from Concentration Camp to the Centre of the Jewish Survivors in Germany', *German History*, 11, 1 (1993), pp.36–59.

Levi, P., *Die Atempause* (Munich: DTV, 1994).

Lipscomb, F.M., 'German Concentration Camps: Diseases Encountered at Belsen', in Sir H. Letheby (ed.), *Inter-Allied Conferences on War Medicine, 1942–1945* (London: Royal Society of Medicine, 1947), pp.462–5.
Longerich, P., *'Davon haben wir nichts gewußt!': Die Deutschen und die Judenverfolgung 1933–1945* (Munich: Siedler, 2006).
Marrus, M.R., *The Unwanted: European Refugees in the Twentieth Century* (New York and Oxford: Oxford University Press, 1985).
McBryde, B., *A Nurse's War* (London: Hogarth, 1986).
McNeill, M., 'Hilfe für Ausländer (DPs)', in M. Kelber, *Quäkerhilfswerk, Britische Zone 1945–1948* (Bad Pyrmont: Friedrich, 1949), pp.85–106.
Moskowitz, M., 'The Germans and the Jews: Postwar Report: The Enigma of German Irresponsibility', *Commentary* (1946), pp.7–14.
Posener, J., *In Deutschland 1945 bis 1946* (Berlin: Siedler, 2001).
The Relief of Belsen, April 1945: Eyewitness Accounts (London: Imperial War Museum, 1991).
'Report of Myrtle Beardwell-Wielzynska, on her Work as a Nurse in the Liberated Concentration Camp Bergen-Belsen', in *Konzentrationslager Bergen-Belsen* (Hanover: Niedersächsische Landeszentrale für Politische Bildung, 1995), p.202.
Rosensaft, J., 'Our Belsen', in *Belsen* (Tel Aviv: Irgun Sheerit Hapleita Me'haezor Habriti, 1957), pp.24–51.
Saunders, H., *The Red Cross and the White: A Short History of the Joint War Organization of the British Red Cross Society and the Order of St John of Jerusalem During the War 1939–1945* (London: Hollis & Carter, 1949).
Schröder, S., *Displaced Persons im Landkreis und in der Stadt Münster 1945–1951* (Münster: Aschendorff, 2005).
Schulze, R., 'A Difficult Interlude: Relations between British Military Government and the German Population and their Effects for the Constitution of a Democratic Society', in A. Bance, *The Cultural Legacy of the British Occupation in Germany: The London Symposium* (Stuttgart: H.-D. Heinz, 1997), pp.67–109.
Smith, L., *Pacifists in Action: The Experience of the Friends Ambulance Unit in the Second World War* (York: William Sessions Limited, 1998).
Sommer, K.-L., *Humanitäre Auslandshilfe als Brücke zu atlantischer Partnerschaft: CARE, CRALOG und die Entwicklung der deutsch-amerikanischen Beziehungen nach Ende des Zweiten Weltkriegs* (Bremen: Staatsarchiv Bremen, 1999).
Steinert, J.-D. and Weber-Newth, I., *Labour and Love: Deutsche in Großbritannien nach dem Zweiten Weltkrieg* (Osnabrück: Secolo, 2000).
Steinert, J.-D., 'British Relief Teams in Belsen Concentration Camp: Emergency Relief and the Perception of Survivors', in Suzanne Bardgett and David Cesarani (eds), *Belsen 1945: New Historical Perspectives* (London and Portland, OR: Vallentine Mitchell, 2006), pp. 62–78.
Steinert, J.-D., 'Food and the Food Crisis in Post-War Germany, 1945–1948: British Policy and the Role of British NGOs', in Flemming Just and Frank Trentmann (eds), *Food and Conflict in Europe in the Age of the Two World Wars* (Basingstoke: Palgrave Macmillan, 2006), pp.266–88.
Steinert, J.-D., *Nach Holocaust und Zwangsarbeit: Britische humanitäre Hilfe in Deutschland: Die Helfer, die Befreiten und die Deutschen* (Osnabrück: Secolo, 2007).
Steinert, J.-D., 'British Humanitarian Assistance: Wartime Planning and Postwar Realities', *Journal of Contemporary History*, 43, 3 (2008), pp 421–35.
Stern, F., *Im Anfang war Auschwitz: Antisemitismus und Philosemitismus im deutschen Nachkrieg* (Gerlingen: Bleicher, 1991).
Stern, H., 'The Aftermath of Belsen', in H.B.M. Murphy (ed.), *Flight and Resettlement* (Luzern: UNESCO, 1955), pp.64–75.
Strang, Lord W., *Home and Abroad* (London: Andre Deutsch, 1956).
Whitworth, R., 'Germany: The Next Step', *The Friend*, 30 November 1945, pp.808–10.
'Work of the Jewish Relief Unit', *British Zone Review*, 29 March 1947, p.17.
Wyman, M., *DPs: Europe's Displaced Persons, 1945–1951* (Ithaca, NY: Cornell University Press, 1989).

NOTES

1. This chapter is based on a research project, which was generously supported by the British Academy. The main outcomes from this project are: J.-D. Steinert, *Nach Holocaust und Zwangsarbei: Britische humanitäre Hilfe in Deutschland: Die Helfer, die Befreiten und die Deutschen* (Osnabrück: Secolo, 2007); J-D Steinert, 'British Relief Teams in Belsen Concentration Camp: Emergency Relief and the Perception of Survivors', in Suzanne Bardgett and David Cesarani (eds), *Belsen 1945: New Historical Perspectives* (London and Portland, OR: Vallentine Mitchell, 2006), pp.62–78; J.-D. Steinert, 'Food and the Food Crisis in Post-War Germany, 1945–1948: British Policy and the Role of British NGOs, in Flemming Just and Frank Trentmann (eds), *Food and Conflict in Europe in the Age of the Two World Wars* (Basingstoke: Palgrave Macmillan, 2006), pp.266–88; J.-D. Steinert, 'British Humanitarian Assistance: Wartime Planning and Postwar Realities', *Journal of Contemporary History*, 43, 3 (2008), pp.421–35.
2. Relief teams were provided by the British Red Cross Society, the Friends Relief Service, the Friends Ambulance Unit, the Young Women's Christian Association, the Save the Children Fund, the Salvation Army, the Catholic Committee for Relief Abroad, the Jewish Committee for Relief Abroad, the International Voluntary Service for Peace, the Boy Scouts Association, and the Guide International Service.
3. Public Records Office, Kew (PRO), FO 936/698, Council of British Societies for Relief Abroad, Report for the Year 1947, p.8.
4. M. Kelber, *Quäkerhilfswerk, Britische Zone 1945–1948* (Bad Pyrmont: Friedrich, 1949), p.17.
5. PRO FO 936/698, Council of British Societies for Relief Abroad, Report for the Year 1947, pp.12–13.
6. F.S.V. Donnison, *Civil Affairs and Military Government North-West Europe 1944–1946* (London: HMSO, 1961), p.221; *The Relief of Belsen, April 1945: Eyewitness Accounts* (London: Imperial War Museum, 1991), p.31.
7. H. Lavsky, 'The Day After: Bergen-Belsen from Concentration Camp to the Centre of the Jewish Survivors in Germany', *German History*, 11, 1 (1993), p.44.
8. R. Collis and H. Hogerzeil, *Straight On* (London: Methuen, 1947), p.53.
9. Friends Library, London (FL), FRS/1992/Box 8, Friends Relief Service. Digest of Overseas Reports No. 3, week ending 5 May 1945.
10. M.C. Carey, 'Progress at Belsen Camp', in *British Red Cross Quarterly Review*, July 1945, p.103.
11. 'Medical Students for Belsen Camp: Treating the Starved', *The Times*, 30 April 1945.
12. M.F. Beardwell, *Aftermath* (Devon: Ilfracombe, 1953), p.40.
13. Carey, 'Progress at Belsen Camp', p.104.
14. British Red Cross Archive (BRC), Acc 96/29, Belsen Letters, letters sent from Miss Margaret Wyndham Ward, MBE, to her mother, Sarah Langlands Ward, from 24 February 1945 to 14 August 1945, here 23 April 1945.
15. Wiener Library, London (WL), Henriques Archive 3/13, Jane Leverson, Bergen-Belsen Concentration Camp, 6 May 1945.
16. WL Henriques Archive 3/13, Jane Leverson, Bergen-Belsen [undated, April 1945].
17. WL Henriques Archive 3/13, Jane Leverson, Bergen-Belsen Concentration Camp, 6 May 1945.
18. P. Levi, *Die Atempause* (Munich: DTV, 1994), p.245.
19. 'Red Cross in Belsen: Battle against Death', *The Times*, 16 May 1945.
20. E. Kolinsky, 'Jewish Holocaust Survivors Between Liberation and Resettlement', in J.-D. Steinert and I. Weber-Newth (eds), *European Immigrants in Britain 1933–1950* (Munich: Saur, 2003), p.123.
21. M. Wyman, *DPs: Europe's Displaced Persons, 1945–1951* (Ithaca: Cornell University Press, 1989), pp.96–7.
22. 'Report of Myrtle Beardwell-Wielzynska, on her Work as a Nurse in the Liberated Concentration Camp Bergen-Belsen', in *Konzentrationslager Bergen-Belsen* (Hanover: Niedersächsische Landeszentrale für Politische Bildung, 1995), p.202.
23. F.M. Lipscomb, 'German Concentration Camps: Diseases Encountered at Belsen', in Sir H. Letheby (ed.), *Inter-Allied Conferences on War Medicine, 1942–1945* (London: Royal Society of Medicine, 1947), p.464.
24. Beardwell, *Aftermath*, pp.54–5.

25. M.R. Marrus, *The Unwanted: European Refugees in the Twentieth Century* (New York and Oxford: Oxford University Press, 1985), p.332; A. Königseder and J. Wetzel, *Lebensmut im Wartesaal: Die jüdischen DPs (Displaced Persons) im Nachkriegsdeutschland* (Frankfurt a. M: Fischer, 1994), p.27.
26. B. McBryde, *A Nurse's War* (London: Hogarth, 1986), p.168.
27. 'Work of the Jewish Relief Unit', in *British Zone Review*, 29 March 1947, p.17.
28. McBryde, *A Nurse's War*, p.92.
29. Wyman, *DPs*, p.133.
30. Marrus, *The Unwanted*, p.308.
31. Ibid.
32. F. Stern, *Im Anfang war Auschwitz: Antisemitismus und Philosemitismus im deutschen Nachkrieg* (Gerlingen: Bleicher, 1991), p.61.
33. A. Lasker-Wallfisch, *Inherit the Truth, 1939–1945: The Documented Experiences of a Survivor of Auschwitz and Belsen* (London: Giles de la Mare, 1996), p.96.
34. J. Rosensaft, 'Our Belsen', in *Belsen* (Tel Aviv: Irgun Sheerit Hapleita Me'haezor Habriti, 1957), pp.25–6.
35. H. Stern, 'The Aftermath of Belsen', in H.B.M. Murphy (ed.), *Flight and Resettlement* (Luzern: UNESCO, 1955), p.71.
36. N. Belton, *The Good Listener: Helen Bamber: A Life against Cruelty* (London: Phoenix, 1999), p.109.
37. Ibid., p.111.
38. R. Abrahams, 'Children of Belsen', in *The World's Children*, November 1945, p.176.
39. R. Klüger, *Weiter leben: Eine Jugend*, 10th edn (Munich: DTV, 2001), p.240.
40. Lipscomb, 'German Concentration Camps', p.464.
41. W. Jacobmeyer, *Vom Zwangsarbeiter zum Heimatlosen Ausländer: Die Displaced Persons in Westdeutschland* (Göttingen: Vandenhoeck & Ruprecht, 1985), p.49. See also, for a rural area, S. Schröder, *Displaced Persons im Landkreis und in der Stadt Münster 1945–1951* (Münster: Aschendorff, 2005).
42. M. McNeill, 'Hilfe für Ausländer (DPs)', in M. Kelber, *Quäkerhilfswerk, Britische Zone 1945–1948* (Bad Pyrmont: Friedrich, 1949), p.89.
43. BRC Acc 96/29, Belsen Letters, letters sent from Miss Margaret Wyndham Ward MBE to her mother, Sarah Langlands Ward, from 24 February 1945 to 14 August 1945, here 15 May 1945.
44. FL FRS/1992/Box 72, Jane E. Leverson to Roger, 6 June 1945.
45. J. Posener, *In Deutschland 1945 bis 1946* (Berlin: Siedler, 2001), p.16.
46. R. Schulze, 'A Difficult Interlude: Relations between British Military Government and the German Population and their Effects for the Constitution of a Democratic Society', in A. Bance, *The Cultural Legacy of the British Occupation in Germany: The London Symposium* (Stuttgart: H.-D. Heinz, 1997), p.74.
47. Lord W. Strang, *Home and Abroad* (London: Andre Deutsch, 1956), p.233.
48. Stern, *Im Anfang war Auschwitz*, p.93.
49. Marrus, *The Unwanted*, pp.310–11.
50. Königseder and Wetzel, *Lebensmut im Wartesaal*, p.29.
51. Beardwell, *Aftermath*, pp.47–8.
52. J.-D. Steinert and I. Weber-Newth, *Labour and Love: Deutsche in Großbritannien nach dem Zweiten Weltkrieg* (Osnabrück: Secolo, 2000), p.55.
53. Salvation Army International Heritage Centre, London (SA), Germany, War-Time/2, G.R. Carpenter, Adjutant, Liaison Officer, Germany Today and the Salvation Army, 8 April 1947.
54. L. Smith, *Pacifists in Action: The Experience of the Friends Ambulance Unit in the Second World War* (York: William Sessions Limited, 1998), p.329.
55. E. Bark, *No Time to Kill* (London: R. Hale, 1960), p.53.
56. FL FRS/1992/Box 73, K.M. Agnew, Deputy Commissioner, British Red Cross Commission (Civilian Relief), A Letter on Non-Fraternisation by the Deputy Commissioner for Civilian Relief, 22 June 1945.
57. FL FAU/1947/3/4, Report, RS8/FAU Essen, 20 November 1945.
58. R. Whitworth, 'Germany: The Next Step', *The Friend*, 30 November 1945, p.808.
59. FL FRS/1992/Box 72, M. Yande, Dortmund, First Impressions of Germany, 12 March 1947.

60. 'Criticism Grows in Germany: British Blamed for Everything Except the Weather: Morale Lowered by Self-Pity', *Manchester Guardian*, 22 January 1947.
61. Bark, *No Time to Kill*, p.65.
62. H. Saunders, *The Red Cross and the White: A Short History of the Joint War Organization of the British Red Cross Society and the Order of St John of Jerusalem during the War 1939–1945* (London: Hollis & Carter, 1949), p.174.
63. FL FRS/1992/Box 35, Roger Wilson, Report on Visit to Germany, October–November, 1945, 31 December 1945.
64. FL FRS/1992/Box 71, Barbara Walker, FRS Oberhausen, to Hugh Jenkins, FRS London, 12 March 1947.
65. K.-L. Sommer, *Humanitäre Auslandshilfe als Brücke zu atlantischer Partnerschaft: CARE, CRALOG und die Entwicklung der deutsch-amerikanischen Beziehungen nach Ende des Zweiten Weltkriegs* (Bremen: Staatsarchiv Bremen, 1999), p.219.
66. 'Germany's Food: Miss Wilkinson's Fear for Winter', *Manchester Guardian*, 8 October 1945.
67. Sommer, *Humanitäre Auslandshilfe*, p.226.
68. Modern Record Centre, University of Warwick (MRC), MSS.157/3/SEN/4, Dr Th. Michaltschoff to Mr Brown, 16 October 1945.
69. K. Gershon (ed.), *Postscript: A Collective Account of the Lives of Jews in West Germany since the Second World War* (London: Gollancz, 1969), p.71.
70. See, for example, E. Johnson and K.-H. Reuband, *What We Knew: Terror, Mass Murder and Everyday Life in Nazi Germany* (London: John Murray, 2005); P. Longerich, *'Davon haben wir nichts gewußt!': Die Deutschen und die Judenverfolgung 1933–1945* (Munich: Siedler, 2006).
71. R. Barer, *One Young Man and Total War (From Normandy to Concentration Camp, a Doctor's Letters Home* (Edinburgh: Pentland Press, 1998), p.228.
72. M. Moskowitz, 'The Germans and the Jews: Postwar Report: The Enigma of German Irresponsibility', *Commentary* (1946), p.7.
73. H. Arendt, *Besuch in Deutschland* (Berlin: Rotbuch, 1993), pp.24–5.

2

'Please report only *true* nationalities': The Classification of Displaced Persons in Post-Second World War Germany and its Implications

LYNNE TAYLOR

In any humanitarian crisis, one of the first challenges facing those wanting to provide assistance is 'counting heads'. The essential question is simple: how many need aid? This question is quickly followed by another: who exactly is eligible for aid? This second question arises because, in most instances, the organization providing the aid is restricted to a particular population or segment of a population by its constitution or mandate. Answering these questions is seldom as easy a task as it might seem at first glance. And in the counting of heads, policy decisions are reflected or even made, while priorities are made stark, in ways that speak volumes about both the decision-makers and the victim population. It was no different in the first post-Second World War humanitarian crisis that saw millions displaced from their homes and in dire need of immediate assistance. A study of the Displaced Persons (DPs) crisis in the American occupation zone of Germany provides a way of exploring those policy decisions, giving an insight into how nationalities were understood at the time and the shaping of the post-war world emerging from the rubble of Europe.

In the evolution of the discussion about who was going to be eligible for assistance, the allied occupation authorities in Germany and the United Nations Relief and Rehabilitation Administration

(UNRRA) effectively granted legitimacy, or denied it, to particular national identities, privileging some and denying the existence of others. This reflected the emerging tensions, primarily between the USSR and the US, that would ultimately become the Cold War, and it helped to shape the nationality question for the latter half of the twentieth century and until today. It began with the decision that, in the first instance, the allied military authorities (SHAEF – the Supreme Headquarters, Allied Expeditionary Forces – and then the various occupying military authorities in the several zones) would provide aid to the anticipated hordes of post-war refugees as the allied forces established control of the conquered territory. In the second instance, at least in theory, UNRRA would also provide aid. In reality, this aid was supplied by the military authorities and distributed and managed by UNRRA. As early as 1944, both were defining who would receive aid, but their definitions were, in hindsight, very rudimentary. Simply put, the crux was about distinguishing between enemy and non-enemy refugees.[1] For UNRRA, aid was to be extended to refugees of United Nations nationalities – that is, citizens of its member nations, which more or less correlated with SHAEF's 'non-enemy refugees.' This very simple definition of eligibility for aid was deemed sufficient because all believed that these refugees would only require assistance for a very short period of time. This was as true of the military authorities as it was of UNRRA. The expectation was that the refugees would all want to return home, and would do so in a very short time. Thus there seemed no need to make sorting them out too complicated. This meant that the first distinctions drawn between DPs were focused on organizing the masses so that they could be returned home expeditiously. Western Europeans and eastern Europeans were separated insofar as western Europeans were directed towards the west, and eastern Europeans to the east, in anticipation of their repatriation. This worked for the vast majority of the refugees who did return home quickly.[2]

The only other group singled out at this point were Soviet citizens. A corollary to the Yalta Agreement required that all Soviet POWs and civilians be repatriated to the USSR, whether they wished to return or not. This repatriation move, involving 2.5 million people, dominated the spring and summer months of 1945. While most returned willingly, a significant minority refused. To the shock of the American troops forcing them onto trucks and trains, many repatriates volubly and sometimes violently protested their forced repatriation. A significant number of those protesting argued that they were not, in fact, Soviet citizens. Thus a question quickly emerged from the field that would have long-term implications: who exactly was a Soviet citizen?

There should have been a simple answer to this question, but there was none, not least because of considerable border shifts in eastern Europe over the course of the war. In 1939, the USSR had invaded Poland and subsequently annexed the eastern half of that country. In 1940, it had formally absorbed the Baltic Republics – Latvia, Lithuania and Estonia. In both cases, the Soviet government considered the inhabitants of the annexed regions to be Soviet citizens and insisted they be included in the forced repatriation. Many from these regions, however, vehemently protested the assumption that they were Soviet citizens and demanded to be registered as Poles, Latvians, Estonians, Lithuanians. Repeated and desperate calls came in to SHAEF headquarters asking for directions about how to handle these refugees – should they be considered Soviets and repatriated, or not? As early as May 1945, SHAEF was quietly instructing those in the field to allow Poles and other east Europeans, other than bona fide Soviet citizens, the choice as to whether they would repatriate or not. If they affirmatively claimed Soviet citizenship, they would be repatriated. If they did not, they would not.[3]

Thus, by May 1945, the list of categories being used by the central authorities had been refined to non-enemy or UN DPs, Soviet citizens, and those not claiming/affirming Soviet citizenship. This was of little help to those in the field actually trying to sort the DPs. There the situation was much more complex, as reflected in repeated memos asking for direction on how to deal with a more complex list of nationalities confronting them: Soviet, Estonian, Latvian, Lithuanian (these three often being lumped together as 'Balts'), Polish, and also Ukrainian, the stateless (admittedly an odd one to see in a list of nationalities), and Jewish.

Initially, 'Jewish' was a term that had not figured at all in the early directives that outlined who qualified for aid. Even SHAEF's Administrative Memorandum No. 39, the definitive guide, failed to include 'Jews' as a category of DPs in its long list of eligible nationalities.[4] As explained in SHAEF's handbook for the occupation of Germany, 'as a general rule, military Government should avoid creating the impression that the Jews are to be singled out for special treatment, as such action will tend to perpetuate the distinctions of

Nazi racial theory'.[5] Ironically, this had unfortunate, often tragic, consequences for the Jews being released from the concentration camps. First, it meant that Jewish DPs received no extra or special care, in spite of their particularly dire condition, having been the special target of the Nazi regime and subjected to particularly brutal conditions in the camps. Second, as they were not considered a distinct category, they were placed in assembly centres with other DPs sharing their citizenship – Soviet Jews with Soviet DPs, Polish Jews with Polish DPs, for example. This often had the effect of putting them in the same camps as their earlier guards and tormentors. Third, as 'Jewish' was not considered a separate category or group, these DPs did not have the benefit of their own representatives – governmental or non-governmental – to protect their own particular interests or to fight on their behalf. Charitable organizations that wished to assist them were initially denied access, as they weren't acting as representatives of any government. Fourth, it meant that German and Austrian Jews were treated as ex-enemy refugees. They often found themselves left to their own devices, denied aid, and having to appeal to German authorities for assistance, a particularly distressing and infuriating situation.[6]

This situation was only corrected after pressure was brought to bear on the US government by US Army rabbis and American soldiers who mobilized and galvanized public opinion by sending home news of the horrific conditions.[7] In the wake of a particularly damning report by Earl Harrison, who inspected the DP camps in Germany in July 1945 at Washington's behest, the military occupation authorities made two changes. First, they immediately improved the living conditions and standard of care for the Jewish population. Second, they recognized the Jews as a special group. As Harrison argued, because they had been more severely victimized than the non-Jewish DPs, they had to be recognized as a separate group with greater needs. He stated that 'the first and plainest need of these people is a recognition of their actual status and by this I mean their status as Jews'.[8] By dint of their treatment at the hands of the Nazis, the Jews had been forged into a new, separate identity. In effect, he implied, 'Jewish' had become a nationality and had to be recognized as such by the American authorities. The response was swift. In a meeting on 25 July, even before Harrison had officially submitted his report to the president of the United States, the deputy military governor of Germany, General Lucius Clay, informed the army commanders that 'Jewish displaced persons would be provided for on the basis of nationality and not on the basis of religion'.[9] Interestingly, provision was made that if DPs of Jewish faith wished to be repatriated to the country 'of which they were nationals', they would be treated as citizens of that nationality. If they were without nationality or chose not to repatriate to their country of origin, with the exception of Soviet Jews, they would be considered Jews.[10] Effectively, Jews were allowed to choose whether they would reassume their nationality/citizenship or not. So, by the end of July 1945, the officially recognized categories had expanded to: UN DPs, Soviet citizens, non-Soviet citizens, and Jews.

It was not until October 1945 that it is possible to talk of UNRRA being operational in the field. Teams had been brought forward beginning in May, but they were few on the ground, very inadequately equipped, and their role carefully circumscribed by the military. During the summer of 1945, it was the military who controlled the handling of DPs. But UNRRA was laying its own plans for its eventual assumption of responsibility for the DPs. UNRRA's understanding of who it was responsible for was, like the military authorities', initially very simple: United Nations nationals who were displaced as a result of the war; persons not of United Nations nationality who were displaced as a result of the war and who were obliged to leave their country or place of origin or former residence by action of the enemy, because of their race, religion, or activities in favour of the United Nations (soon to be known as persecutees); and the stateless who had been displaced.[11] For UNRRA, the initial preoccupation was the geographical and chronological limits to its assistance – in which territories would it operate, and what would be the chronological boundaries for defining 'displaced as a result of the war'? Would it be the beginning of hostilities in 1939 or would it be 1933 and the advent of the Nazi regime? And what would be the end date?[12] The second preoccupation was the definition of 'stateless,' as that did not seem as obvious a 'UN nationality' as it had at first glance. 'Nationality', other than as a means of differentiating between enemy and non-enemy refugees, was of little concern at this point.

When UNRRA finally began to assume control of the camps, it faced the same challenges that had confronted the military authorities. Unexpectedly, after the dust settled, there were some 600,000 DPs remaining in the camps in Germany who either refused or were not able to return home, or had no home to return to.

They were largely from eastern Europe, and the majority were Poles, although a considerable number were from the Baltic Republics as well. The question then was what to make of this remnant, how to determine which were eligible for care, and how, ultimately, to dispose of them. The situation was made even more complicated by the growing influx of refugees fleeing westward from Poland, the Baltic Republics and the rest of eastern Europe, beginning in the fall of 1945. These 'infiltrees' (as they became known) were people who had not been displaced during the war but were now, in the immediate post-war months, fleeing westward to avoid persecution and economic hardship. It was thus unclear whether UNRRA had a mandate to care for them. However, they were predominantly Jewish. The pressure on the already overtaxed resources of UNRRA and the camps was mounting in size and seriousness. Getting a clear picture of this very fluid situation was crucial, as well as addressing quickly the issue of who was eligible for aid. As the director for the US zone of UNRRA, A.R. Guyler noted astutely, 'this may very well develop into a problem of considerable dimensions and is rendered particularly difficult by its close connection with the entire maze of questions relating to sovereignty, citizenship and statelessness in the east of Europe'.[13]

Information coming in from the field was very problematic. As Rebekah Taft, chief of the newly-formed Reports and Statistics Branch of the US Zone, UNRRA, complained, the reports she was getting from the field were all but useless. In spite of having forms to fill out with categories of DPs clearly delineated, the field workers insisted on creating new categories and adding new columns to the reports, resulting in chaotic and inconsistent reporting. Without effective and accurate reporting, she argued, the district headquarters would be unable to be of much service to those in the field, and she pleaded that they 'please report only *true* nationalities'. This was a rather revealing statement, if unhelpful, given that it was very unclear just what *was* a 'true' nationality.[14]

In November, the American military authorities issued a directive entitled 'Determination and Reporting of Nationalities', intended to lay out exactly who was eligible for assistance and who was not. This directive had two objectives: first, to eliminate the rampant confusion in the field; and second, to reduce the cost of the DPs' maintenance, which was mounting astronomically, by removing from the DPs those getting assistance who didn't qualify for it. The preamble to the directive made stark the confusion. It stated bluntly that, based on the evidence provided by weekly reports from assembly centres, as well as other reports, 'considerable confusion exists regarding the definition of nationalities and the assignment of individuals to their appropriate category. In many cases there has been a tendency to identify persons by reference to their religion, to geographical regions, to national sub-division, to ethnological groupings, and to other unrecognized categories, rather than by reference to the political state of which they are citizens or nationals'. The directive's purpose, then, was to provide a comprehensive list of the acceptable categories of DPs.[15]

It began with a long list of those nations considered United Nations, whose nationals were eligible for assistance, followed by a list of Neutral Nations and Ex-Enemy Nations. Then came a set of special categories. First, the Baltic Republics were listed as 'Political Entities', the only ones in that category, reflecting the US government's impasse regarding their status. It had refused to acknowledge the Republics' absorption into the USSR and so would not acknowledge these DPs' purported Soviet citizenship. This allowed the US to refuse the Soviet demands for their forcible repatriation. On the other hand, the United States was also not willing to take action to liberate the Baltic Republics. Later in the directive, the military authorities explained how they were to be dealt with: those who 'affirmatively claimed Soviet citizenship' would be repatriated. Those who 'cannot or do not desire to be repatriated' were to be treated as 'assimilated United Nations displaced persons'. Being categorized as 'Political Entities', the Balts were put in an ambiguous position – not quite a nation, but some other undefined 'thing'. It did, however, make them a recognized, acknowledged category, which had important advantages, primarily in the form of access to aid and to protection from Soviet designs.

This was followed by another section entitled 'Special Categories': Jews who could not or would not repatriate; other persecuted persons of ex-enemy nationality; and the stateless. For the first time in a directive, Jews were given their own, privileged category, privileged in the sense that Jews were the only DPs who were given the right to choose their nationality – either their pre-war citizenship or Jewish nationality. 'Jewish' was now recognized as a nationality category, and this would be reflected in every form sent into the field, either by the military authorities or UNRRA, from this point on.[16] Protection was also effectively enshrined for non-Jewish persecuted persons of ex-enemy nationality, as it ordered that they be counted separately from the other ex-enemy DPs. The stateless were now officially recognized as a category or equivalent of a nationality, defined as all persons other than Jews and ex-enemy persecutees who 'de jure or de facto, have been deprived of the protection of a government'. Only those impossible to classify according to these categories could be classified as 'doubtful'. Finally, the directive explicitly stated that 'Ukrainian' was *not* recognized as a nationality and instead these DPs would be dealt with 'according to determined nationality status as Soviet, nationals of other countries of which they may be citizens, or as stateless persons'.[17]

While the directive enshrined the special status of the Jewish DP population, it did little to resolve the issues surrounding the treatment of the Balts, the Ukrainians, or the stateless. And so the confusion continued. In March 1946, another instruction was issued to field offices, accompanying yet another new form for weekly assembly centre reports, explaining that categories such as Arabs, Mongolians, Gypsies, Kalmycks, South Americans and White Ruthenians were incorrect and unacceptable. Instead, nationalities were to be reported by reference to the country of which they were nationals or citizens, the only exception being Jews.[18] In August 1946, J.H. Whiting, UNRRA director of the US zone, issued yet another instruction, once again trying to clarify how DPs should be classified and emphasizing that it was not permissible to report them only by ethnic groups. If their citizenship was impossible to determine, they were to be reported as 'undetermined'.[19]

The concern about enumerating DPs and their proper categorization arose because the agencies responsible for their care and ultimate disposition needed to determine just how many of the remaining DPs were repatriable and how many were not, as well as to ensure that only those eligible for aid were receiving it. The objective in 1946 still was to encourage them all to return home, although, after the disastrous forced repatriation of Soviet citizens in the summer of 1945, no one was to be forcibly repatriated. That didn't mean, however, that the ultimate goal of liquidation of the camps had changed. After all, these camps were expensive to maintain. Some resolution to the situation had to be found. As few foreign countries were yet ready to take them in any quantity, resettlement was not yet an option (as it was not part of UNRRA's mandate). This left repatriation as the only apparent solution. This required two things, according to those dealing with the DPs: identifying those who were potentially repatriable, and separating them from those who were vehemently opposed to repatriation (and who often worked to actively dissuade people from repatriating), so that efforts to encourage repatriation would have more chance of success. All this meant sorting the DPs and confirming their eligibility.

Two problems made this difficult. The first was a very practical problem, but one which had made the process of identification a serious challenge from the start. Few DPs had any identity papers, so there was little objective evidence to verify their nationality or citizenship. Instead, those doing the registration in the camps and transit centres had to rely on the DPs' testimony. The DPs, of course, had a vested interest in presenting themselves as holding a nationality that would entitle them to aid. For them, it was a matter of figuring out what nationalities were eligible, and as those were refined, it was not uncommon for the DPs to modify their identities. For many others, the declaration of their nationality was also a political statement – a denial of the absorption of their homeland into the USSR, for example, or a declaration of their belief in their nationality's right to be recognized. The registration process itself facilitated and encouraged this in a way that was probably unanticipated, but that validated this perceived right on the part of the DPs to choose their nationality. The DP2 cards used to register the DPs when they first showed up at a camp had a blank for 'claimed nationality'. The word 'claimed' is crucial. It was felt that the registrar was obliged to put down whatever nationality the DP asserted.[20] Finally, since UNRRA's policy was that it did not determine nationality (that was the responsibility of the military authorities[21]), then this was the nationality upon which it had to base its reports. When it was unclear what to do with someone, they were put into 'other and unclassified', which soon became 'doubtful or undetermined'. Inevitably, this was a category that was growing steadily in size, as the confusion grew over how to handle many of the east Europeans.[22]

A second problem that compounded the first was the confusion over what constituted a nationality. Instructions to field operatives issued in the fall of 1945 explicitly equated 'nationality' with 'citizenship', explaining that the use of the term 'national' in UNRRA resolutions is equivalent to the term 'citizen' in American practice. Country of citizenship and nationality were considered synonymous, both referring to a legal claim on a country.[23] The displaced persons generally saw it differently. As one reports officer explained, 'It is my experience that Eastern Europeans customarily distinguish between nationality (in their eyes an ethnic concept, based on cultural factors) and citizenship (corresponding to the concept of nationality, based on legal status following political boundaries).'[24] Nonetheless, at least UNRRA and military policy-makers held fast to the argument that only citizenship was a valid source of national identity, if its practice tended to be less clear-cut. Citizenship, of course, proved very difficult to ascertain, for the reasons mentioned earlier. If a DP refused to reveal their citizenship and the registrar was suspicious of their claimed nationality, the best the registrar could do was put the person in the 'undetermined' or 'doubtful' category (the words were used interchangeably).

Another challenge was that, due to the border changes, a considerable portion of the remaining DPs population either did not know for certain what their citizenship was any longer, or refused to accept the change. The Baltic Republics had remained intact as political entities within the USSR, so there was little confusion about whether someone was from those regions or not. But it was unclear how to classify someone of Ukrainian ethnicity from east of the Curzon Line.[25] Indeed, Ukrainians proved to be a rather intractable problem. This was because of the enormous shift westward of the Soviet border to the Curzon Line in Poland, as a result of the Soviet invasion of eastern Poland in 1939. At the war's end, all the land occupied by the USSR east of the Curzon Line remained in Soviet hands and was recognized as part of the USSR. The question then became this: what was the citizenship or nationality of those DPs who came from east of the Curzon Line? Was a Ukrainian deemed to be Polish based on the national status of the area in which he was born as of mid-1945 or as of 31 August 1939? It did not help that a ruling from the Polish government was not forthcoming until November 1946, leaving it to the individuals filling out the DP cards to guess as to how to classify these people. They generally claimed Ukrainian nationality, to avoid admitting that they were Soviet citizens and so avoid forcible repatriation. This meant that the category of 'Ukrainian' continually showed up on reports, in spite of repeated instructions from on high that 'Ukrainian' was not recognized as a nationality.

When the Polish government finally did give UNRRA a statement on nationality, it flew in the face of UNRRA's position (and the position of the military authorities, which was the same). Poland

and the USSR had seized the moment during the chaos of the immediate post-war period to ethnically cleanse their respective territories, Poland transferring Ukrainians to the Ukrainian SSR, and the USSR shifting Poles – and others – to Poland. Reflecting this, the Polish government made clear in its statement, finally issued in November 1946, that

> persons of Polish citizenship in 1939 but of Ukrainian nationality, formerly domiciled in the territories east of the Curzon Line ceded to the Ukrainian Republic, have lost their Polish citizenship. Those of Polish nationality retain their Polish citizenship ... All persons of Ukrainian nationality acquire Ukrainian citizenship, including those subject to repatriation out of present Polish territory into the Ukraine ... Ukrainians, Byelorussians [*sic*] and Lithuanians at present outside the Polish boundaries ... are not acceptable for repatriation to Poland.[26]

This meant that, if they repatriated, the Polish Ukrainians would be sent to the Ukrainian SSR, not Poland, unlike the Poles from former eastern Poland. The Polish government had made a clear distinction between its citizens, based on ethnic lines. This made things much more difficult for UNRRA and the military authorities, as they now had a definitely unrepatriable population identified by an ethnic identity whose legitimacy they had steadfastly denied, but which had been formally recognized by the Ukrainian DPs' country of citizenship, Poland. It now became urgent to identify the Polish Ukrainians among the DPs, in order to know how many could no longer be considered repatriable. The problem, of course, was that UNRRA had no idea how many Polish Ukrainians it had in its camps, as it had been telling its people continuously not to count them. As a result, the reporting was completely unreliable. It was especially embarrassing because various Ukrainian organizations had been pressing UNRRA to recognize the size of the Ukrainian problem, quoting a figure of 300,000 Ukrainians in Europe but outside the USSR who needed assistance, a number UNRRA was unable either to confirm or refute.[27]

One of the first options for dealing with those who were of an unrecognized claimed nationality such as Ukrainian, Belorussian, Kalmyck, and Mennonite had been to consider them 'stateless'. In international law, at least initially, it was believed this category was very straightforward. This was a group who had lost their nationality as a result of the peace treaties following the First World War and the border shifts that resulted from them; whose governments had passed laws which denationalized them, usually as a consequence of what their governments deemed 'bad conduct'; or whose naturalization was cancelled due to changes in nationality laws. The largest group prior to the war was made up of Russians who had fled the Bolshevik regime and had had their citizenship revoked as a result. None of these people had acquired another nationality. Those deemed 'stateless' were, thus, those who did not enjoy the diplomatic protection of any state: this 'statelessness' arose when the 'state removed itself from the individual'. It is important to note that it was not possible for an individual to unilaterally declare themselves stateless. To address the serious problems created by this situation, the League of Nations had established a special identity and travel document, the Nansen passport, named after Dr Nansen, the League's high commissioner for refugees. It was later extended to other specific groups, but the list was very carefully delimited.

By 1946, this narrow definition of 'stateless' seemed increasingly unworkable. Were Polish Ukrainians who were denied their citizenship as well as the right to return to Poland (whether they wanted to go or not) by the Polish government now rendered stateless? What about those Poles who did not wish to return to Poland? At what point did someone who was non-repatriable become stateless? These questions had important ramifications, not just for counting heads but ultimately for figuring out what to do with these people. It did not help that this category had become the proverbial 'kitchen junk drawer', containing, as the chief of Reports and Statistics Branch complained, 'persons with recognized legal "statelessness", persons with good claims to legal "statelessness", and persons in merely self-declared "stateless" category'. The problem, according to the chief, was that at this time almost any DP in Germany had as much right to claim de facto statelessness as those non-Nansen DPs currently counted as stateless. Failing to distinguish between them would only make their final disposition that much more difficult to determine.[28] 'Undetermined' was as unsatisfactory an alternative, not least because of considerable consternation at the upper levels of UNRRA, even as far up the administrative chain as the Central Committee of the General Council where, by late 1946, there was considerable frustration with this category. It was felt that this long after the war's end, there was no reason for having an 'undetermined nationality'.[29]

So yet again, instructions were issued to officers in the field, slightly changing the categories for reporting purposes. Those whose nationality was undetermined were to be broken down as follows. Those claiming no nationality but clearly of Ukrainian extraction (they spoke Ukrainian rather than Polish; they belonged to the Orthodox, not Catholic Church) and who came from former Polish territory that was now part of the Ukrainian SSR should be shown as Ukrainian (thus undermining the argument that nationality was determined solely by citizenship and enshrining the concept of an ethnic-based national identity). Those with Nansen passports should be listed as stateless. Those claiming to be Nansen passport holders, but having lost their documents, should be classified as 'Claim Nansen status'. All others of undetermined nationality should be classified by their last permanent residence or residence as of 1 January 1938; in most instances, then, by their citizenship.[30]

The obvious question was finally posed to UNRRA's legal counsel: why didn't UNRRA simply stop using the term 'nationality' when what it really meant was 'citizenship'. The answer was what one might have expected from a bureaucrat. All military government and army legal officers, as well as all international bodies using the English language, used the word 'nationality' to mean 'citizenship'. It would 'cause no little inconvenience' if UNRRA began to use terminology all its own, especially since this seemed to be a particular concern only in the US zone. Second, if UNRRA were absorbed into another international organization, something very likely to happen as the end of its mandate drew near (UNRRA was soon to be replaced by the International Refugee Organisation), confusion over terminology would inevitably erupt and complicate matters. Finally, the argument was made that while it was possible to talk about a Kalmyck nationality, for example, from a legal and political point of view, it was not possible to talk about a Kalmyck citizenship. To acknowledge the Kalmycks would imply that UNRRA recognized the existence of a Kalmyck state 'which of course is not only nonsense but grounds for political gripes', in the words of the counsel.[31] This got to the heart of the issue. To acknowledge ethnic identities in the process of counting heads would be to recognize those ethnic identities formally as nations, which might well be construed as support for possible claims to statehood. Thus, the legal counsel insisted that nationality had to be based on citizenship, with the exception of the stateless and the Jews.

It was a strategy doomed to failure, because those in the field refused to abide by the fresh instructions. A close look at the

'Summary of DP Population, District No. 5, as of 28 December 1946' compiled by the Statistics and Reports Branch, UNRRA HQ District No. 5, Munich, suggests as much. The summary, put together by mid-level bureaucrats whose job it was to compile the statistics (and who therefore should have understood the system of categories if anyone did), reflected which 'nationalities' were now deemed acceptable to report. The list had now expanded considerably, to a total of eight-eight categories. It is worth lightly deconstructing the list as a way of getting a sense of how 'nationality' was understood by late 1946. 'Jews' are the very first category listed, broken down by nationality into four subcategories (Polish, Hungarian, German, Other). Evidently this was one category that was well understood. This simplicity held true for the west European nationalities, which were listed straightforwardly. Confusion set in, however, when dealing with Ukrainian, stateless, and undetermined. Unlike the Jews, 'Ukrainian' is scattered throughout the report. We find eleven classifications for Ukrainian spread throughout the list of eighty-eight: Polish Ukrainian; Ukrainian Undeterm; Ukrainian; Russian Ukrainian; Ukrainian Stateless; Ukrainian Czech; Ukrainian Roumanian; Ukrainian French; Ukrainian Yugoslavian; Ukrainian USA; and Ukrainian Iranian. As well, there were four categories of stateless: Stateless; Ukrainian Stateless; Russian Stateless; and Nansen Stateless. Finally, there were four categories of Undetermined: Undetermined; Ukrainian Undetermined; Russian Undetermined and Undetermined Lithuanians.[32] Other categories that were surprising to see, in light of the repeated instructions not to use them, were Kalmuck (*sic*), White Ruthenian, Russian Mennonite, Mongolian, Arabian, Russian Bessarabian, and German Gypsy. The reasons for the lack of compliance were several. The practical problems of identification continued, as had UNRRA's policy that its officers did not make determinations of nationality. This left the UNRRA workers conducting the registration with no choice but to record the nationality that the DPs gave them. Directives to stop burying the problematic DPs in the 'stateless' or 'undetermined' category meant that the ethnic categories had to be used, as citizenship was undeterminable. Furthermore, many UNRRA workers were decidedly sympathetic to the DPs' fears, and so inclined to help them use the system to their advantage.

Without trying to read too much into this particular document, there are several things that can be drawn from this report. First, by late 1946, accounting for the Jewish population and the west

European nationalities had become clear. These identities were either well established and uncontested, or now accepted. The same could not be said about others. White Ruthenian, Mennonite, Arabian, and so on – these were not supposed to show up, but show up they did. The way in which 'Ukrainian' was handled, with eleven different possible categories haphazardly scattered throughout the list, suggests a degree of confusion, no doubt heightened by the sudden about-face by the administration after the Polish government's disavowal of responsibility for those Ukrainians of pre-war Polish nationality from areas now annexed to the USSR. However, the fact that the report's compiler could create categories such as 'Undetermined Lithuanian' and 'Russian Undetermined', when 'undetermined' was supposed to indicate that an individual's nationality was impossible to determine, suggests that confusion was rampant.

At the heart of this confusion was the clash between the definition of nationality as something based on citizenship, insisted upon by the upper levels of administration at UNRRA and the military authorities (who provided direction to UNRRA), and a definition of nationality based on ethnic identity used by the DP population. As so astutely pointed out by Liah Greenfeld, by the late nineteenth century there existed two types of nationalism – one for which the basis of membership was 'civic' – that is, identical with citizenship – and one that was 'ethnic', based on a set of attributes or commonalities from which was constructed a particular ethnic identity.[33] The tension between the two was never resolved. The searing experiences of the chaotic post-First World War period, when new nations were carved out of the European landscape wholesale, as well as the vicious racism of the Nazis, reinforced a deep ethnic self-awareness among the various national populations of Europe, especially among east Europeans. This sense of ethnicity was carried forward into the immediate post-war period and informed the way in which they identified themselves. They had thoroughly absorbed the language of ethnicity and national identity and mobilized it in an effective and surprisingly sophisticated manner. The failure of the various international agencies to understand this language or to recognize that the DPs identified themselves in those terms, meant that they were completely unprepared for the caustic reaction that erupted when they denied the conventionally pre-determined identities.

It appears, then, that the concept of 'nationality' was very much in a state of flux in the late 1940s. The immediate post-war period was a time of tremendous fluidity in many ways. At the risk of overstating the case, the Second World War had caused a fundamental rupture with the pre-war era on many levels. The notion of national identity was one such rupture. With the enshrinement of the Wilsonian concept of national self-determination in the post-First World War peace treaties, a Pandora's box had been opened. The Second World War and its immediate aftermath saw the mobilization of national identity and national self-determination for a variety of purposes and political motives that had little to do with the more abstract intellectual debate over what constituted a nationality, but was happy to borrow from it. We see in the debate over what constituted a nationality, and which nationalities would be recognized, a clash between the legalistic definition of nationality in terms of citizenship and the more abstract – but in the end much more powerful – definition of nationality as something broader, determined by ethnic and cultural boundaries. At this time of great uncertainty, groups fought to take advantage of this post-war caesura to carve out for themselves a new identity and a new space in the post-war world and, in so doing, establish the legitimacy of their claimed nationality. In the rather banal exercise of counting heads, and in the arguments over what categories would be used, the bean-counters made these battles real. As both UNRRA and the military authorities recognized, in the decision whether to grant the various groups the status of a column-heading on their field reports, they were effectively deciding on their legitimacy as a nationality. In the mundane task of counting heads, then, we see nationalities being created, confirmed, and denied.

By early 1947, the question of the DPs' nationalities had become increasingly less important, as it was clear that the remaining DP population was not repatriable. As attention shifted to resettlement, the resettlement missions that came from across the western world to tour the DPs camps were less interested in the nationality of the DPs than in their age, marital status, state of health, and vocational training. These missions were largely looking for workers and it was the DPs' brawn and skills that were important, not their national identity. Yet, the nationality issue did not go away. While the Cold War may have driven the question underground, with its end these same tensions re-emerged with a vengeance, as nascent national identities picked up again the fight for recognition and legitimacy.

REFERENCES

Archives

United Nations Archives, Record Group PAG (United Nations Archives Record Group) 4 (S-0425 and S-0412).

National Archives and Records Administration (NARA), Washington, DC, Records Groups 331 and 260.

Published Sources

Dinnerstein, Leonard, *American and the Survivors of the Holocaust* (New York: Columbia University Press, 1982).

Greenfeld, Liah, *Nationalism: Five Roads to Modernity* (Cambridge, MA: Harvard University Press, 1993).

Grossman, Atina, *Jews, Germans, and Allies: Close Encounters in Occupied Germany* (Princeton, NJ: Princeton University Press, 2007).

Königseder, Angelika and Wetzel, Juliane, *Waiting for Hope: Jewish Displaced Persons in Post-World War II Germany* (Evanston, IL: Northwestern University Press, 2001).

NOTES

1. UNRRA PAG 4/1.0.1.0.0:32 no.3 Displaced Persons 1945–1946, 'Statement on Displaced Persons: Displaced Persons with whom UNRRA is at present Authorized to Deal', Standing Technical Committee on Displaced Persons, UNRRA, 6 April 1945; National Archives and Records Administration (NARA) RG 331 Supreme Headquarters Allied Expeditionary Forces (SHAEF), Office of the Chief of Staff, Secretary, General Staff, Decimal File May 1943 – Aug 1945, Entry 1, box 88, '383.7 vol. 1' (Refugees and Displaced Persons of European nationality, memo, T.J. Davis, Brigadier General, SHAEF to 'all concerned', 18 December 1944.
2. NARA RG 260 Civil Administration Division, PW&DP Branch, Records Relating to DPs in Germany and Other Countries, 1945–49, box 140, 'Headquarters US Group CC – Policy Book – PoW&DP Division', cable from SHAEF Main, signed SCAEF to C in C 21 Army Group; CG 12 Army Group; CG 6 Army Group; CG Com Zone, ref no. S-87880, paraphrased, dated 22 May 1945.
3. NARA RG 331 General Staff, G-1 Division, Administrative Section, Decimal Correspondence File, 1944–45, Entry 6, box 28, '383.6/8 Russian Prisoners of War, General', cable WX-63626, from AGWAR from the Joint Chiefs of Staff to SHAEF Main to Eisenhower, dated 5 April 1945.
4. NARA RG 260 Office of the Adjutant General, General correspondence & other records, 1945–49, 390/40/21/2 box 92 file AG 383.7 Displaced Persons. Vol. 1. Omg 1945–46, Administrative Memorandum No. 39, issued by SHAEF, dated 16 April 1945 (revised).
5. As cited in L. Dinnerstein, *America and the Survivors of the Holocaust* (New York: Columbia University Press, 1982), p.13.
6. NARA RG 331 General Staff, G-5 Division, Secretariat, Numeric File August 1943 – July 1945, Entry 47, box 54, 'Displaced Persons Branch. SHAEF/G-5/2814. DPs Welfare–Children', letter, PM Malin, Vice-Director, Intergovernmental Committee on Refugees (IGCR), SHAEF to chief, DP Branch, and Executive, DP Branch, 12 June 1945.
7. A. Grossman, *Jews, Germans, and Allies: Close Encounters in Occupied Germany* (Princeton NJ: Princeton University Press, 2007), p.138; A. Königseder and J. Wetzel, *Waiting for Hope: Jewish Displaced Persons in Post-World War II Germany* (Evanston, IL: Northwestern University Press, 2001), pp.18–19.
8. Report submitted by Earl G. Harrison to President Truman, 22 August 1945: can be found online at http://www.ushmm.org/museum/exhibit/online/dp/resourc1.htm (22 May 2008).
9. NARA RG 260 OMGUS, Civil Administration Division, PW&DP Branch, Records Relating to DPs in Germany and Other Countries, 1945–49, box 140, 'Headquarters US Group CC – Policy Book – PoW&DP Division', minutes of second meeting of the Deputy Military Governor with Army Commanders, held 25 July 1945, dated 26 July 1945.

10. NARA RG 260 Civil Administration Division, PW&DP Branch, Records Relating to DPs in Germany and Other Countries, 1945–49, box 165 '383.7 Stateless Persons', letter, from H.H .Newman, Col AGD, Acting Adjutant General, to Commanding Generals: Eastern and Western Military Districts, dated 22 August 1945.
11. PAG 4/1.0.1.0.0:32 File no. 3 Displaced Persons 1945–1946, 'Statement on Displaced Persons: Displaced Persons with whom UNRRA is at present Authorized to Deal', Standing Technical Committee on Displaced Persons, UNRRA, 6 April 1945.
12. PAG 4/1.0.1.0.0:32 File no. 3 Displaced Persons 1945–1946, memorandum, 'The Scope and Application of Resolutions No. 57 and 60', Wm. G. Rice to A.H. Feller, 14 June 1945; file no. 2 Displaced Persons November 1944 – January 1945, 'Directives of Displaced Persons Operations,' United Nations Relief Administration – European Regional Office, first issued October 1945; PAG 4/1.3.1.1.0:12 P300.12 'A Study on "Stateless Persons"', 21 February 1945.
13. UNRRA S-0425-0002, Administrative – Correspondence – Divisions in Zone Headquarters, memo, Director, US Zone, UNRRA to Deputy Director i/c German Operations, UNRRA, 12 October 1945.
14. UNRRA S-0425-0050, Statistics – Statistics and Reports 1/5, memo, Rebekah L. Taft to Mr Whiting, 30 October 1945.
15. RG 260 1945-49 Box 91 'AG 383.7 Displaced Persons (Refugees, Expellees, Internees)' 2 of 2, 'Determination and Reporting of Nationalities', directive issued by Headquarters, US Forces, European Theater OMGUS, 16 November 1945.
16. UNRRA S-0425-0002 Administrative – Correspondence – Divisions in Zone Headquarters, letter, Rebekah L. Taft for J.H. Whiting, Zone Director, US Zone, UNRRA to Alex Squadrilli, Wiesbaden District Office, 9 January 1946.
17. NARA RG 260 1945–49 Box 91 'AG 383.7 Displaced Persons (Refugees, Expellees, Internees)' 2 of 2, 'Determination and Reporting of Nationalities', directive issued by Headquarters, US Forces, European Theater OMGUS, 16 November 1945.
18. UNRRA S-0425-0001 Administrative – Administrative Orders – Instructions – Reports and Statistics Division, Administrative Order No. 23, 'Weekly Population Report', by J.H. Whiting, Zone Director, US Zone UNRRA, 11 March 1946.
19. UNRRA S-0425-0001 Administrative – Administrative Orders – Instructions – Reports and Statistics Division, Administrative Order No. 127, 'Weekly Population Report Forms', issued by J.H. Whiting, Zone Director, US Zone, UNRRA, 7 August 1946.
20. PAG 4/1.0.1.0.0:32 DP File No. 4 1946–1947, interoffice memo, R.J. Youdin to A.H. Robertson, 16 July 1946.
21. UNRRA PAG 4/3.0.11.0.0:5 013.0/A Displaced Persons – Instructions to the Field on Eligibility for UNRRA Assistance, Administrative Order No. 29, UNRRA German Operations, 4 March 1946.
22. UNRRA PAG 4/1.0.1.0.0:32 DP File No. 4 1946–1947, interoffice memo, R.J. Youdin to A.H. Robertson, 16 July 1946.
23. UNRRA S-0412-0012, European Regional Office – Instructions from ERO on Reports – Supplement No. 3 to ERO Administrative Order No. A-120, 'Instructions to Chiefs of Missions for Reporting to ERO (Additional Information on Displaced Persons Operations in Germany and Austria) on UNRRA Forms MSR-2 and MSR-3'.
24. UNRRA S-0425-0004, Administrative – Reporting Procedures (15), memo, E.S. Seldon, Reports Officer, for District Director to Chief, Reports and Statistics Branch, UNRRA, US Zone HQ, 8 June 1946.
25. The Curzon Line was the border between Poland and the Soviet Union proposed in December 1919 by the British foreign secretary, George Curzon, in an attempt to settle a border dispute between the two countries. It reflected, roughly, the ethnic frontiers. The 1920 border was ultimately established elsewhere under the Treaty of Riga. However, the Curzon Line was used in subsequent renegotiations of the border.
26. UNRRA PAG 4/3.0.11.0.0:6 013.1/C Displaced Persons – Ukrainians, memo, Paul N. Carter, Legal Adviser, Office of the Legal Adviser to Acting Chief of Operations, UNRRA Germany, 10 December 1946.
27. UNRRA PAG 4/1.0.1.0.0:33 DPs – Legal and Policy Decisions 1946 #2, cable 1989 London to Warsaw, originated by Repatriation Division, Mr Linney, 20 November 1946.
28. S-0425-0040 Reports Branch, Including Administrative Files, Monthly Reports and Special Reports – US Zone Headquarters Inter-Office, memo, E.S. Seldon, Chief,

Reports and Statistics Branch, UNRRA US HQ, Germany to Deputy Zone Director, Department of Field Operations, 11 April 1947.

29. UNRRA – Central Committee of the Council, memo CC (46) 113, Director General to the Central Committee, 25 October 1946; PAG 4/1.0.1.0.0:33 Displaced Persons – Legal and Policy Decisions 1946, cable 16047, Washington to London, 25 October 1946; PAG 4/1.0.1.0.0:36 Displaced Persons – undetermined nationality – DPs of, memo, A.E. Davidson to C.T. Lloyd, 21 October 1946.
30. S-0412-0012 European Regional Office – Instructions from ERO on Reports, cable London to Arolsen 491, Vienna 255, repeated to Washington Savingram 2628, 7 December 1946.
31. UNRRA S-0425-0019, Legal Matters – Eligibility, carrier sheet, Legal Department to R.W. Collins, 9 December 1946.
32. UNRRA S-0425-0050 Statistics – Special Surveys – Statistical Reports Prepared by Statistics and Reports Branch – US Zone HQ, Summary of DP Population, District No. 5 as of 28 December 1946, Statistics and Reports Branch, UNRRA HQ, District No. 5, 28 December 1946.
33. L. Greenfeld, *Nationalism: Five Roads to Modernity* (Cambridge, MA: Harvard University Press, 1993), pp.11–13.

3

From Illustrations to Sources: A Survey of Photographs of and about Displaced Persons

STEFAN SCHRÖDER

Photographs depicting the Holocaust or concentration camps right after liberation are known worldwide. Due to their ample distribution – at least in western societies – it is nearly impossible not to have seen some of them.[1] The photographs that document Displaced Persons (DP)[2] and the DP camps in the post-war years are a completely different case. Although such photographs have been shown more recently – for example in museums and memorials such as the United States Holocaust Memorial Museum (USHMM)[3] or in small exhibitions on DPs,[4] and especially on the Internet[5] – photographs illustrating the history of DPs and DP camps had no publicity for decades. With few exceptions, it was only in 1995, on the fiftieth anniversary of the end of the Second World War, that in some publications and exhibitions photographs on DPs became visible again or, in some cases, for the first time. It is only speculation, but there might be a certain correlation between the long-forgotten experience of the DPs and the absence of relevant visual media. This survey of photographs showing the DPs' lives in Germany is intended as a preliminary exploration of a vast subject which has been neglected until now.

In recent years, historical research has turned a lot of its attention to visual sources, and among them also to photographs. This process is fundamentally changing the role of images, because they are no longer seen exclusively as illustrations in books, exhibitions and museums.[6] I want to apply this new methodology to DP photography. First, I will demonstrate by whom and under which circumstances these photos came into being. I will continue with a survey of where these pictures are kept today and show their use as illustrations in historical publications. I will then conclude by suggesting future opportunities and some implications of these possibilities.

FROM 1945 TO THE 1950S: PHOTOGRAPHS ABOUT DPs AND PHOTOGRAPHS OF DPs

The first photos of DPs in Germany were taken during their liberation in the spring of 1945 by allied soldiers. Special units had been established for documenting the Allied war effort. It was the task of the US Signal Corps and the British Army Film and Photographic Unit (AFPU). The Canadian Army made photographs as well.[7] In the course of their work, these soldiers armed with cameras shot hundreds of thousands of pictures.[8] The chief motifs in images shot by the US Signal Corps were: relief activities by US Army detachments, DPs preparing their repatriation in their camps, documentary photographs showing liberated forced labourers, and the scars resulting from mistreatment or bad conditions while they were working for the Germans, but also street scenes with DPs and Germans engaged in plundering. The US National Archives and Records Administration (NARA) is unable to make an estimate of the number of photographs referring to DPs,[9] but given the millions of DPs liberated in 1945, these photos must amount to thousands at least. Creators of these pictures were, on the one hand, soldiers who had to work as photographers, and, on the other hand, professional photographers recruited for the relevant army units. Therefore, these images might originate from professional, semi-professional or even amateur photographers.[10] This situation was the same with British and Canadian troops.[11] Furthermore, photojournalists had been accredited as reporters from the diverse theatres of war with the purpose of taking pictures for newspapers and illustrated magazines such as *LIFE* or *Picture Post*.[12]

To some extent, these journals also obtained material from army photographers[13] and from the United Nations Relief and Rehabilitation Administration (UNRRA). UNRRA had its Public Information Division, which charged photographers to take pictures explicitly of UNRRA relief and welfare work. The intention was to assist the press and to give public information. Especially with regard to the DPs, the press was very critical of the organization's administration, as

George Woodbridge, chief historian to UNRRA, judged in 1950.[14] This may indicate that UNRRA photographs had a hidden intention: even if they were not taken for PR reasons, a bad press was not intended either. This probably influenced the decision about what was to be shown in the photos that were handed to the press, while certain images were ignored when they did not seem to fit the UNRRA information guidelines. We could add the question: which – of all the photos taken – found their way from the photographers through UNRRA's Visual Information Office to the press and public. This question sheds light on the choice of images and censorship by UNRRA. One example of this selectivity is the only photograph from Greven DP camp (No. UNRRA/1598) included in the UNRRA photographs from Germany (now series S-1058) held by the UN Archives in 1997. It shows an UNRRA team director watching two DP children taking a meal.[15] When researching for this article, I found out that the Imperial War Museum (IWM) held the same image (together with others) and that it was taken by UNRRA's photographer Norman Weaver (1913–89).[16] On her website, www.normanweaver.com, Weaver's daughter also presents other images from Greven that were not included in the UNRRA photo collection of the UN Archives. This is not only an example of a censored output, but also shows the importance of documentation in the archives, because in October 2008 the UN Archives still did not know who took the picture.[17]

Besides the army photographers, UNRRA photographers and photojournalists who produced the majority of official pictures of the DPs, soldiers and relief workers also took photographs probably showing a completely different part of the DPs' everyday lives.[18] In exceptional cases, German amateur and professional photographers took pictures of DPs, too.[19] Eventually the DPs themselves began photographing and collecting photos. It is one characteristic of privately owned DP photographs that it is often impossible to know who owned the camera and who shot these pictures. Infrequently, stamps on the photos' reverse side hint at DPs who had a photographic business in the camps.[20] It is no surprise that many images in these private photographs show a family context. Aside from this, these pictures also show the highlights of camp life, such as religious or political festive days and sporting events.[21] Motifs like these are sometimes also to be found in DP camp newspapers. Unusually, the professional photographer Karl Hintzer, an Estonian DP, produced more than 9,000 negatives which show scenes of everyday life in various Estonian DP camps. They document the reality of the camps: for example, by photographing food rations per person/per day. Hintzer earned his living partly by selling his pictures.[22]

In 1945 official photographs seem to predominate, but the majority of photos showing DPs made in the following years are of a private character and present a contrast to the official motifs. Many of these images seem to show the self-perception of the DPs: for instance, when posing for a family photo is used to express normality despite the camp life[23] or, in contrast, to document a depressing camp reality.[24] In any case, the statement about the DPs we read in these photographs – whether official or private ones – is dependent on the context of their production and diffusion, as far it is known to us. But it is not an easy task to reconstruct the context of a photograph, least of all with DP photos.

THE WHEREABOUTS OF DP PHOTOS

A systematic search for these photographs is connected with the nature of the images themselves: photos of the liberation are to be found in archival series of the Allied armies, which means in the national archives and related institutions of the countries involved. The organizational work of a British Army team in a Hamburg DP camp in 1945, for example, is in the custody of the IWM,[25] where the majority of the official British photographic production in question is to be found. Welfare work is portrayed by UNRRA images that are kept in the UN Archives,[26] while the archives of other welfare organizations possibly keep similar photographic material.[27] Depictions of everyday DP life are found in the private photography of welfare workers and Allied soldiers, while this aspect from the DPs' point of view is kept in their family photo collections and albums.

Publicly accessible today, and in some cases already searchable on the Internet, are the photographs held by NARA, the IWM, the USHMM and the National Archives of Canada (now Library and Archives Canada).[28] By now also accessible online are photo collections of individual photographers (such as the Estonian Karl Hintzer, kept by the Herder-Institut in Marburg, Germany)[29] or collections documenting particular nationalities (such as the Latvian online project *DP albums*).[30] Since November 2008, Google started to bring the photographic archive of the magazine *LIFE* to the

Internet, thus also showing how *LIFE* photojournalists wanted to make the DPs visible to their readers. With ten million photos or 20 per cent of the whole collection online, I found about 200 hits for the term 'displaced'.[31] This might be a good starting point for research on photojournalistic features of the subject.

Nevertheless, despite these publicly accessible collections, the biggest proportion of existing photographs are almost certainly still in the private possession of former DPs and their descendants. The quantity in question could amount to hundreds of thousands of photographs. This is a very rough estimate and the result of a non-representative query I made in the autumn of 2008 by sending emails to 110 DPs or their descendants, whose families live in western countries today.[32] With about 700,000 DP resettlers from 1947 to 1951 (of whom half a million went to the USA, Australia and Canada)[33] just a small number of private photos per DP adds up to an enormous quantity. I should add that DPs repatriated to western Europe,[34] Poland and the USSR, too, were in possession of photographs.[35] These examples comprise images of the repatriation by train, school classes, leisure activities or family groups. So my conclusion is that worldwide there are still many more photographs of DPs or DP camps in private possession than the total of those held by public institutions. The pictures used until now in magazines, books or on the Internet mostly come from institutions, only because of easier access.[36]

PHOTOGRAPHS ABOUT DPs AS ILLUSTRATIONS

Since the war, how have historians and the public gained a visual impression of the DP experience? Generally, historical research is based on written texts. In the 1970s and 1980s photographs were rarely printed in reference books. By contrast, photos were printed regularly in popular history books. Therefore it is no wonder that in the 1970s, it was in photographic documentations of the end of the Second World War that DPs first appeared in visual form, but marginally, as the DPs had not yet become the focus of contemporary history.[37] Since the mid-1970s, some reference books have included relevant photographs, for example Earl F. Ziemke's work, *The US Army in the Occupation of Germany*. It contains at least five photographs of DPs (from a total of seventy-five photographs, taken by US Army detachments).[38] This might not be representative, but it hints at future developments. Wolfgang Jacobmeyer's standard work on DPs, published in 1985, does not contain any photographs; it was addressed to scholars.[39] Soon after, DPs as participants in the regional history of Westphalia in 1945 show up in photographs in textbooks published in 1985 and 1986,[40] and also in 1988 in Martin Caiger-Smith's photographic history, *The Face of the Enemy*, edited in a German and an English version.[41] The use of captions in Caiger-Smith's book shows the author's interest in and sensitivity to photo history, although he was primarily concerned with the history of art, and not DPs or post-war history.[42]

Since the end of the 1980s, a wave of publications exclusively about DPs and illustrated with photographs has appeared. This development reflects a greater interest amongst the public, including the former DPs and their descendents. In 1989 Mark Wyman's book on *Europe's Displaced Persons* contained twenty-five photographs, fourteen of them of UNRRA origin, and in 1990 Ulrich Müller published his study on DPs in Stuttgart (containing twenty-five photographs of DPs and DP camps), aimed at a regional audience.[43] It is typical of works published in the last twenty years on this subject that these books contain descriptions of the photographs and copyright information, but no context information about the photographers or original captions. Wyman, for instance, does not inform the reader about the purpose of the UNRRA photos he uses.[44] I would now like to discuss some exceptions to this tendency.

When Patrick Wagner's book on DPs in Hamburg was published in 1997, it contained an annotated series of forty-two photographs taken in June 1945 by British Army photographers in the 'Zoo' DP camp.[45] This series originated from the Imperial War Museum's photo archive. Even though the original captions of these photographs have been omitted in the interpretation, because Wagner classified them as 'meagre' or 'laconical', these pictures show – in an idealized way – how British soldiers carried out their relief work between the reception of DPs in the camp and their repatriation. Despite the chapter's innovative character, important information is lacking, for example on the photographers and their background, or which of the pictures seem to be posed. A comparison with similar photographic series from other DP camps might have given deeper insights into photographs as sources. But these photographs were still primarily used as illustrations for the situation in Hamburg, and only secondarily as important sources in their own right.

I would like to give two more examples of books constructed

around photograph collections. In both publications the provenance of the photo albums and the identities of the photographers are given, but even so there are limitations. The photo album from Bergen-Belsen was published in 2004 and it contains only a fraction of the original 1,117 photographs. The full album was much too big for a complete edition in print. Moreover, the photos were sorted thematically, so that the original context of the album is lost in the publication. The book on the photo album from Zeilsheim DP camp, published in 1995, also uses topical chapters, but in this case the whole album, consisting of fifty-two pages, was reprinted in reduced scale so that the readers may read the original captions and see the composition of the photos.[46]

I must admit that it is nearly impossible to cover all the diverse aspects of photographs in using them as historical sources in a publication in printed form. The examples I have chosen did not pave the way to the kind of visual history that has been proposed in recent years. In these books, photographs are used as illustrations, and although sometimes the authors go one step beyond and add some commentary or interpretation it is always mainly to arouse interest in the reader about the history of the DPs.

FROM ILLUSTRATIONS TO A VISUAL HISTORY

With the cultural turn in historiography, photographs have attained more interest as sources, and are regarded as more than mere illustrations. While in Germany it is only in the last few years that research into contemporary history has shown interest in photographic sources, in the Anglo-American context of cultural studies the field of visual culture is well-established.[47] Many theories, often multidisciplinary, offer ways of reading photographs but those doing contemporary history seem to be late in joining this development.

I would like to end by considering a few possibilities that are already practicable. A study of the perception of published photographs, similar to the study of Holocaust pictures by Barbie Zelizer,[48] could possibly also be made in respect of DP photos. Yet, as I have shown, most of these photos have not been published. So alternatively, it might also be fruitful to compare the images produced by known individual photographers to those not chosen for publication. There are at least two UNRRA photographers, Norman Weaver and Maxine Rude,[49] whose pictures seem to be suitable for such a comparison because they have survived in different contexts: in the official selection of UNRRA photographs and also in private collections or in the care of other institutions.[50] A history of perception might also be used especially in relation to pictures held by former DPs and their families. In this case the role these photos played in the family narratives about the DP era – possibly in the creation of identity – would be worth investigating. What role do these images have for the younger generations, who sometimes did not get much or any information from their parents on their fate during the war and post-war period? It might also be interesting to compare the photographs made by Allied soldiers, welfare workers, photojournalists and DPs in reference to the same DP camp.

Research on the photographic history of DPs is confronted with the difficulty of finding the vast numbers of as yet uncollected and undocumented photographs in private hands. However, the accessibility of the photographic collections kept by public institutions worldwide is improving, above all by using database and website technology. The Imperial War Museum's website, www. iwm.org.uk, is one example. Photographs in the online collection come with catalogue number, item name, production date, maker, object type, format description, description of the image and further information.[51] It is obvious that not only the image but also basic context information is important, and while we still have to see the original photo in paper form for reliable research, with photo collections including adequate context information online, wherever we are sitting we can now judge if a journey to the IWM might be worthwhile.

On the Internet there are also collections of private photographs of DPs. Unfortunately, their use for historical research is limited for several reasons. One paradigm of such a private initiative is the website www.dpcamps.org, where DPs and their families post their questions and share information. Despite the interesting photos presented there, the lack of sufficient context information hinders their use for serious research. Another privately initiated project – for Latvian DP photos – is www.dpalbums.lv, with 4,090 images by 27 January 2009. Browsing for different aspects – single camps or topical selections – is possible, but knowledge of the Latvian language is necessary for using the context information properly. For scientific research the information given is not enough to make it possible to avoid contacting the holders of the original photographs, so the advantages of online collections are reduced or even nullified.

If DP photos are simply collected, not much more can be done with them, other than using them as illustrations. So compiling sufficient and adequate context information is necessary, but this is a very laborious task that has to be done by archives and similar institutions at the moment of acquiring photo collections. Later on, this might no longer be possible, as information that goes beyond the material form – such as the size of the photograph or motif – often is not there, but has to be obtained from those people who hand their photos over. Oral history interviews may be necessary to reconstruct details such as the photographer's name and the circumstances of the photo production, provenance and reception. Especially with photo collections of former DPs, even stories connected with single images might be fruitful for research by telling us something about how the DP families dealt – and still deal – with this past.

As I have argued, the majority of surviving DP photos are in private hands, scattered worldwide. Up to now, we have seen only the tip of an enormous iceberg. A virtual collection of DP photos to a high academic standard on the Internet might be an answer to this problem, provided that adequate attention is given to the collection of context information. I have concluded that there are so many difficulties connected with DP photos that, on the one hand, there might be other subjects easier to handle for writing visual histories, while, on the other, the images of DPs are there and we already use them. So it might be advisable from this point onwards to do it more carefully and more thoughtfully.

REFERENCES

Bachmann-Medick, Doris, *Cultural Turns: Neuorientierungen in den Kulturwissenschaften* (Reinbek bei Hamburg: Rowohlt, 2006).

Caiger-Smith, Martin, *Bilder vom Feind: Englische Pressefotografen im Nachkriegsdeutschland* (Berlin: Verlag Dirk Nishen, 1988).

Caiger-Smith, Martin, *The Face of the Enemy: British Photographers in Germany 1944–1952* (London: Nishen, 1988).

Danys, Milda, *DP: Lithuanian Immigration to Canada after the Second World War* (Toronto: Multicultural History Society of Ontario, 1986).

Dinnerstein, Leonard, *America and the Survivors of the Holocaust* (New York: Columbia University Press, 1982).

Giere, Jaqueline and Salamander, Rachel (eds), *Ein Leben aufs Neu: Das Robinson-Album. DP-Lager: Juden auf deutschem Boden 1945–1948* (Wien: Brandstätter, 1995).

Goeze, Dorothee M., 'Alltag estnischer DPs in Deutschland: Die Sammlung Hintzer im Herder-Institut Marburg', in Christian and Marianne Pletzing (eds), *Displaced Persons:*

Flüchtlinge aus den baltischen Staaten in Deutschland (München: Martin Meidenbauer, 2007), pp.29–61.

Jacobmeyer, Wolfgang, *Vom Zwangsarbeiter zum Heimatlosen Ausländer: Die Displaced Persons in Westdeutschland 1945–1951* (Göttingen: Vandenhoeck & Ruprecht, 1985).

Lembeck, Andreas, *Befreit, aber nicht in Freiheit: Displaced Persons im Emsland 1945–1950* (Bremen: Edition Temmen, 1997).

Lütkemöller, Bernhard, 'Drei "schwarze Tage" im Frühjahr 1945: Schicksalsschwer für Oelder Bevölkerung', in Kreisheimatverein Beckum-Warendorf (ed.), *Heimatkalender des Kreises Warendorf 1995* (Warendorf: Darpe, 1995), pp.68–72.

McNeill, Margaret, *By the Rivers of Babylon: A Story of Relief Work among the Displaced Persons of Europe* (London: Bannisdale Press, 1950).

McNeill, Margaret, *An den Wassern von Babylon: Erfahrungen mit Displaced Persons in Goslar zwischen 1945 und 1948* (Bielefeld: Verlag für Regionalgeschichte, 1995).

Müller, Helmut, *Fünf vor null: Die Besetzung des Münsterlandes 1945*, new and revised edn (Münster: Aschendorff, 2005; 1st edn 1971).

Müller, Ulrich, *Fremde in der Nachkriegszeit: displaced persons – zwangsverschleppte Personen – in Stuttgart und Württemberg-Baden 1945–1951* (Stuttgart: Klett-Cotta, 1990).

Muncke, Thomas, *Nachkriegsjahre im Kreis Steinfurt* (Steinfurt: Kreis Steinfurt, 1986).

Paul, Gerhard, *Bilder des Krieges – Krieg der Bilder: Die Visualisierung des modernen Krieges* (Paderborn: Schöningh, 2004).

Paul, Gerhard (ed.), *Visual History: Ein Studienbuch* (Göttingen: Vandenhoeck & Ruprecht, 2006).

Schröder, Stefan, 'Das Schicksal der Displaced Persons in Warendorf nach 1945', in Paul Leidinger (ed.), *Geschichte der Stadt Warendorf*, vol. 2 (Münster: Ardey, 2000), pp.307–12.

Schröder, Stefan, *Displaced Persons im Landkreis und in der Stadt Münster 1945–1951* (Münster: Aschendorff, 2005).

Schröder, Stefan 'Zwangsarbeiter und Displaced Persons in fotografischer Überlieferung', *Westfälische Forschungen*, 58 (2008), pp. 471–87.

Schulze, Rainer and Wiedemann, Wilfried (eds), *AugenZeugen: Fotos, Filme und Zeitzeugenberichte in der neuen Dauerausstellung der Gedenkstätte Bergen-Belsen: Hintergrund und Kontext* (Celle: Stiftung Niedersächsische Gedenkstätten, 2007).

Schwarze, Gisela, *Gefangen in Münster: Kriegsgefanene – Zwangsarbeiter – Zwangsarbeiterinnen 1939 bis 1945* (Essen: Klartext, 1999).

Somers, Erik and Kok, René (eds), *Jewish Displaced Persons in Camp Bergen-Belsen 1945–1950: The Unique Photo Album of Zippy Orlin* (Seattle, WA: University of Washington Press, 2004).

Sturken, Marita and Cartwright, Lisa, *Practices of Looking: An Introduction to Visual Culture* (New York: Oxford University Press, 2001).

't Hoen, Henk, *Zwei Jahre Volkswagenwerk: Als niederländischer Student im 'Arbeitseinsatz' im Volkswagenwerk von Mai 1943 bis zum Mai 1945* (Wolfsburg: Volkswagen AG, Unternehmensarchiv, 2002).

Trees, Wolfgang et al., *Stunde Null in Deutschland: Die westlichen Besatzungszonen 1945–1948: Ein Bild/Text-Band* (Bindlach: Gondrom, 1989), originally edited in three vols with differing titles (Droste-Verlag: Düsseldorf, 1978–1980).

Wagner, Patrick, *Displaced Persons in Hamburg: Stationen einer halbherzigen Integration 1945 bis 1958* (Hamburg: Dölling und Galitz, 1997).

Wiethege, Dieter, *Und als der Krieg zu Ende schien ... Krieg, Überrollung und Ausländerlager in Voerde, 1939–1948* (Meinerzhagen: MD&V, 1985).

Woodbridge, George, *UNRRA: The History of the United Nations Relief and Rehabilitation Administration*, 3 vols (New York: Columbia University Press, 1950).

Wyman, Mark, *DPs: Europe's Displaced Persons, 1945–1951* (Philadelphia, PA: Associated University Presses, 1989).

Zelizer, Barbie, *Remembering to Forget: Holocaust Memory through the Camera's Eye* (Chicago and London: Chicago University Press, 1998).

Zelizer, Barbie (ed.), *Visual Culture and the Holocaust* (New Brunswick, NJ: Rutgers University Press, 2001).

Zelizer, Barbie, 'Gender and Atrocity: Women in Holocaust Photography', in Barbie Zelizer, (ed.), *Visual Culture and the Holocaust* (New Brunswick, NJ: Rutgers University Press, 2001), pp.247–71.

Ziemke, Earl F., *The US Army in the Occupation of Germany, 1944–1946* (Washington, DC: Center of Military History, United States Army, 1975).

NOTES

1. See B. Zelizer, *Remembering to Forget: Holocaust Memory through the Camera's Eye* (Chicago and London: Chicago University Press, 1998); B. Zelizer (ed.), *Visual Culture and the Holocaust* (New Brunswick, NJ: Rutgers University Press, 2001).
2. The term 'Displaced Person' is used in its legal connotation. Therefore it does not exclusively comprise survivors of the Holocaust. At this stage of scarce research on DP photography, a further distinction of subgroups – such as Jewish DPs, national groups, survivors, refugees or even perpetrators – and their specific relation to photography might lack distinct clarity.
3. The exhibition *Life Reborn: Jewish Displaced Persons 1945–1951* was shown in the USHMM between December 1999 and May 2000: see http://www.ushmm.org/museum/exhibit/online/dp/eventstxt.htm (accessed 26 November 2008).
4. Examples: *Ein Leben aufs Neu* (a touring exhibition created in 1995 by the Fritz-Bauer-Institut, Frankfurt am Main, Germany), http://www.fritz-bauerinstitut.de/ausstellungen.htm#Ein%20Leben%20aufs%20neu (accessed 20 January 2009); the exhibition *Rebirth after the Holocaust: The Bergen-Belsen Displaced Persons Camp, 1945–1950* was shown in the B'nai B'rith Klutznick Jewish National Museum, Washington, DC, from January to September 2000, http://www.ushmm.org/museum/exhibit/online/dp/events.htm (accessed 20 January 2009), and toured the US, e.g. New York from 9 September 2002 to 3 July 2003, http://www.huc.edu/newspubs/pressroom/2002/bergenbelsonNew3.shtml (accessed 26 November 2008), and Florida Atlantic University (Boca Raton) from 12 January to 11 February 2006, http://www.huc.edu/newspubs/pressroom/2005/11/rebirth1.shtml (accessed 26 November 2008); *Befreit, aber nicht in Freiheit: Displaced Persons zwischen Weser und Ems 1945–1950* (a touring exhibition created in 2007), www.diz-emslandlager.de/wander.htm (accessed 20 January 2009).
5. Examples: the virtual version of the USHMM special exhibition *Life Reborn*, http://www.ushmm.org/museum/exhibit/online/dp/menu.htm (accessed 29 January 2009); the virtual exhibition on the Zeilsheim DP camp, http://www.ifs.tu-darmstadt.de/fileadmin/ueberlebende-zeilsheim/index.html (accessed 20 January 2009); *Displaced Persons Camp Exhibit*, an exhibition to commemorate the sixtieth anniversary of the US DP Act of 1948, by the Ukrainian Museum-Archives, Cleveland/Ohio: http://www.umacleveland.org/DPC/index.php (accessed 18 January 2009).
6. See, for example, R. Schulze and W. Wiedemann (eds), *AugenZeugen: Fotos, Filme und Zeitzeugenberichte in der neuen Dauerausstellung der Gedenkstätte Bergen-Belsen: Hintergrund und Kontext* (Celle: Stiftung Niedersächsische Gedenkstätten, 2007); and http://www.bergenbelsen.de/de/ausstellung/displaced-persons-camp/ (accessed 18 November 2008).
7. For the US Signal Corps, see G. Paul, *Bilder des Krieges – Krieg der Bilder: Die Visualisierung des modernen Krieges* (Paderborn: Schöningh, 2004), pp.248–9; for the AFPU see M. Caiger-Smith, *Bilder vom Feind: Englische Pressefotografen im Nachkriegsdeutschland* (Berlin: Verlag Dirk Nishen, 1988), pp.7–11; English version: *The Face of the Enemy: British Photographers in Germany 1944–1952* (London: Nishen, 1988). Eight examples of Canadian photographs are in A. Lembeck, *Befreit, aber nicht in Freiheit: Displaced Persons im Emsland 1945–1950* (Bremen: Edition Temmen, 1997), p.220.
8. Quantities for the US Signal Corps in Zelizer, *Remembering*, p.23; 55,000 still photos had already been taken on the European front by April 1945. The descriptions for Record Group 111 (US Signal Corps) of NARA (National Archives and Records Administration) still reflect these quantities: RG 111 contains about 377,000 photos (alternatively, more than 7,700 photo albums) from the period 1941–1954: see http://www.archives.gov/research/arc/ (accessed 20 January 2009) by using the ARC Identifiers 530707 or 531473. The British Ministry of Information's Photographic Division had to classify and censor up to 40,000 photographs per week: see Caiger-Smith, *Bilder*, p.8.
9. I owe thanks to Holly Reed, NARA Still Picture Reference, for her information given online on 4 November 2008 to my reference request made one day earlier.
10. See B. Zelizer, 'Gender and Atrocity: Women in Holocaust Photography', in B. Zelizer

(ed.), *Visual Culture and the Holocaust* (New Brunswick, NJ: Rutgers University Press, 2001), p.249; Caiger-Smith, *Bilder*, pp.7–9.

11. See also P. Wagner, *Displaced Persons in Hamburg: Stationen einer halbherzigen Integration 1945 bis 1958* (Hamburg: Dölling und Galitz, 1997), pp.23–42; Lembeck, *Befreit*, p.220; Caiger-Smith, *Bilder*, pp.7–8.
12. See Paul, *Bilder*, p.248. One example: *LIFE*, 30 July 1945, pp.13–19.
13. See Zelizer, *Remembering*, p.22.
14. See G. Woodbridge, *UNRRA: The History of the United Nations Relief and Rehabilitation Administration* (New York: Columbia University Press, 1950), vol. 1, pp.280–92.
15. Printed in S. Schröder, *Displaced Persons im Landkreis und in der Stadt Münster 1945–1951* (Münster: Aschendorff, 2005), p.450 (picture twenty-four). I got a bad quality reprography (in fact, a reversed image of the original) from the UN Archives in 1997, but when asking, in 2004, for a better version to be published in my above-mentioned book, they were unable to trace it again. The text on the photo's reverse side read: 'UNRRA/1598 Greven, Germany (British Zone). UNRRA cares for displaced Polish children in British Zone of Germany. UNRRA team director Oswald Jerusalem (Czech) watches two of his young wards tuck away their midday meal, stew made of potatoes, beans and bits of meat.' A stamp on the back read: 'Received from UNRRA Visual Information Office, Washington, under agreement of March 10, 1947 by UN Dept of Public Information. Visual Information Section. Catalogued by UN Archives. Property of the United Nations. Credit: UNRRA photograph from United Nations.' No name was given for the photographer.
16. I am very grateful to Laura Clouting, Curator of the IWM photo archive, for her help which I received via email in October 2008. The photograph in question here is on the Internet in two versions, courtesy of Weaver's daughter: http://www.normanweaver.com/page5.htm [slide four] 'Mr O. Jerusalem (Czech), director of UNRRA Team 11, at Greven, chats with two young diners in the large children's feeding centre, of which he is justly proud.' (accessed 20 January 2009); and http://www.chgs.umn.edu/museum/exhibitions/displaced/N005.jpg (accessed 20 January 2009).
17. To be fair, the UN Archives are still progressing their work with the UNRRA photo collection, containing about 5,000 photographs from twenty-eight countries. My point here is that in the private legal estates of these photographers, it might be possible to find additional motifs to those held by the UN Archives in the UNRRA photo collection.
18. One example is M. McNeill, *An den Wassern von Babylon: Erfahrungen mit Displaced Persons in Goslar zwischen 1945 und 1948* (Bielefeld: Verlag für Regionalgeschichte, 1995), containing nine photographs of a former member of McNeill's Friends Relief Team. Original title without photographs: *By the Rivers of Babylon: A Story of Relief Work among the Displaced Persons of Europe* (London: Bannisdale Press, 1950).
19. Examples in S. Schröder, 'Das Schicksal der Displaced Persons in Warendorf nach 1945', in P. Leidinger (ed.), *Geschichte der Stadt Warendorf*, vol. 2 (Münster: Ardey, 2000), p.309; S. Schröder, 'Zwangsarbeiter und Displaced Persons in fotografischer Überlieferung', *Westfälische Forschungen*, 58 (2008), p.480; B. Lütkemöller 'Drei "schwarze Tage" im Frühjahr 1945: Schicksalsschwer für Oelder Bevölkerung', in Kreisheimatverein Beckum-Warendorf (ed.), *Heimatkalender des Kreises Warendorf 1995* (Warendorf: Darpe, 1995), p.72.
20. Photos in a private photo album of Mr A.N., Australia, a former inhabitant of DP camp Reckenfeld – which he showed me during his visit to Germany in mid-2007 – had stamps on their reverse sides: 'Foto Sobejko Waclaw Reckenfeld 36', indicating a professional Polish DP photographer in the camp.
21. See, for example, the pictures in http://www.dpalbums.lv (accessed 26 November 2008) from Latvian DPs.
22. See the introductory article on Karl Hintzer (1895–1967) with forty-eight of his photographs: D.M. Goeze, 'Alltag estnischer DPs in Deutschland: Die Sammlung Hintzer im Herder-Institut Marburg', in C. and M. Pletzing (eds), *Displaced Persons: Flüchtlinge aus den baltischen Staaten in Deutschland* (München: Martin Meidenbauer, 2007), pp.29–61. More of his images are online: http://www.herder-institut.de/index.php?lang=de&id=10 (accessed 26 November 2008). The combination of the collection *Hintzer* with a full-text search (*Volltextsuche*) for 'Displaced' adds up to 293 hits.
23. See, for example, Schröder, 'Zwangsarbeiter', p.482, picture eight.

24. See Goeze, 'Alltag', p.43.
25. Edited with a commentary in Wagner, *Displaced*, pp.23–42.
26. The UNRRA photographs are kept in three series: S-0800 (all UNRRA missions except Germany and China), S-1058 (Germany), S-0801 (China). I owe thanks to Shelley Lightburn, UN Archives, for emailing information in October 2008.
27. See, for example, the photographic collection of the British Society of Friends: http://www.quaker.org.uk/Templates/Internal.asp?NodeID=90019 (accessed 28 November 2008).
28. Online: http://www.nara.gov; http://www.iwm.org.uk; http://www.ushmm.org; http://www.collectionscanada.gc.ca/index-e.html (accessed 20 January 2009).
29. See http://www.herder-institut.de/index.php?lang=de&id=10 (accessed 2 January 2009).
30. See http://www.dpalbums.lv (accessed 2 January 2009).
31. Research can be done by browsing Google Images http://images.google.com/ (accessed 21 January 2009) with a search for 'displaced source:life'. The example I used in my lecture for the 'Beyond Camps and Forced Labour' conference on 9 January 2009 was http://images.google.com/hosted/life/l?imgurl=1479010d93399742&q=displaced%20source:life&prev=/images%3Fq%3Ddisplaced%2Bsource:life%26start%3D18%26gbv%3D2%26ndsp%3D18%26hl%3Den%26sa%3DN (accessed 21 January 2009) and comprises the image and additional information: 'Russian displaced persons boarding a train to return to their homeland through the bomb-damaged Ruhr Valley. Location: Duisburg, Germany. Date taken: July 1945. Photographer: Margaret Bourke-White. Size: 1280 x 903 pixels (17.8 x 12.5 inches).' By using the full-size version it is even possible to read the Russian inscriptions of the flags displayed outside the boxcars.
32. I traced the emails on http://www.dpcamps.org, a privately administered website for people interested in the subject. For thirty-two emails, I received a failure notice. Ten of the seventeen answers I got provided me with information on quantities of photographs. Three people had no photographs at all. Five of the answers said that they still possess about five photos from the DP era and in two cases the families still hold collections of, respectively, fifty and one hundred and fifty photos. My own experiences with DPs and their descendants, made as an archivist in a town where two large DP camps existed from 1945 to 1949/50, also shows that very often at least some photographs and documents have survived in the DPs' families until now.
33. See W. Jacobmeyer, *Vom Zwangsarbeiter zum Heimatlosen Ausländer: Die Displaced Persons in Westdeutschland 1945–1951* (Göttingen: Vandenhoeck & Ruprecht, 1985), pp.173–5.
34. See, for example, H. 't Hoen, *Zwei Jahre Volkswagenwerk: Als niederländischer Student im 'Arbeitseinsatz' im Volkswagenwerk von Mai 1943 bis zum Mai 1945* (Wolfsburg: Volkswagen AG, Unternehmensarchiv, 2002), p.129.
35. Examples in G. Schwarze, *Gefangen in Münster: Kriegsgefanene – Zwangsarbeiter – Zwangsarbeiterinnen 1939 bis 1945* (Essen: Klartext, 1999), p.160 (USSR); Schröder, *Displaced*, pp.448–9, 454 (pictures 19–21, Poland).
36. A rare counter-example is M. Danys, *DP: Lithuanian Immigration to Canada after the Second World War* (Toronto: Multicultural History Society of Ontario, 1986). She interviewed Lithuanian-Canadians about their experiences as DPs. Some of the photographs in her book came from her interviewees.
37. See H. Müller, *Fünf vor null: Die Besetzung des Münsterlandes 1945*, new and revised edn (Münster: Aschendorff, 2005; 1st edn 1971). W. Trees *et al.*, *Stunde Null in Deutschland: Die westlichen Besatzungszonen 1945–1948: Ein Bild/Text-Band* (Bindlach: Gondrom, 1989), originally edited in three vols with differing titles (Droste-Verlag: Düsseldorf, 1978–1980).
38. See E.F. Ziemke, *The US Army in the Occupation of Germany, 1944–1946* (Washington, DC: Center of Military History, United States Army, 1975).
39. Jacobmeyer, *Vom Zwangsarbeiter*. A counter-example, but maybe rather clarifying the difference between publications in the United States and in Germany, is L. Dinnerstein, *America and the Survivors of the Holocaust* (New York: Columbia University Press, 1982). Dinnerstein focuses on Jewish DPs, but he also describes the other groups of DPs. His book contains nineteen photographs; eleven of them show a DP context. In the combination of research on DPs presented in textual form and visual illustrations, it seems to be hybrid. This might be explained by the fact that publications in the United States could take advantage of an easier access to images on the subject, and that they

undoubtedly had a mixed public of historians and former DPs who came to the USA or other Anglophone countries. In Germany, on the contrary, the subject not infrequently aroused feelings of guilt or repression and attracted little attention, even among professional historians during the 1980s.

40. See D. Wiethege, *Und als der Krieg zu Ende schien ... Krieg, Überrollung und Ausländerlager in Voerde, 1939–1948* (Meinerzhagen: MD&V, 1985); T. Muncke, *Nachkriegsjahre im Kreis Steinfurt* (Steinfurt: Kreis Steinfurt, 1986), pp.123–7.
41. See Caiger-Smith, *Bilder*, pp. 48–69.
42. Biographical information online: http://www.courtauld.ac.uk/people/caigersmith-martin.shtml (accessed 21 January 2009).
43. See M. Wyman, *DPs: Europe's Displaced Persons, 1945–1951* (Philadelphia, PA: Associated University Presses, 1989); U. Müller, *Fremde in der Nachkriegszeit: displaced persons – zwangsverschleppte Personen – in Stuttgart und Württemberg-Baden 1945–1951* (Stuttgart: Klett-Cotta, 1990).
44. Typical of that is his commentary on the photographs he uses without giving further context information; see Wyman, *DPs*, p.72: 'Return to Poland. Repatriation trains generally left with great fanfare, with branches and flags adorning the cars, and songs competing with the rumble of the locomotive. These Polish youths were typical of the joyful return. Some others went back apprehensively, however. (*UNRRA photo.*)'
45. See Wagner, *Displaced*, pp.23–42.
46. J. Giere and R. Salamander (eds), *Ein Leben aufs Neu: Das Robinson-Album: DP-Lager: Juden auf deutschem Boden 1945–1948* (Wien: Brandstätter, 1995); E. Somers and R. Kok (eds), *Jewish Displaced Persons in Camp Bergen-Belsen 1945–1950: The Unique Photo Album of Zippy Orlin* (Seattle, WA: University of Washington Press, 2004).
47. See D. Bachmann-Medick, *Cultural Turns: Neuorientierungen in den Kulturwissenschaften* (Reinbek bei Hamburg: Rowohlt, 2006), pp.329–80; M. Sturken and L. Cartwright, *Practices of Looking: An Introduction to Visual Culture* (New York: Oxford University Press, 2001), p.2. Examples: G. Paul (ed.), *Visual History: Ein Studienbuch* (Göttingen: Vandenhoeck & Ruprecht, 2006); Zelizer, *Visual Culture*; Zelizer, *Remembering*.
48. See Zelizer, *Remembering*.
49. For Maxine Rude, see http://www.chgs.umn.edu/museum/exhibitions/displaced/index.html (accessed 12 January 2009); for Norman Weaver see http://www.normanweaver.com/ (accessed 12 January 2009).
50. Norman Weaver's photos are kept by his daughter and also by the IWM. Maxine Rude left her UNRRA negatives in Europe after the war and it was only in 1997 that she found out that her negatives are held by the USHMM; see http://www.chgs.umn.edu/museum/exhibitions/displaced/index.html (accessed 3 January 2009).
51. As an example, for my lecture on 9 January 2009 I chose photograph BU 6633 from the War Office Second World War official collection, produced on 18 May 1945 by Sergeant J. Mapham of No. 5 AFPU, showing Leon Wasrcruk, a DP child who arrived at No. 17 Displaced Persons Assembly Centre in Hamburg Zoological Gardens, with his parents and sister, being treated with anti-louse powder. The photo was published before by Wagner, *Displaced*, p.27.

PART 2
RECEPTIONS AND RESENTMENTS

4

Minorities, Violence and the Establishment of Communist Rule in Poland

MICHAEL FLEMING

This chapter presents a synthetic understanding of violence in Poland in the immediate aftermath of war. To date, the anti-minority violence which swept across the country has been generally approached on a minority-by-minority basis, Germans and Ukrainians being victims of 'revenge', Jews being victims of anti-Semitism.[1] One consequence of the domination of these narratives is the marginalization of the experience of members of minorities who were victims of violence that cannot be explained by 'revenge' or anti-Semitism. It is no accident that the killing of Belorussians in post-war Poland has largely been omitted from accounts of the post-war period. This chapter argues that by comparing the experience of minorities in Poland, a more nuanced understanding of post-war violence is gained. It is contended that the Polish Workers' Party (PPR) tolerated subjective violence against minorities in order to manage social anger.[2] Minority populations were positioned as *homines sacri* despite proclamations condemning anti-Semitism and chauvinism.[3] So while exploration of the violence against each minority has to be sensitive to its specificity, this chapter aims to show that a broad comparative approach has considerable merit, offering insight into the ascendancy of communism in Poland and demonstrating that the violence which minorities experienced had a unifying logic beyond that hitherto articulated in work focusing upon singular minority population groups.

Anita Prażmowska's[4] contention that 'the party which was most constrained in its attempt to formulate a nationality policy ... was the PPR' requires significant qualification. The difficulty in conceptualizing the nationality policy of the PPR stems from the practice of thinking and writing about Poland's post-war minority populations in isolation. Each of the minorities in post-war Poland has been thought and written about as though it had a unique and specific history, ignoring or marginalizing common experiences and pressures. In the most literal sense, of course, minorities did experience specific and unique histories, but such awareness should not deter detailed and rigorous comparative analysis. Indeed, a deeper understanding of the history of minorities in the post-war period and of the functioning of PPR nationality policy can be gained by viewing minorities as subject to the same underlying forces and tensions. So while each minority had specific relations with the wider population, the forces of the communist security apparatus, and Polish underground partisans, and was burdened by the legacy of the events of the Second World War in a different way, it is also true that minorities, of whatever nationality, posed a significant challenge to the emerging Polish state, dominated by the PPR, and its ethno-nationalist project, that was endorsed by the allies, ofcreating a nationally homogeneous nation state.

This chapter explores the contours of how the PPR reconciled the drive to national homogeneity with the existence of minority populations, and shows that nationality policy, rather than being a mere marginal issue, was at the centre of the PPR's struggle for hegemony in the immediate aftermath of war.

RECREATING THE POLITY

During the last years of the Second World War, the issue of who was to be included within the new Polish state was discussed by the three main allied powers – the USSR, the USA and the UK, as well as amongst Poles, both those based in London around the government in exile, and those who were based in or looked towards Moscow. Part of the discussions amongst members of the Grand Alliance focused upon the physical shifting of Poland, the relinquishing of her eastern border areas and the gaining of areas of Germany to the north and west. The rationale for such radical border changes was the contention that nationally-mixed states were unstable and that minorities were liable to be disloyal to the state in which they lived; the desire to create a more durable system of nation states for the post-war period; and Stalin's geo-political desire to secure a rim of 'friendly' states to the west of the Soviet Union.

The internationally sanctioned project of creating national homogeneity through population expulsions and transfers had significant social support within Poland. Several reports received by the government in exile noted the decline in toleration for national plurality during the course of the Second World War. Examples include the Karski report of 1940 and the 'secret' letter from Roman Knoll, director of the Commission for Foreign Affairs of the Government Delegation, to Polish Foreign Minister Tadeusz Romer in 1943. Indeed, Knoll wrote in the summer of 1943 that 'the prevalent mood amongst the peasant population is that a post-war Poland has to be purely ethnically Polish'.[5] The redrawing of Poland's borders was more problematic. The Polish government in exile protested against the loss of Poland's eastern regions. The loss of the territories east of the 'Curzon line' agreed by the UK, US and USSR at the Tehran Conference of late 1943 was particularly traumatic. It led to Prime Minister Stanisław Mikołajczyk leaving the government in exile when he could not persuade other ministers to accept the new reality in November 1944.[6] By this point, population transfers were already underway in eastern Poland, with Ukrainians and Belorussians being moved to 'their' respective Soviet Socialist Republics, and Poles being shifted to within the new frontiers of Poland.[7]

The evolution of the Polish Workers' Party to the ethno-nationalism that was later to characterize it was heavily influenced by Stalin's vision of the post-war international settlement.[8] In autumn 1941, the initiative group which was later to become the PPR was created in Moscow at the behest of Stalin. According to the minutes of the initiative group, it did not call itself communist in order that, amongst other reasons, 'the masses see in our party an organization linked with the Polish nation and its most vital interests and that our enemies will not be able to refer to us as agents of a foreign power'.[9] This sensitivity to how communists were perceived in Poland did not deter PPR leader Władysław Gomułka from calling, as late as December 1943, for Polish-German understanding amongst those opposed to Nazism.[10] However, with the failure of this 'liberal' position to garner support and with a less tolerant line coming from Moscow, the PPR leadership began to push a harder ethno-nationalist agenda.

This shift was not merely one policy position amongst several, but was a defining moment in the PPR's bid for hegemony. It clearly identified those who were to be included within the emerging polity and those who were to be excluded. The agreements made between the Polish Committee of National Liberation (PKWN) and the various Soviet Republics in September 1944 gave this policy concrete form, and population transfers/expulsions in eastern Poland began in the autumn of 1944.[11] The only minority that was permitted to remain in Poland and return to the country was the Jewish minority.[12] And although the PPR affirmed the equality of citizens, it was not prepared to intervene strenuously when Polish Jews were attacked and marginalized as a result of anti-Semitic sentiment.

SOCIAL ANGER

Social anger describes the negative emotions and the frustrations which any social system creates. David Ost, exploring the situation in post-communist Poland, shows how in the 1990s Solidarity activists redirected anger at the decline in living standards onto symbolic and mythical figures such as 'communists, crypto-communists, liberals, non-believers, "foreigners" (often defined as Poles who did not fit "Polish Catholic" norms), criminals and other assorted "aliens".'[13]

The model of social anger that is advanced here has three main components. First and perhaps most important is the role played by the economic and political systems that give rise to social anger; second is the effect of social sedimentation – that is, established practices and memories which help guide social anger; and third is the crucial role played by elites in directing social anger. The interaction of these components helps explain how social anger is actually manifested. What is clear is that social anger can take many forms, but not any form. Embedded social practice and elite guidance are crucial controlling elements.

The task facing the PPR was to create a narrative which was believable to the population and would redirect social anger away from itself and its Soviet ally. It also had to take into consideration the prejudices, stereotypes and the social knowledge of society, since any attempt to subvert established myths would increase the difficulty of redirecting social anger. Thus, the ethno-nationalism of the PPR, illustrated by its drive to national homogeneity through population expulsions and transfers and later by programmes of assimilation, 'polonisation' of autochthonic populations and the rigid limits placed upon minorities' self expression, was not merely putting into practice the Soviet geopolitical vision of nation state congruence. Rather, the PPR's ethno-nationalism played an important function in both managing social anger in society and securing from society an uneasy acquiescence to its hegemony.

It is therefore crucial to distinguish between the centrifugal and centripetal aspects of the PPR's nationality policy. To date, scholarly attention on communist nationality policy in Poland and elsewhere has focused on how communists attempted to link themselves with the population through nationalist rhetoric and propaganda, and the general conclusion has been that since the population continued to view communists as 'agents of Moscow' then nationality policy largely failed.[14] However, this conclusion is only valid if the centripetal aspects of policy (drawing the population and communist party closer together) is emphasized, while the centrifugal aspect of policy (exacerbating ethnic and national cleavages in society) is marginalized. The centrifugal aspect of nationality policy, I argue, was the primary mechanism for securing social acquiescence, as it provided 'legitimate' targets for social anger. By dividing the core population from national minorities, animosity against the PPR and its Soviet allies could be, and was, redirected to minorities. From this perspective, PPR nationality policy looks somewhat more successful. And although centrifugal and centripetal aspects of ethno-nationalism are linked (overvaluing the in-group implies an undervaluing of the out-group), it was the centrifugal tendencies that were of primary importance. The attempt of the PPR to define itself as Polish and the mobilizing of Polish traditions and history to gather social support was important and necessary, but of secondary importance. This is clearly seen if we consider the various forms of violence that took place in Poland in the immediate aftermath of war.

VIOLENCE

The post-war period in Poland witnessed a high level of violence, part of which saw anti-communist groups engage in a prolonged campaign against the emerging domination of the PPR. Forces loyal to the PPR and the allied Soviet Army conducted mass arrests, deportations and summary executions, including some performed on the spot by military firing squads.[15] Between 1944 and 1945 some 8,000 death sentences were passed, of which 3,100 were carried out. In addition, there were 2,830 casualties of combat in 1945; 3,383 in 1946; 2,149 in 1947; and 306 in 1948.[16] Between 1946 and 1948, 32,477 people were sentenced for 'crimes against the state'.[17] Prażmowska[18] has argued that the period up until 1947 can be characterized as a civil war. There is a great deal to recommend this view.

However, it is also necessary to explain the violence directed against minority populations. As argued in the introduction, traditional explanations of the violence – including murder, robbery, rape and beatings – that was inflicted on members of minority communities, such as 'revenge' in relation to the German and Ukrainian minorities and anti-Semitism (and 'fear') in relation to Jews are partial (for figures outlining the scale of this violence, see below).

The problem with these conceptualizations is that each minority is divorced from its wider historical context and seen in isolation. In short, the experience of each minority is fetishized so that the wider experience of minorities is overlooked. By comparing the violence directed against minorities in Poland in the immediate aftermath of war we can come to a deeper understanding of the forces and tensions in operation and offer a more nuanced account of the upsurge in ethno-nationalism. To this end, it is necessary to isolate the type of violence which effected minorities. By drawing out the different characteristics of two types of violence – subjective and structural violence – it is possible to analyse how violence, social anger and PPR ethno-nationalism were related.

The main contention made here is that in the period up until late 1947, subjective violence dominated, while after 1947 structural violence was increasingly pervasive. Subjective violence is conceptualized as unnecessary violence that has an identifiable author, whereas structural violence inheres within the set of social relations which define a particular society, or explicitly aims to sustain those social relations. Structural violence has three elements. First is the violence concomitant with the dominant social relations. In contemporary western society, unemployment seems to be a structural necessity to the continuation of profitable accumulation, for instance.[19] Second is the violence that is necessary to ensure the continuation of a particular set of relations, but requires direction or intent (intentional structural violence). For example, the anti-union legislation and other mechanisms to control workers' collective aspirations that are often claimed to be required for the continuation of capitalism in many western countries are forms of intentional structural violence. In the aftermath of the Second World War in Poland, the appropriation of private property was a structural necessity, as was the removal of opposition.[20] Third is the violence that inheres within language – for example, stereotypes and various idées fixes. This is known as representational violence.[21] Representational violence played an important role in creating an environment conducive for outrages to take place. As Leszek Kołakowski argued in 1956:

> A necessary condition for bloody Jewish pogroms, slaughters and atrocities has always been a social atmosphere of emotional tolerance of anti-Semitism, even in its mildest watered-down form. Wherever atrocities occurred, the system of discrimination and suspicion, even if apparently harmless, always gathered reserves of destructive social energy beforehand which nourished and bred criminals.[22]

The negative stereotypes of non-ethnic Poles in the immediate aftermath of war played an important function in permitting attacks, murders and rapes against minority members to take place. Such stereotypes included the characterization of both Jews and Belorussians, for example, as 'communists'. Both groups were victims of Polish underground activity in which several hundred people lost their lives.

In total, 422 Belorussians are thought to have been killed in the mid- to late 1940s in the Białystok *voivodship*. Of these, 296 were civilians, sixty-six were members of the security forces (citizens' militia and Office of Public Security) and sixty were members of the PPR/PZPR (Polish United Workers' Party).[23] January and February 1946 were particular violent. The Special Action Group National Army Association (PAS-NSW) under the command of Romuald Rajs (pseudonym 'Bury') coerced Belorussians to leave Poland, killed eighty-seven and 'pacified' six Belorussian villages.[24] To this subjective violence one has to add the structural violence inhering within the state project of creating a nationally homogeneous state through population transfers. Between 1944 and 1946, as part of the 1944 population transfer agreement, 27,409 Belorussians[25] left the Białystok *voivodship*. The great majority was coerced to leave.[26]

Engel[27] argues that 'it does not seem possible to determine with any reasonable degree of certainty the total number of Jews killed by Poles in the years following the liberation' (1944–46), and suggests that the total number of fatalities falls in the range of 500–600, 'with the probability of a greater or lesser figure declining sharply with distance from that range'.

The murder of Jews on the railway network, the pogroms of 1945 and 1946, or the slaughter of Belorussians in the Białystok *voivodship* in 1946, for example, constituted manifestations of subjective violence, since they were unnecessary and did not inhere within the structure of social relations. This is not to say that the social offensive against minorities did not play a wider function. Indeed, the relatively muted response from the PPR and the state more generally indicate that these organs were prepared to accept the existence of widespread subjective violence with the proviso that it did not undermine the drive to communist hegemony.

Subjective violence against minorities had the imprimatur of sanction through the policy of the PPR. Firstly, the programme of population transfers and expulsions clearly showed to the Polish public that minorities had no place in Poland and, secondly, the concomitant rhetoric of senior PPR figures made sure there was no misunderstanding. For example, Władysław Gomułka contended at the PPR's Central Committee plenum in May 1945 that, 'countries are built on national lines and not on multinational ones'.[28] Furthermore, PPR propaganda drove home the message that Poland was for Poles. Minority populations were clearly shown to society to be in the 'wrong' place, and those populations which the Polish state was later to claim as Polish, such as Kashubians, Silesians and Mazurians – the so-called autochthones – were, in the immediate aftermath of war, similarly engulfed in the anti-minority sentiment, as they were seen as German, or having pro-German sympathies. The subjective violence of the population often did not distinguish between the autochthones and Germans, and religion was often used as evidence of German nationality. As late as 1949 the view that 'a Pole is a Catholic, an Evangelical is a kraut' (Polak to katolik, a ewangelik to szwab) remained fairly widespread, and was to some extent encouraged by the Catholic Church's ethno-religious project.[29] In addition, as Strauchold[30] points out, there were cases where people were expelled from the 'Recovered Territories' because the ethnically Polish new arrivals from areas incorporated into the Belorussian SSR and Ukrainian SSR wanted their property.

The PPR's enthusiasm for the population transfer programmes was a result of its desire to direct social anger away from itself, and of its strong desire to be seen as a Polish party and thereby counteract oppositionist contentions that it was a mere front for Soviet interests. By using every opportunity to demonstrate its Polishness and by excluding minorities, the PPR could not then come out strongly against those groups and individuals who harmed minorities on their own account. To use Giorgio Agamben's[31] language, the PPR positioned minorities as *homines sacri* – people who could be killed but not sacrificed. They were not Polish and had no place in the new Poland.

For example, during the population transfer to the Ukraine, Szcześniak and Szota[32] maintain that 2,268 families were victims of robbery, over 3,000 farm animals were confiscated, forty-seven people were either hanged or drowned, and over 4,500 civilians killed. And while the high level of violence has to be placed in the context of ongoing military action, in which communist forces fought sections of the Polish underground and Ukrainian nationalists, the violent and coercive nature of the 'transfers' has to be recognized. Those who remained in Poland were resettled in the 'Recovered Territories' through Action Vistula. Around 140,000 people were moved in this military-backed resettlement operation. In the Jaworzno camp, 3,873 Ukrainians were exposed to further violence. Even those whom many Polish officials and senior politicians such as the PPR leader and deputy prime minister Władysław Gomułka considered loyal to the state, such as Łemkos, were 'resettled' as 'Ukrainians'.

The number of German victims of post-war violence remains highly contested, but the figure is sure to run into tens of thousands. Between May and August 1945, the Germans in Poland were exposed to widespread subjective violence as the Soviet Army and, to a lesser degree, Poles coerced them to leave through assault, murder and widespread rape.[33] This is known as the period of 'wild expulsions'. Even after the Potsdam conference in late July and early August 1945, violence against Germans continued. As late as August 1946, five months after the start of the programme transferring Germans from Poland to the British zone of occupation in Germany – 'Operation Swallow' – and twelve months after the agreement at Potsdam, Germans expelled from the Liegnitz district complained of being robbed and suffering poor treatment.[34] Gomułka's 1945 demand that 'the kinds of conditions should be created so they [Germans] won't want to remain' was satisfied through both structural and subjective violence.[35] One-and-half million Germans were shifted from Poland to the British zone of occupation in Germany alone in the period from February 1946 to the suspension of 'Operation Swallow' in December 1946.[36]

THE PPR AND ANTI-SEMITISM

The PPR condemned anti-Semitism on several occasions. Yet it attempted to balance two countervailing policies that impacted on the status of Jews in Poland. It proclaimed 'the full equality of all citizens regardless of race, nationality and creed,' while at the same time maintaining that 'In the face of the tragedy suffered by the Jewish nation, Jews who wish it should have their national aspirations in Palestine facilitated.'[37] The tension between assisting Jews to emigrate and providing resources to help those Jews who chose to remain and re-establish their lives in Poland was uneasy. Indeed, as early 1945, the Jewish section of the PPR identified a link between the advocacy of a homogenized nation state, the displacement of minorities and anti-Jewish actions.[38] The government did establish the 'Office of the Government Commissar relating to the Productivisation of the Jewish Populace,' which aimed to train Jews for work in mainstream manufacturing and agriculture: that is, to redirect Jews from occupations seen by society as 'Jewish'. This policy, most probably derived from ideas circulating in the USSR during the 1930s, had a further difficulty – there were relatively few Jews to be made 'productive', given that most of Polish Jewry had been murdered in the Holocaust, while pre-war stereotypes of Jews remained potent and in widespread circulation.

It was clear by 1945 that post-war Jewish life in the new Poland was to be inflected by majoritarian norms, though in the period up until 1948 the Jewish communities enjoyed some autonomy, with thirty-six Jewish schools functioning by 1 August 1946.[39] However, from late 1947 to early 1948, the community came under increasing assimiliatory pressure as the hard ethno-nationalism of population transfers and expulsions gave way to a soft ethno-nationalism characterized by 'polonisation' programmes and greater state control of all social organizations.

Engel[40] argues that the 'peak periods of violence [against Jews] – March–August 1945 and February–July 1946 – both appear to have coincided with periods during which the number of Jews in

Poland was increasing'. The Central Committee of Jews in Poland (CKŻP) responded by encouraging Jews to abandon small towns and rural landholdings, and move to the cities, which were more secure. This policy also removed Jews from the reach of those who felt threatened by the possible restitution of property belonging to Jews.

The ambiguity of the PPR's position in relation to the Jewish minority is illustrated by the actions of the Kielce Communist Party secretary on the day of the Kielce pogrom. He had refused to address the crowd to diffuse its anger, as he 'didn't want people saying that the PPR is a defender of the Jews'. Furthermore, Itzhak Klajnerman, the legal expert to the provisional parliament (KRN – Homeland National Council), rebuked Adolf Berman's entreaties to enhance the legal protection of Jews and to combat anti-Semitism, by arguing that such action would be 'counterproductive, perhaps even harmful, as such a decree would certainly become an excellent pretext for energized agitation against the Jews and against the government'.[41] The policy that the government adopted towards Jews who intended to remain in Poland was one which sought to promote assimilation and integration. Nevertheless, as early as November 1945, the British ambassador to Poland, Victor Cavendish-Bentinck, concluded that the Polish government's policy was to 'encourage emigration of Jews and prevent emigration of Poles except in exceptional cases'.[42] When Jews became victims of violence, the government response was fairly muted. The government actually provided arms to Jews so they could defend their own institutions. Following the pogrom in Kielce in July 1946, the CKŻP[43] organized a Special Commission which aimed to provide 'adequate protection and defence of Jewish institutions and thereby assist the authorities in their defence of the lives of the Jewish population in the country'.[44]

Though the arming of Jews may have been related to a possible lack of security manpower, for the PPR it also had the distinct advantage in that it helped it to avoid the 'accusation' that the PPR was pro-Jewish, as Jews were now able to defend themselves and their institutions from attack. Jews guarded Jewish institutions and a de facto Jewish militia existed in Lower Silesia.[45] In short, Jews posed a serious strategic problem for the PPR, a dilemma that was manifested in its policy ambiguity and its unwillingness to energetically combat anti-Semitism.

The PPR sought to define the 'We/They' boundary on the basis of nationality. This demarcation had significant social support. So while the opposition to the PPR sought to maintain that boundary, especially in relation to the Germans, the opposition also wished to create a further axis dividing society from the PPR through the well-founded assertion that the PPR was an instrument of Moscow. However, sufficient segments of the population, weary from several years of brutal war, found enough within the PPR programme to at least acquiesce to its emerging hegemony. In this the PPR's enthusiasm for ethnic homogeneity played a crucial role. The slogan 'Man in the Right Place' was widely promulgated, and continual reference to Polish historical figures such as Bolesław Chrobry, Henryk Dąbrowski, Tadeusz Kościuszko helped the PPR challenge oppositionist rhetoric on its Polishness.[46]

However, the centrifugal aspects of the post-war ethno-nationalist project were not orchestrated by the PPR alone. It had an influential ally that had deep roots amongst broad swathes of the Polish population. The Roman Catholic Church played a key role in shaping the discursive environment and endorsing national homogeneity.

THE ROLE OF THE ROMAN CATHOLIC CHURCH

An important factor contributing to the anti-minority discourse (or, more precisely, anti-minority representational violence) which framed post-war subjective violence was the ethno-religious ambitions of the Roman Catholic Church in Poland. Contemporary Polish scholarship on the Catholic Church in Poland in the immediate aftermath of the Second World War contends that the Catholic Church was a victim of sustained communist oppression with minimal scope for manoeuvre. For instance, Dudek and Gryz[47] suggest that the communists pursued a 'salami strategy' against the Church, whereby the state made continuous 'cuts' into the Church's position and weakened it.

However, this perspective overemphasizes the Church's defensive posture, and radically underestimates its scope for independent action prior to 1947. In that period the Polish primate August Hlond pursued an unambiguous ethno-religious agenda. Hlond's use of the special plenipotentiary powers granted to him by Pope Pius XII on 8 July 1945 enabled him to swiftly take control of the Catholic Church in former German lands in the west and north of Poland. For example, on 12 August 1945 in Wrocław, Hlond informed

German Catholic bishops that the Pope had agreed to replace the Breslau metropolitan with apostolic administrators, whereas in reality Pius XII had not explicitly consented to Hlond's plan.[48] Hlond made it clear to the German clerics that they had no future in Poland. Hanna Diskin[49] rightly argues that 'Church activity in the western territories was highly successful and made a genuine contribution to the settlement project in these territories and to the re-establishment [*sic*] of their Polish character.'

Today the Catholic Church is widely viewed as having been firmly anti-communist and a beacon for oppositionists, but its ethno-religious ambitions echoed the ethno-nationalist policy of the PPR. Where the PPR sought to exclude Ukrainians and Belorussians on national grounds, the Catholic Church sought to exclude the same people on religious grounds. Even Catholic Germans were problematic for the 'Polish' Roman Catholic Church, as they hindered its bid for domination in the 'Recovered Territories'. The PPR excluded people on the basis of nationality; the Catholic Church, on the other hand, largely, but not entirely (as its dealings with the German Catholic clergy illustrate), sought to marginalize people on the basis of faith/denomination.

The state transferred German Protestant churches to the Catholic Church. As early as October 1945, deputy bishop Jan Szeruda of the Evangelical Augsburgian Church clearly perceived collaboration between the Polish government and the Roman Catholic Church in marginalizing the Evangelical Augsburgian Church. Szeruda wrote to Prime Minister Edward Osóbka-Morawski on 12 October 1945, contending that state institutions (state government, local government, militia and public security organs) in collaboration with Catholic clergy were seizing Augsburgian property, were identifying members of the Augsburgian Church as German and were attempting to convert the faithful to Roman Catholicism.[50]

In relation to the Greek-Catholic (Uniate) Church, the Roman Catholic Church represented a path towards 'polonisation', and the 'battle for souls' had a strong nationalistic element. Of the approximately 140,000 people relocated in Action Vistula in 1947, for example, approximately two-thirds were Greek-Catholic.[51] For many Ukrainian Greek-Catholics, the 'Catholic religion was more important than Eastern ritual, they baptized their children, buried their dead and were wed in Roman Catholic churches.'[52] In addition, Uniate clerics were permitted to perform the lower functions of a reverend, but a large proportion of the Uniate clergy abandoned their ministry. It is moot whether Roman Catholic policy towards the Greek-Catholic Church was helpful or the exploitation of circumstance to complete the domination of a Church virtually destroyed by oppression. As Syrnyk[53] suggests, the sentiment guiding many within the Roman Catholic Church was both related to the issue of nationality (Pole versus Ukrainian) and to a sense of superiority as expressed in the Latin phrase: 'greca fides nulla fides' (Greek faith is no faith).

The Catholic Church in the main did not hinder the expression of anti-Semitism (there were a few exceptions amongst senior clerics, such as Bishop Kubina of Częstochowa). It refused to speak honestly about the myth of ritual murder, and attempted to rationalize it by blaming Jews themselves for encouraging anti-Semitic sentiment within society through their actions. Indeed, in 1946 Stefan Wyśzynski, Bishop of Lublin, met with Jewish representatives and argued that 'the matter of blood was not definitively settled', a reference to the myth of ritual murder.[54] This was 700 years after Pope Innocent IV declared in his 1247 papal bull that the accusations of ritual murder against Jews were false.

The cumulative effect of the Church's interventions was to support, rather than challenge, the form of polity that the PPR was creating. By endorsing the notion that some people did not belong within the Polish polity due to their ethnic/national/religious background, and by over-valorizing the identity 'Pole–Catholic', the Church contributed to the orchestration of centrifugal ethno-nationalism.

Thus the PPR's use of ethno-nationalism to steer social anger away from itself and its Soviet ally was assisted by one of its main opponents, the Roman Catholic Church. The Church, for its part, by agreeing that some people had to be excluded, fostered illiberality in the political culture and, despite its declared intentions, undermined efforts to create a more plural polity. After autumn 1947, when it was identified as enemy number one by the PPR, the Roman Catholic Church became a victim of the illiberal polity established.

CONCLUSION

The violence which was unleashed on minority communities in the aftermath of the Second World War in Poland had a unifying logic which sheds lights upon the emergence of communist hegemony. The argument presented here has three main points.

Firstly, the PPR was able to secure sufficient acquiescence to its emerging hegemony through its nationality policy in the immediate aftermath of war. Contrary to much recent scholarship, this policy was dominated by its centrifugal aspects rather than by its centripetal aspects.

Secondly, by positioning minority populations as *homines sacri*, the PPR created legitimate targets for the population to vent their frustrations and anger on (and it thereby redirected anger from itself to minority populations). This allowed subjective violence to flourish in the period up until late 1947, by which time the party had established sufficient control to reign in the physical attacks on the relatively few remaining members of minority groups. Its tolerance of subjective violence was much reduced by late 1947, as such violence now undermined its contentions that it was in control and that life for the population would improve. By late 1947 subjective violence had decreased substantially. The intentional structural violence of state agencies was also reduced, but it remained at a fairly high level.[55] After late 1947 the careful marshalling of representational violence helped to divert criticism away from the party. The targets were also frequently minorities.[56] From early 1948 onwards minorities were exposed to strong and increasing assimilatory pressures.

The third contention is that the ethno-religious ambitions of the Catholic Church, rather than challenge the form of polity which the PPR sought to create, actually supported it. The Church's intolerance of minorities was aligned with, and supported, the social anger regime which the PPR wished to orchestrate.

Thus, the violence which erupted in the immediate aftermath of the Second World War and was directed at minority communities has to be recognized as playing an important function in the PPR's drive to dominance, both by diverting social anger and by legitimating the notion that 'non-people' exist: that is, affirming illiberality in the political culture. The irony, of course, is that those who attacked, discriminated against and murdered members of minority population groups often saw themselves as fighting for the 'true' Poland. In the mid-1940s, after several years of brutal occupation, tolerance and belief in pluralism were in short supply when they were needed most.

REFERENCES

Archives

New Documents Archive (AAN), Warsaw.
State Archive in Łódź (APŁ).
Polish Institute and General Sikorski Museum (PISM), London.
The National Archives, London (TNA).

Published Sources

Agamben, G., *Homo Sacer: Sovereign Power and Bare Life*, trans. D. Heller Roazen (Stanford, CA: Stanford University Press, 1998).

Datner, H., 'Szkoły Centralnego Komitetu Żydów w Polsce w latach 1944–1949', *Biuletyn Żydowskiego Instytutu Historycznego*, nr 1–3 (169–171) (1994), pp.103–20.

Diskin, H., *The Seeds of Triumph: Church and State in Gomułka's Poland* (Budapest: CEU, 2001).

Dudek, A. and Paczkowski, A., 'Poland', in K. Persak and Ł. Kamiński (eds), *A Handbook of the Communist Security Apparatus in East Central Europe 1944–1989* (Warsaw: IPN, 2005).

Dudek, A. and Gryz, R., *Komuniści i Kościół w Polsce 1945–1989* (Kraków: Znak, 2006).

Egit, J., *Grand Illusion* (Toronto: Lugus, 1991).

Engel, D., 'Patterns of Anti-Jewish Violence in Poland, 1944–1946', in *Yad Vashem Studies*, 26 (1998), pp.43–85.

Engel, D., 'After the Holocaust: Polish–Jewish Conflict in the Wake of World War II', in C. Freeze *et al.* (eds), *Polin: Studies in Polish Jewry, Vol. 18: Jewish Women in Eastern Europe* (Oxford: Littman, 2005), pp. 424–9.

Fleming, Michael, *Communism, Nationalism and Ethnicity in Poland (1944–1950)* (London: Routledge, 2009).

General Sikorski Historical Institute, *Documents on Polish–Soviet Relations 1939–1945* (London: GSHI, 1961 and 1967).

Gontarczyk, P., *Polska Partia Robotnicza: Droga do Władzy (1941–1944)* (Warszawa: Fronda, 2003).

Gross, J.T., 'Stereotypes of Polish-Jewish Relations after the War: The Special Commission of the Central Committee of Polish Jews', in A. Polonsky (ed.), *Polin: Studies in Polish Jewry, Vol. 13: Focusing on the Holocaust and its Aftermath* (Oxford: Littman, 2000), pp.194–205.

Gross, J.T., *Fear – Anti-Semitism in Poland after Auschwitz: An Essay in Historical Interpretation* (Princeton, NJ: Princeton University Press, 2006).

Gutman, I., *Więź – Thou Shalt Not Kill: Poles on Jedwabne* (Warsaw: Więź , 2001).

Hałagida, Igor, *Ukraińcy na zachodnich i północnych ziemiach Polski 1947–1957* (Warszawa: IPN, 2003).

Harvey, D., *The Limits to Capital* (Oxford: Blackwell, 1999).

Iwaniuk, S., 'Represje polskiego podziemia wobec ludności białoruskiej na Białostocczyźnie po lipcu 1944', in J. Milewski and A. Pyżewska (eds), *Stosunki Polsko-Białoruskie w Województwie Białostockim w Latach 1939–1956* (Warszawa: IPN, 2005).

Kemp-Welch, A., *Poland under Communism: A Cold War History* (Cambridge: Cambridge University Press, 2008).

Kersten, K., *The Establishment of Communism in Poland, 1943–1948* (Berkeley, CA: University of California Press, 1991).

Kopka, B., *Obozy pracy w Polsce 1944–1950: Przewodnik encyklopedyczny* (Warszawa: Nowa Karta, 2002).

Mevius, M., *Agents of Moscow: The Hungarian Communist Party and the Origins of Socialist Patriotism 1941–1953* (Oxford: Clarendon Press, 2005).

Micgiel, J., 'Coercion and the Establishment of Communist Rule in Poland 1944–1947' (unpublished PhD thesis, Columbia University, New York, 1992).

Michlic-Coren, J., 'Anti-Jewish Violence in Poland, 1918–1939 and 1945–1947', in Polonsky (ed.), *Polin, Vol. 13*, pp.3–61.

Michlic, J., *Poland's Threatening Other: The Image of the Jew from 1880 to the Present* (Lincoln, NE: University of Nebraska, 2006).

Mironowicz, E., *Białorusini w Polsce 1944–1949* (Warszawa: PWN, 1993).

Mironowicz, E., *Polityka narodowościowa, PRL* (Białystok: Wydanie Białoruskiego Towarzystwa Historycznego, 2000).

Naimark, N.M., *Fires of Hatred: Ethnic Cleansing in Twentieth-Century Europe* (Cambridge, MA: Harvard University Press, 2001).

Nitschke, B., *Wysiedlenie czy wypędzenie? Ludność niemiecka w Polsce w latach 1945–1949* (Toruń: Marszałek, 2004).
Ost, D., *The Defeat of Solidarity: Anger and Politics in Postcommunist Poland* (London: Cornell University, 2005).
Polonsky, A. and Drukier, B., *The Beginnings of Communist Rule in Poland* (London: Routledge, 1980).
Polubiec, Z., *Polska Partia Robotnicza: Dokumenty 1942–1948 programowe* (Warszawa: Książka i Wiedza, 1984).
Prażmowska, A., *Civil War in Poland 1942–1948* (London: Palgrave, 2004).
Siebel-Achenbach, S., *Lower Silesia: From Nazi Germany to Communist Poland 1942–1949* (New York: Macmillan in association with St Antony's College, Oxford, 1994). Sienkiewicz, W. and Hryciuk, G., *Wysiedlenia, wypędzenia i ucieczki 1939–1959, Atlas Ziem Polski: Polacy, Żydzi, Niemcy, Ukraińcy* (Warszawa: Demart, 2008).
Strauchold, G., *Autochtoni Polscy, Niemieccy czy ... Od Nacjonalizmu do Komunizmu 1945–1949* (Toruń: Marszałek, 2001).
Syrnyk, J., *Ludność ukraińska na Dolnym Śląsku 1945–1989* (Wrocław: IPN, 2007).
Szcześniak, B.A. and Szota, Z.W., *Droga do nikąd. Działalność Organizacji ukraińskich Nacjonalistów i jej likwidacja w Polsce* (Warszawa: MON, 1973).
Ther, P. and Siljak, A., *Redrawing Nations: Ethnic Cleansing in East-Central Europe, 1944–1948* (New York: Rowman and Littlefield, 2001).
Toranska, T., *'Them': Stalin's Polish Puppets* (New York: Harper and Row, 1987).
Urban, K., 'Kościół Ewangelicko-Augsburgski w Polsce 1945–1950 (z zagadnień kształtowania się struktury diecezjalno-parafialnej)', *Zeszyty Naukowe Akademii Ekonomicznej w Krakowie*, nr 437 (1994), pp.65–80.

NOTES

1. Jan Gross has argued that anti-Jewish actions were the result of how Poles treated Jews during the course of the Second World War, and of the fear that returning Jews would seek to reclaim the property and status lost during the occupation, which had been assumed by Poles. See J.T. Gross, *Fear – Anti-Semitism in Poland after Auschwitz: An Essay in Historical Interpretation* (Princeton, NJ: Princeton University Press, 2006).
2. Subjective violence is unnecessary violence which has an identifiable author. It is discussed more fully below.
3. *Homo sacer* is a figure from archaic Roman Law, situated at the 'intersection of a capacity to be killed and yet not sacrificed, outside both human and divine law'. See G. Agamben, *Homo Sacer: Sovereign Power and Bare Life*, trans D. Heller-Roazen (Stanford, CA: Stanford University Press, 1998), p.73. Agamben elaborates on the connection between the sovereign and *homo sacer*, contending that they have the same structure: 'the sovereign is the one with respect to whom all men are potentially *homines sacri*, and *homo sacer* is the one with respect to whom all men act as sovereigns'.
4. A. Prażmowska, *Civil War in Poland 1942–1948* (London: Palgrave, 2004), p.168.
5. Polish Institute and General Sikorski Museum (PISM), A9.Ie/15 doc 55, 'Uwagi o naszej Polityce międzynarodowej'.
6. K. Kersten, *The Establishment of Communism in Poland, 1943–1948* (Berkeley, CA: University of California Press, 1991), p.113.
7. The Polish government in exile was dismayed by the population exchanges being carried out under the agreements signed by the Committee of National Liberation (PKWN). Polish Foreign Minister Tadeusz Romer, wrote to the British government on 7 October 1944, arguing that those agreements 'do not cover the repatriation of Polish citizens deported into the interior of Russia in 1939–1941 which seem to indicate that in this case the Soviet Government had a purely political effect in view'. He also protested against the 'unilateral decision to change the traditional ethnographical face of these territories by arbitrarily moving masses of millions of people': letter from Polish Foreign Minister T. Romer to the British government, 7 October 1944, PISM A.11.49/Sow/6, reprinted in *Documents on Polish–Soviet Relations* (*DPSR*), vol. 2, no. 235, p.400.
8. Stalin justified the Soviet occupation of eastern Poland between 1939 and 1941, in part, by suggesting that the USSR was merely supporting legitimate Belorussian and Ukrainian

national aspirations. To this end, the USSR released ethnographic data which claimed that the region was inhabited by seven million Ukrainians, three million Belorussians and only one million Poles. In fact the region contained, according to analysis of updated 1931 census data, 4.5 million to just over 5 million Poles, a similar number of Ukrainians, 2.5 million Belorussians, a million Jews and a small number of other nationalities. Poland's ally, Britain, was keen to sustain relations with the USSR and looking for reasons to rationalize the Soviet invasion of Poland. As early as 30 September 1939, the British ambassador to Moscow, Sir William Seeds, suggested to colleagues at the Foreign Office that British flexibility on Polish territorial integrity, so long as the Soviet occupation followed 'ethnographical and cultural lines', could be consistent with Britain's treaty obligation to Poland in the face of Soviet aggression: see TNA, FO 371/23103/237–8. This view was subsequently endorsed by senior official Sir Ivone Kirkpatrick, and on 19 October 1939, R.A. Butler, Undersecretary of State for Foreign Affairs, maintained – in a statement to the House of Commons – that the British–Polish Treaty in which Britain agreed to defend Poland from aggression was understood as meaning aggression from Germany alone: see TNA, FO 371/23097/ 203–209. The extent to which British amenability to ethnographically-based Soviet territorial claims in 1939 further encouraged Stalin to pursue national homogeneity in east-central Europe in the post-war period requires further scholarly attention.

9. Quoted in A. Polonsky and B. Drukier, *The Beginnings of Communist Rule in Poland* (London: Routledge, 1980), p.128. For a discussion of the foundation of the initiative group see P. Gontarczyk, *Polska Partia Robotnicza: Droga do Władzy (1941–1944)* (Warszawa: Fronda), p.78.
10. See Z. Polubiec, *Polska Partia Robotnicza: Dokumenty 1942–1948 programowe* (Warszawa: Książka i Wiedza, 1984), pp.174–9, doc. no. 24, 'O nasz stosunek do Niemców' (*sic*).
11. The transfer agreements between Poland, Belarus and Ukraine were signed on 9 September 1944 by Edward Osóbka-Morawski, head of the department of Foreign Affairs, representing the PKWN; Panteleimon Ponomarenko, representing the Belorussian Soviet Socialist Republic; and Nikita Krushchev, representing the Ukrainian Soviet Socialist Republic. The Polish–Belorussian agreement sought to transfer Belorussians to Belarus from Poland, and Poles to Poland from Belarus, and envisaged a transfer operation lasting from 15 October 1944 to 15 February 1945. However, this was not achieved, and a subsequent supplementary protocol was signed on 25 November 1945. Similarly, the tight time frame envisaged in the Polish–Ukrainian agreement was revised by the supplementary protocol of 14 December 1945, which extended the registration period for 'evacuees' until 15 January 1946 and the resettlement deadline until 15 June 1946. The agreement between the PKWN and the Lithuanian SSR was signed on 22 September 1944 by Osóbka-Morawski and Mečislovas Gedvilas, head of the Council of People's Commissars of the Lithuanian SSR. This agreement was also modified on 10 December 1945 to extend the period of resettlement to 15 June 1946. The agreement with the Soviet Union itself was signed by Zygmunt Modzelewski and Andrei Wyszynski in Moscow on 6 July 1945, nine months after the other agreements, and served to regulate the movement of Poles from the USSR to Poland.
12. After the period of expulsions and transfers, relatively small numbers of several minority groups remained in Poland, including Jews, Belorussians, Ukrainians, Germans and Lithuanians amongst others, constituting just less than 3 per cent of the population in 1950. Prior to the Second World War, minorities constituted about one-third of the population.
13. D. Ost, *The Defeat of Solidarity: Anger and Politics in Postcommunist Poland* (London: Cornell University, 2005), p.180.
14. M. Mevius, *Agents of Moscow: The Hungarian Communist Party and the Origins of Socialist Patriotism 1941–1953* (Oxford: Clarendon Press, 2005).
15. J. Micgiel, 'Coercion and the Establishment of Communist Rule in Poland 1944–1947' (unpublished PhD thesis, Columbia University, New York, 1992).
16. These figures do not refer exclusively to ethnic Poles, but we must assume that they constituted the majority by some margin.
17. A. Dudek and A. Paczkowski, 'Poland', in K. Persak and Ł. Kamiński (eds), *A Handbook of the Communist Security Apparatus in East Central Europe 1944–1989* (Warsaw: IPN, 2005), p.273.

18. See Prażmowska, *Civil War in Poland.*
19. D. Harvey, *The Limits to Capital* (Oxford: Blackwell, 1999), pp.32, 159–60.
20. State violence to deal with opposition ranged from 'education' programmes to imprisonment and, at the extreme end, execution of those whose actions and views were inimical to the social order being created. A prison camp complex was created and many of these camps housed those classified as 'anti-state'. See B. Kopka, *Obozy pracy w Polsce 1944–1950: Przewodnik encyklopedyczny* (Warszawa: Nowa Karta, 2002) for an overview. A report by the Ministry of Internal Affairs from 1979 states that in 1944, 11,063 were arrested; 45,148 in 1945; 44,411 in 1946; 30,521 in 1947; 24,443 in 1948; 22,848 in 1949; and 20,727 in 1950. Almost half of the figure for 1945 is made up of arrests for war crimes, so as Dudek and Paczkowski contend (see Dudek and Paczkowski, 'Poland', p.272), if Germans and alleged collaborators are excluded, 1946 was the peak year for arrests. These figures do not include the 80,000–100,000 who were detained prior to the election in January 1947, or those incarcerated by the Soviet Army/NKVD.
21. This conceptualization of violence helps to highlight that only some forms of violence can be overcome within the confines of a specific set of social relations, and it may help inform normative judgement about the justice of particular social relations.
22. Cited in I. Gutman, 'Introduction', in *Więź – Thou Shalt Not Kill: Poles on Jedwabne* (Warsaw: Więź, 2001), p.16.
23. S. Iwaniuk, 'Represje polskiego podziemia wobec ludności białoruskiej na Białostocczyźnie po lipcu 1944', in J. Milewski and A. Pyżewska (eds), *Stosunki Polsko-Białoruskie w Województwie Białostockim w Latach 1939–1956* (Warszawa: IPN, 2005), p.101.
24. Noted in E. Mironowicz, *Polityka narodowościowa PRL* (Białystok: Wydanie Białoruskiego Towarzystwa Historycznego, 2000), p.45. Records can be found at the State Archives in Białystok (APB UWB 234, 117 and 5). Also see APB UWB 515, 'Spalenie wsi Szpaki, Zanie, Wólka Wygonowska, Zaleszany, Końcowizna. Meldunki i korespondencje.'
25. W. Sienkiewicz and G. Hryciuk, *Wysiedlenia, wypędzenia i ucieczki 1939–1959, Atlas Ziem Polski: Polacy, Żydzi, Niemcy, Ukraińcy* (Warszawa: Demart, 2008), p.233.
26. Mironowicz notes that the source data is problematic as there seem to be discrepancies in the figures. However, the limited number of Belorussian transferees is not in question. It was initially planned to remove a greater number of Belorussians from Poland. See E. Mironowicz, *Białorusini w Polsce 1944–1949* (Warszawa: PWN, 1993).
27. D. Engel, 'After the Holocaust: Polish–Jewish Conflict in the Wake of World War II', in C. Freeze *et al.* (eds), *Polin: Studies in Polish Jewry, Vol. 18: Jewish Women in Eastern Europe* (Oxford: Littman, 2005), p.425.
28. See Polonsky and Drukier, *Beginnings of Communist Rule*, p.425.
29. New Documents Archive, Warsaw, Archiwum Akt Nowych (AAN): PZPR 237/VII/2619/111 (point 3) Voivodship Committee of the PZPR in Olsztyn 6/11/1949.
30. G. Strauchold, *Autochtoni Polscy, Niemieccy czy ... Od Nacjonalizmu do Komunizmu 1945–1949* (Toruń: Marszałek, 2001), p.53.
31. See Agamben, *Homo Sacer.*
32. B.A. Szcześniak and Z.W. Szota, *Droga do nikąd. Działalność Organizacji ukraińskich Nacjonalistów i jej likwidacja w Polsce* (Warszawa: MON, 1973), pp.421–32.
33. It is worth noting that most rapes occurred during the final push to Berlin and in the immediate post-war period, with Soviet troops largely responsible. By May 1946, a British official reported: 'In direct contrast to the stories told by Honeybee refugees [from the Russian Zone] against the Russians, very few cases of rape are reported against the Poles. In fact only eight cases have come to the notice of this HQ since the start of Operation Swallow.' TNA, FO 1052/324/18F.
34. TNA, FO 1052/475/24.
35. Cited in N.M. Naimark, *Fires of Hatred: Ethnic Cleansing in Twentieth-Century Europe* (Cambridge, MA: Harvard University Press, 2001), p.125.
36. In June 1947, the British advised the Poles that the agreed 1.5 million people had been accepted – 1.4 million from Polish administered territories and 100,000 via the American zone. See TNA, FO 1052/473 195, 211, 222.
37. Speech of Prime Minister Osóbka-Morawski on 29 April 1946 at the plenary session of the Homeland National Council – Krajowa Rada Narodowa (KRN).
38. J. Michlic, *Poland's Threatening Other: The Image of the Jew from 1880 to the Present* (Lincoln, NE: University of Nebraska, 2006), p.208.

39. H. Datner, 'Szkoły Centralnego Komitetu Żydów w Polsce w latach 1944–1949', *Biuletyn Żydowskiego Instytutu Historycznego*, nr 1–3 (169–171) (1994), p.105.
40. D. Engel, 'Patterns of Anti-Jewish Violence in Poland, 1944–1946' in *Yad Vashem Studies*, 26 (1998), p.77.
41. Cited in Gross, *Fear*, p.155. Adolf Berman was a leading figure in the Marxist Zionist party Poalei Zion-Left and had been active in Jewish resistance during the war.
42. TNA, FO 371/51127 (WR 3418), Cavendish-Bentinck's despatch to the Foreign Office 19 November 1945.
43. The CKŻP represented the various political orientations of Polish Jews and provided social, cultural and welfare support to Polish Jews in the aftermath of the Second World War and the Holocaust.
44. J.T. Gross, 'Stereotypes of Polish-Jewish Relations after the War: The Special Commission of the Central Committee of Polish Jews', in A. Polonsky (ed.), *Polin: Studies in Polish Jewry, Vol. 13: Focusing on the Holocaust and its Aftermath* (Oxford: Littman, 2000), p.195.
45. J. Egit, *Grand Illusion* (Toronto: Lugus, 1991), p.65.
46. APŁ KWPPR 1022/164/1, Polish Army Political Education Main Board publication no. 4, 28 September 1944.
47. A. Dudek and R. Gryz, *Komuniści i Kościół w Polsce 1945–1989* (Kraków: Znak, 2006), p.13.
48. S. Siebel-Achenbach, *Lower Silesia: From Nazi Germany to Communist Poland 1942–1949* (New York: Macmillan in association with St Antony's College, Oxford, 1994), p.203.
49. Hanna Diskin, *The Seeds of Triumph: Church and State in Gomułka's Poland* (Budapest: CEU, 2001), p.13.
50. See K. Urban, 'Kościół Ewangelicko-Augsburgski w Polsce 1945–1950 (z zagadnień kształtowania się struktury diecezjalno-parafialnej)', in *Zeszyty Naukowe Akademii Ekonomicznej w Krakowie*, nr 437 (1994), pp.65–80; letter from Jan Szeruda to Edward Osóbka-Morawski, New Documents Archive (AAN), MAP 1053.
51. Igor Hałagida, *Ukraińcy na zachodnich i północnych ziemiach Polski 1947–1957* (Warszawa: IPN, 2003), p.53.
52. J. Syrnyk, *Ludność ukraińska na Dolnym Śląsku 1945–1989* (Wrocław: IPN, 2007), p.244.
53. Ibid., p.245.
54. Gross, *Fear*, p.148.
55. A. Kemp-Welch, *Poland under Communism: A Cold War History* (Cambridge: Cambridge University Press, 2008), p.42.
56. This managed reservoir of negative sentiment was tapped through the course of the Polish People's Republic by the party and factions within it, for example in the anti-Semitic/'anti-Zionist' campaign of 1968.

5

Returning Home after Forced Labour in the Reich: The Example of the French of *Service du Travail Obligatoire*

RAPHAËL SPINA

> '*When I'm tired, I have a nightmare, always the same. I have to catch the train to leave Germany, and I miss the train. It means I'm tired and that I've got to have a rest. For 50 years, I've been having the same nightmare.*'[1]
>
> Jean Dardel (1920–2005), forced worker at Bielefeld from August 1943 to April 1945, later Bishop of Clermont-Ferrand.

From September 1942 to June 1944, the Vichy government's laws sent between 600,000 and 650,000 French forced workers to Germany's war factories. A further 200,000 went willingly (generally pressed by harsh economic conditions and persuaded by propaganda). No comprehensive study has ever been made of their return. The participants in the *Service du Travail Obligatoire* (STO, Compulsory Work Scheme) – have been forgotten, their fate neither horrible nor exceptional enough to warrant concern. Indeed, the STO were accused of having agreed too readily to go to Germany, and quite often were unfairly confused with those who *had* gone willingly. The memory of the STO is therefore marked by ambiguity and disquiet.

None of the twenty-six witnesses interviewed by Walter Zambon for a regional study in 1999 wanted to dwell on the reception they had had on their return – indeed, if the interviewer broached this topic, their reaction could be violent.[2] The journalist Jean-Pierre

Vittori did much to popularize the idea that the STO had been ill-received on their return, ignored and despised. His pioneer book about this marginalized community of war victims ends with a harsh scene: a railway worker, during the mass return to France of April–May 1945, asks the passengers of a cattle wagon whether they are prisoners of war or ex-concentration camp inmates. When told that they are civil workers, he withdraws his hand from the respondent's shoulder and walks away.[3] On the other hand, a study of STO memories in Lorraine fifty years later suggested that the workers themselves had only tenuous memories of their repatriation. Time had passed, and their return was to them less important than the long-awaited reunion with their families: 'Difficulties or incidents, if any, were quickly forgotten.'[4]

So what was the reality of the experience of this group? The Fédération Nationale des Déportés du Travail (FNDT), the former STO's mass organization founded in 1945, has consistently exaggerated the number of its members who died in Germany. The figure of '60,000' comrades who never returned has entered the organization's mythology, and '15,000' is usually given for those 'shot, hanged, beheaded for acts of resistance'. Research suggests that the death toll was in fact less than half that figure, and that what repression occurred was in response to mild transgressions and criticisms rather than active, organized resistance. It now seems that the 35,000 civil workers who died in Germany lost their lives mainly because of allied bombing.[5] Many were buried in simple local cemeteries. In 1945, for example, 110 were recorded in the cemetery of Rastfuhl at Sarrebrück. The remains of those killed were in some cases repatriated. In 1954, for example, the victims of the Bittermark massacre in Dortmund were returned to France. As late as the late 1970s, the Federation repatriated the corpses of 293 'DT' (Déportés du Travail, Labour Deportees) who had been buried in the USSR. At the national necropolis of Montauville, 619 identified DT are buried and identified by name.[6] Others remain permanently in Germany or Poland, depriving their families of any normal mourning. Among the young victims of the Bittermark massacre was Daniel Ribes, a 23-year-old law student: his parents died of grief when they realized that their son would never return.[7]

The movement of DT was in fact extremely erratic. Some 2,000 jumped out of the trains to Germany. Thousands escaped after their arrival, going through chequered and even amusing adventures to reach the borders of France or Switzerland, often with the help of railway workers or farmers. If discovered, they were sent to an *Arbeitserziehungslager* (AEL, Work Educative Camp), whose conditions could be close to those of the concentration camps, although the periods of incarceration were limited (however, some died there). The number who escaped is difficult to know (it is certainly not 80,000, as the FNDT claimed), but the minister Henry Frenay,[8] as well as historians Michel Boivin and Patrice Arnaud, estimate it to be around 20,000 to 25,000.[9] Several hundred priests or Catholic activists were expelled for illegal religious activities among their fellow exiled workmates – others were jailed or sent to concentration camps, and were later venerated as martyrs, a process of beatification that is still in progress.[10] Between 10,000 and 20,000 workers were sent back 'disabled' – many dying shortly after their return.[11]

Table 1. Permissions as a Way to Escape from Germany: A Chronological Evolution

Period	Permissions granted	Returned to Germany	Defaulters stayed in France
1 May to 14 July 1943	46,418	26,780	19,638
15 July to 30 August	43,140	14,362	28,778
November 1943 to 2 April 1944 (after two months of suspension)	90,702	38,702	52,005

In fact, most workers simply waited for their promised leave of absence and never went back. Germany actually lost more than 100,000 *permissionaires défaillants* in a year: a mass phenomenon, whose details are today properly known (Table 1). So from May 1943 to April 1944, out of more than 180,000 leaves-of-absence granted to French civil workers, 104,419 at least (55.7 per cent) were used to escape. No less than a quarter of French manpower in Germany registered in June 1943 returned home by legal ways, long before the fall of the Reich, and about 15 per cent of the total French voluntary or forced manpower exiled during the war.[12]

The number of defaulters increased with time. As the tide of the war turned and the Wehrmacht met defeats, the DT felt less inclined to stay in Germany. The proportion could also vary from a French area to another and from one German factory to another.[13] The earlier one had been called up, the earlier one got leave and could go back home. The first law of 4 September 1942 had tacitly drafted industrial workers only – men who were often older, married and with families, for they had a qualification, whereas the more famous law of 16 February 1943 addressed itself to all young Frenchmen born between 1920 and 1922, and proposed sending them to Germany as an alternative to military service. As married people were given leave more readily and had been called earlier, a greater proportion of the 1942 draft were able to return. Workers used every form of cunning to obtain a leave: relatives would write to say that a parent was about to die, weddings were concocted and illnesses fabricated.

Some escapers, such as the future singer Georges Brassens, felt remorseful to have let their friends in Germany and to have shirked the common fate.[14] Some forged or were given false papers to work and live normally until the liberation. Others were given amnesties provided that they agreed to work in France in Albert Speer's protected enterprises which produced exclusively for Germany. Others joined the Resistance and the Maquis, or even made the journey to join de Gaulle's army. But most stayed hidden at home, or lay low, working on farms.

For most civilian workers *la Quille* (the demob) – was a constant obsession. Why was it, though, that some of the workers on leave readily agreed to return to Germany? After the war, these decisions were taboo. Unfairly accused of having been a volunteer, Georges Marchais, the leader of the Communist Party from 1970 to 1994, felt he had to at least pretend he had escaped when on leave in June 1943, whereas it is most likely he went voluntarily back to Germany, and returned only in 1945, like so many others.[15] Some were simply unlucky, failing to find the right helpers at the right moment. There were many among their neighbours or their comrades' jealous parents ready to denounce workers who shirked their 'duty'. Some returnees felt they had to respect the word given to the German employer or to the civil servant who had let them go. Most frequently, the moral pressure of the group was decisive. At the end of 1943, the Vichy authorities suggested to Berlin that any worker on leave should be responsible for the leaves of three comrades designated by their names. Some sacrificed their leave to allow a friend to remain with his family, even advising against return in case the consequences were grim. But many more did not want to sacrifice their leave in this way and felt sincerely relieved when the comrade came back. Last but not least – and this was a strong taboo in the post-war years – the German wages had been quite attractive; the strength of the mark meant that money could be put away and savings built up.[16]

Escape, leave and health repatriation were not possible after the summer of 1944: France was freed, and the Reich's borders had become a front line. Many STO had departed in 1943 with the hope that Germany would be defeated before the end of the year. In mid-1944, there were hopes that the war would be over before Christmas. They were bitterly disappointed. Sadness and disillusion combined with the growing difficulties of the daily life in a besieged Reich turned the winter of 1944/45 into the worst year of exile. After the D-Day landing, almost all relations and communications with France were cut: for endless months, they had no news from their families, and vice-versa: 'My mother didn't even know if I was alive or dead.'[17] What is more, whereas in France 1944 had seen the fiercest repression and the traumatic impact of the Allied invasion, in Germany the hardest year was 1945. Thus there was a discrepancy of experience, as the returning workers were excluded from the collective jubilation of the liberation, and unable to make their fellow citizens understand the terrible inferno they had witnessed on the very eve of their repatriation.

Indeed, during this last period, civil workers suffered from the lack of tobacco, garments and food, frequently stealing beets that had been set aside as cattle-fodder, or potatoes stored in silos. Henri Barès remembered eating potatoes raw: 'I even cried because of my hunger and despair.'[18] Never had death been so close. More than one million tons of bombs were dropped onto Germany during the last year of the war.[19] Millions of East Germans were displaced by the Red Army's advance after January 1945, reminding many drafted workers of what they had seen in France in June 1940. Some had to flee with the Germans and walk hundreds of miles to find fresh shelter. On the eastern front also, civil workers were often ordered by cruel SS to dig *Schanzarbeiten* (useless trenches), in the harsh, cold winter. The nervous SS or Gestapo agents didn't hesitate to shoot at some STO; thirty-five were killed in the notorious mass shooting of forced workers (mainly from Russia and Poland) in Dortmund on Good Friday 1945.[20] On both front lines, the STO faced shells and fires right up to the moment at which they were freed. Bearing witness to the violent and chaotic last days of the Reich, they endured enforced rubble clearance and saw sights – dead bodies and terribly wounded people – which would haunt them for decades to come. When the end of the war finally came, their situation changed: there was no work to be done and the Germans didn't care about them anymore. Many were given shelter by farmers and spent a comfortable few months in the countryside.[21] But in the cities, the breakdown of the rationing system and lack of policing meant that life was lived on a knife-edge.

Some escaped this chaos, walking for days in the harsh winter in the search for safety. Georges Toupet, aged 24, who had resourcefully organized and protected 2,500 young and older civil workers at Auschwitz, obeyed the order on 21 of January 1945 to evacuate the camp; they had to walk from Silesia to Saxony, fortunately helped by friendly Polish and Czech peasants who gave them some food, hot drinks and places to sleep. Then, when the allies approached at the end of April, they agreed to move again twice to the Bohemian mountains, the Wehrmacht's last pocket of resistance, and were freed only when the Reich capitulated. This was a controversial choice and many of Toupet's young protégés, fed up with walking and eager to be free, deserted his columns alone or in small groups, so that by the time he reached France half of his troop had abandoned him, but the Americans paid tribute to this resourceful group of boys and repatriated them by plane as early as 14 May;[22] many other young workers had to wait for weeks or months.

In total it is thought that some 400,000 French civil workers were still in the Reich in 1945.[23] We know very little about the 10,000 French (and the respective proportion of POWs and civilians among them) who stayed in Germany to start a new life. Usually they met a German girl or war widow, and took over the family's farm or shop. A few had struck up relationships with women forced labourers, so the decision to return home could be heartbreaking. The future writer Cavanna lost forever Maria, his young Russian lover.[24] On the other hand, the young Jean Munsch, from Lorraine, went to Ukraine with the young wife he had met in Silesia, forgot his past life, and only returned to France for a visit in 1997.[25] Some others had no particular scruples about cynically leaving their lovers.

So in April 1945, the mass return of STO started spontaneously. Alone or in groups, they wandered through a devastated country, on foot, in carriages or lorries or by train, eating whatever they could, thieving food and other goods – either because that was the only way to survive or, frequently, out of revenge. The background was apocalyptic: destroyed bridges and bombed stations, twisted rails, collapsed buildings, erased streets and ruined towns, the ditches and the sides of the roads filled with corpses. Thirty million homeless or exiled people wandered the German roads. Crime flourished on a scale not seen before. When Louis Eemans and his friends entered a deserted mansion, they found the body of the woman who lived there, her throat cut, and banknotes all over the floor. Since money no longer had any value, they played football with them.[26] After years of exile and 'slavery', the French were often pleased to take home a symbol of revenge: garments, money, jewels, food: when I interviewed Roger Monnier at his home in 2004, he showed me on his bookshelves examples of fine antiquarian books he brought back during the chaos.[27] But these were principally hard times, when the former workers' main concern was to find enough to eat. Mme Courtil's husband and his comrades had to eat raw potatoes from the fields.[28] Others caught chickens and pigs in the farms, bludgeoning them with elementary tools, and cooking them on open fires. Occasionally these modern nomadic migrations bore a semblance of organization. Robert Barde, aged 24, head of the clandestine Catholic action for Potsdam, led the return of 350 DT who walked and rode by bicycle back to France in late May 1945; this motley procession eventually reached Paris in June.[29] The returning French did virtually no harm to the German civilians they passed; indeed, some even protected their former German workmates, hosts or bosses against the angry Russians.

The vengeful Red Army, eager to punish the Germans for the brutal war they had led against their country, were the source of terrifying memories for many STO. They often witnessed or heard of mass rapes and summary executions, their own suffering generally being confined to thefts of valuables such as watches and other personal goods. In the words of Louis Eemans, the dreadful 'Mongolians' were used as an avant-garde to terrorize civilians, free to plunder and to brutalize whoever crossed their path, so that two days after, when the main troops arrived, people were too scared to resist, and even felt relieved. For being freed by the Soviets generally meant that the journey back to France was long, boring and uncomfortable, involving as it did the land-route through Poland and the USSR to the port of Odessa, followed by a sea journey. Most of the STO freed by the Soviets in January did not arrive in Marseille until the summer of 1945, a few as late as

August or September! Only a minority, however, of the 302,000 French freed by the Soviets (POWs, concentration camp inmates, STO) took the maritime route: between March and August 1945, just 43,000 were repatriated by boat, the others returning by train.[30]

If possible, the DT chose to walk – even for several weeks – if this brought contact with American troops, who had no reason to scare them, and who were less far from the French borders than the Red Army.[31] They generally cheered their western liberators, often helping them to hunt down suspected Nazis and to disarm German soldiers. A spirit of cooperation prevailed and some delayed their own return to help the Americans to organize their comrades' repatriation. Many were impressed by the Americans' displays of power and wealth – gauging from the notion that perhaps the age of Europe was over. There was some resentment – not helped by the fact that their own situation was neglected and misunderstood. Prejudice against America was not far below the surface, and many later accounts of the encounters with American troops have been retrospectively influenced by Cold War representations and by the ambiguous post-war relations between France and the USA. Quite often, relations were easier with the Afro-American soldiers.[32]

The wandering STO were gathered by the Americans in enormous meeting centres, where the wait for repatriation could be frustratingly long. Relations were not always easy. The POWs and the STO, who had known each other well for two years now, usually got along well. Many STO were sensitive enough to realize that priority needed to be given to the concentration camp survivors, whose sufferings had been far worse and whose need for medical care was urgent. But there were some unedifying scenes, as there were competitions to be the first to be repatriated. At any rate, during the summer of 1945, a few planes, a large number of lorries and passenger trains, and an even greater number of cattle wagons, brought back to France hundreds of people from all three categories mixed together. The usual route was across the Rhine on a strange, groaning, hazardous American makeshift bridge of boats. After that, the Dutch and Belgian railways – comparatively intact compared to the French networks – brought the men back to France. There are unanimous memories of how the Benelux people welcomed them, cheering them loudly on the station platforms, offering them drinks and food: this was often their best memory of repatriation.

On the French side, repatriation was the job of the new ministry of Prisoners, Deportees and Refugees (Ministère des Prisonniers, Déportés et Réfugiés) led by Henry Frenay, a great pioneer underground leader. Repatriating one to two million citizens (two to three times the number after the First World War) was a gigantic task for a country whose economy and transports lay in ruins. Improvization was the order of the day and mistakes, wastes and delays were not infrequent. Frenay was the target of a violent press campaign accusing his ministry of carelessness, incompetence and corruption, and of reinstating former Vichy civil servants. The communists were especially fierce in their complaints, as Frenay was very anti-communist and tried to prevent the Resistance from being seduced by the party. In June, the ex-POWs' leaders, together with some STO, held a big demonstration in front of Frenay's office.[33] Relations with the allies were also sometimes quite uneasy. At first, the Gaullist government, wanting as much independence as possible, did not want to cooperate with UNRRA and with the Allied armies, preferring that the repatriation of the French should be the work of France alone.[34] But eventually the task was shared. No one was neglected: besides the big *Mission française de rappatriement en Allemagne*, Frenay also sent missions to Switzerland, Denmark, Norway, Sweden and the USSR to take care of the exiled French who were there. The speed with which repatriation took place is testament to Frenay's efforts – even if a part of the STO had indeed to wait for a long time. Out of a group of 357 STO from Bordeaux, 113 were home just a fortnight after liberation, 106 took between sixteen and thirty days; seventy-nine needed thirty-one to forty-five days, and for sixty-nine the journey home took more than forty-five days![35]

The returnees had first to go to welcome centres, for administrative formalities, where they were given their official *carte de rapatrié*. Their German money had to be given up: only a maximum of 100 marks (2,000 Francs) could be changed and a receipt was given in order to get the remainder later. In fact, it took long years of quarrels before their German savings were refunded, and they lost a great part of them since the government refused to respect the 1944 change toll, fixed by the Germans at one mark for twenty Francs. They usually got a shave and a shower, a very superficial medical examination, and were disinfected with DDT. They were given some money, tobacco, garments, shoes, food and drink. They rediscovered hygiene: 'For the first time for two years, we could sleep into sheets, proper true ones.' Marseille was the gateway for workers coming back from Russia. Paris – with the Gare d'Orsay, the Rex, the Gaumont and other big requisitioned cinemas – was the central hub for repatriation.

With difficulty, volunteers were sorted out from forced workers. The authorities were also on the look out for collaborators or war criminals who had disguised themselves as civil worker. In a recent literary echo, the fictitious French-speaking SS Max Aue, Jonathan Littel's narrator in his bestseller, *The Kindly Ones*, escaped justice by pretending he was an STO and by mixing with the flood of repatriated French. It is often said the genuine forced workers felt annoyed and humiliated by the interrogations and by the notion that they were under suspicion. In fact, most were so pleased to see their country again that they accepted the need for questions and other formalities. Out of a panel of sixty-eight ex-STO from Lyons, three out of four accepted the sorting, half of them recognized its legitimacy or shrugged it off – although one in three admitted that it had been 'unpleasant'.[36]

Witnesses do not readily confess to feelings of vengefulness and violence. But it is certain that the return of POWs, STO and concentration camp inmates led to a renewal of demands for *Epuration* – the rooting-out of collaborators. Many were eager to denounce and punish those who had been responsible for their long exiles, and were impatient for the measures against collaborators to be finished. Some, thirsting for justice, were ready to take the law into their own hands. Volunteers often came back to France in the same trains as the emaciated, exhausted, concentration camp inmates; their arrival shocked public opinion and lead to violent incidents at the Gare d'Orsay, especially against women volunteers. They had, after all, been exempt from the labour draft, so every returning female worker could only be a volunteer – an object of hatred and a scapegoat for public anger and shame.

Chantal Le Bobinnec, aged 18, and her sister Mathilde, aged 15, had accompanied their mother to Germany as voluntary labourers, having little choice in the matter. Their mother – a woman from the aristocracy, ruined by her husband – whom the girls describe as partly mentally disturbed and exceptionally selfish, abandoned them there as guarantors of her own return, remaining nevertheless in France once her leave had expired. For two years Chantal worried about what her return would be like: even if she survived the bombings, how could she prove to her fellow citizens that she was neither a traitor nor a prostitute? When she eventually arrived, haggard and apprehensive, at the border's repatriation centre, she was just given a slap on her face, and was then set free. Others that day were punished more harshly: some French soldiers were said to have followed a group of returned women into the showers, and rumours had it that they had been raped.[37]

There were many more stories of abuse of returning women. In Epinal, in May 1945, female workers had to be protected by police from attacks by a crowd at the station, while in Rambervilliers, a group of former concentration camp inmates and STO held a mock trial and then publicly shaved the heads of a dozen women, then started to hunt collaborators.[38] In Belfort, the prefect had a car with loudspeakers driven along the streets to explain that an ill-treated female worker, the respectable wife of a communist resister who had been imprisoned for his activities, had had to leave France because of persecution.[39] In Angers, a crowd hurled abuse at twenty women, not realizing that they had been illegally sent to the Reich by local collaborators who had organized a 'slave labour' racket.[40]

Male volunteers were not spared. At Givors, on 5 of June, nine out of twenty ex-volunteers summoned by the mayor for examination were given over to former concentration camp inmates who were given free right to assault them outside the town hall, with 300 people watching.[41] At Grenoble, the prefect had volunteers interned, to avoid them being manhandled; hundreds were thus protected, the majority of them men. By October they had all been released and were left in peace. In factories, workers protested and strikes erupted when former volunteers returned to their former jobs. Under the pressure of public opinion, the authorities even considered punishing them by submitting them to a kind of forced labour draft (those strange projects were forgotten after 1945).[42] A minority had to face a trial by the *Chambres civiques*, but these courts proved to be lenient[43] and the government was understanding; except for a minority known to have had sympathy with the Nazi cause, the minister Frenay took the line that that most of the volunteers had been forced to depart because of unemployment, low wages, family or personal problems, or influenced by the propaganda of the time. The post-war quest for national unity produced a lenient response to the STO; they were even referred to as 'the so-called volunteers'.

After some public debates, the government chose not to wait

for the full return of all the exiled French to organize the first post-war free polls, on 29 April 1945. The political inmates were the focus of much public admiration. The few Jewish survivors were ignored – for no one was aware yet of the specificity of their fate. The POWs, so much celebrated by Vichy as a symbol of expiation, were now an irritating reminder of France's defeat. The STO's symbolic capital was even weaker; they were seen as cowards, losers or disguised volunteers, and raised nothing but indifference. No specific attention was paid to their fate by the press or the authorities. Quite often, they arrived mixed with other categories of war victims, or gradually, in small groups, so as to play down their role and diminish any attention.

Despite the black legend about the civil workers' return, and the incidents recounted above, all the former STO interviewed by Jasmyne Jouvin recalled receiving a proper welcome, and went back to their jobs after a prescribed fifteen days of rest.[44] The reception committees complete with brass bands that had been a feature of the weeks immediately following the end of the war tended to diminish somewhat after the end of May, and sometimes no one was on the platform to welcome them home, but most of the time a celebration was offered. The joy of being reunited with their families made most forget the discomforts and sights of their time away. In rural areas, it was common knowledge that there had been little choice but to depart, so they had a warm welcome, even if the absence of the comrades they had left dead in Germany tarnished the collective joy.[45]

Compared to other returning groups, the STO integrated with their families relatively easily. The older and the married had often been the beneficiaries of leave, so had been exiled for no more than six, eight or ten months. The youngest and the unluckiest, who had had to depart in 1943 and come back in 1945, had stayed a maximum of two years in Germany, less than half of the period of captivity endured by POWs. Unlike the concentration camp survivors, they had not been traumatized or dehumanized, but rather had been able to maintain relatively normal social relations; they did not suffer the isolation of those who had gone through an unspeakable experience. Most were still young, full of energy, and eager to catch up on the lost time. With careers as yet not established, they had not suffered any loss of social standing during their exile.

Most went back to their previous jobs. Laws and shortages of manpower constrained employers to keep the same staff as before.

Just a week after his return, Louis Eemans was back working at the same bank as before his departure. A small minority used the rupture in their personal and professional life to get new jobs offering greater security and higher pay. They became civil servants and joined the public sector, vastly swollen after the nationalization programme of the immediate post-war months. In the closing scene of Claude Autant-Lara's famous comedy, *La Traversée de Paris*, Jean Gabin meets again on a station's platform Martin (Bourvil), the unemployed taxi driver whom he had been unable to avoid being sent to the STO. Martin has joined the SNCF and become a luggage carrier, so that he no longer has to fear unemployment. The police in the Loire estimated that 30 per cent of the repatriated would renounce their former jobs in favour of the stability of the public sector.[46] This trend would contribute substantially to the decline of France's rural population in the post-war years.[47]

Some of the STO had lost their parents during their time in Germany, only learning the bad news once they were back. Some had lost weight and were almost unrecognizable. It was a strange feeling, too, to see their babies and children again, who had grown up without them for two years. For some – those with ambitions to study – the dull toil inflicted on them in Germany had a demoralizing effect. Some had lost goods through theft: Jean-Louis Forest, later the leader of the FNDT for half a century, considered himself lucky, for only his bike had disappeared.[48] Others discovered that their houses or even their entire village or town had been destroyed. Some men met their wives in Germany, came back with them, and started a family – whose very existence was owed to the period of exile. Others discovered that their wives had been unfaithful, or that children of whom they were not the fathers had been born. Divorces reached an historic peak in 1945/46.

An unknown number returned mutilated in some way. Thousands had to stay in sanatoriums for weeks or months because of tuberculosis and other diseases caught in the Reich. The FNDT's own sanatoriums were still operational at the beginning of the 1950s. M.G., forced by the Germans to work when he was already sick, had been an invalid since 1963.[49] Twelve per cent of repatriated workers were said to suffer from tuberculosis, 9 per cent from heart problems, and 3 per cent from curvature of the spine.[50] According to the FNDT, 50,000 returned with tuberculosis and 59 per cent with pre-tuberculosis; 20 per cent per cent died prematurely because of diseases contracted or worsened in

Germany – these figures are, of course, impossible to check. According to the more reliable Pr Dessaille, who attended the Nuremberg Trials as a witness, 25,000 STO died of diseases before repatriation, and 30,000 after, but no one can know how many died as a direct result of their exile.[51] The FNDT never managed to have an official inquiry investigate into the 'pathology of labour deportation'.

When the forced labourers returned, a powerful federation had already been formed to welcome them. As early as the autumn of 1944, the underground movement MNPGD (Mouvement National des Prisonniers de Guerre et Déportés – National Movement of POW and Deportees) led by François Mitterrand melded with the Vichy government's social assistance department to found what would become, on 15 October 1945, the Fédération Nationale des Déportés du Travail. It still exists, united and active and seemingly impervious to political events. The federation's first years were the most dynamic, hopeful and altruistic. The survivors, frustrated by the tensions over definitions, wanted to contribute to reconstruction, and to maintain the solidarity which had helped them survive in the German camps – hence the FNDT's major efforts and achievements in social assistance. The federation established a pattern of rites, involving pilgrimages back to both West and East Germany (impressive places of collective executions: Brandenburg, Dortmund, Grossbeeren). The style of remembrance and the nature of official speeches would hardly vary for sixty years. But by the 1950s, the FNDT's dynamism was wearing thin; physical resources were running low, and the predominance of middle class leaders meant an abandonment of the earlier crusading social spirit. Most of the STO from the same areas, factories or camps lost sight of each other. Some refused to overstate or embellish the nature of their exile; some hardly mentioned it throughout their lives. Others kept a vivid memory of this experience, but only within their family circle. After an initial flurry of immediate post-war accounts, it was only in the 1980s and 1990s that a substantial number of memoirs began to appear.[52]

Any sense of solidarity which had existed between the different communities of the repatriated French broke down quite early, when the death camps' deportees began to contest their official name of '*déportés du travail*', pointing out rightly or not that it could lead to a confusion between their terrible ordeal and that of the STO. During the occupation, everyone had described the drafted workers' experience as a 'deportation' (the underground propaganda, the BBC, de Gaulle, the Nuremberg court and even, privately, some ministers at Vichy, or Albert Speer himself). As early as late 1945, some survivors of the Nazi camps expressed their anger at the civil workers claiming the term 'deportees' without any clarification of the nature of their situation. In Chambery, the prefect of the town banned a charity ball which was to have taken place for 'labour deportees', because the furious concentration camp inmate deportees had denounced it – considering it to usurp their own very different experience. Violent clashes were feared, which might have placed the police in the invidious position of protecting the event against Auschwitz survivors.[53]

August 1946 was the last time that the STO were included in a national commemorative gathering, at Compiègne, where First World War veterans, prisoners of war, STO and concentration camp deportees came together for a joint ceremony. Shortly after that, a contest for recognition began which has continued to this day. The FNDT alternated successes and defeats in the parliament, then in the courts. In 1992, the use of the title of 'labour deportees' was finally ruled illegal. The loss of this 'battle for the title', a central plank of the survivors' collective identity, served to bring together the members of this socially and politically very heterogeneous group, whose past experiences in Germany had been too complex and ambiguous for an acceptable narrative to have been agreed.

Meanwhile, both the public and the authorities refuse to take any interest in the history of the former STO. A wall of indifference persists, even as the last survivors approach their final days.

REFERENCES

Archive Sources

Archives départementales (AD) du Rhône

Archives Nationales, Paris (AN)

Records of the Fédération Nationale des Déportés du Travail (FNDT), 6 rue Saint-Marc, Paris.

Published Sources

Arnaud, Patrice, *Les travailleurs civils français en Allemagne pendant la Seconde guerre mondiale (1940–1945)* (thesis, Université Paris-I, 2006).

Berbiguier, Dominique, *Histoire et mémoire du travail obligatoire en Allemagne à travers quelques cas héraultais* (mémoire de maîtrise, Université de Toulouse-Le Mirail, 2000).

Bergere, M., *Une société en épuration* (Rennes: PUR, 2004).

Brune, René, *La Déportation du travail: Le droit au titre: un combat pour l'honneur* (Paris: Publibook, 2001).

Cavanna, F. *Les Russkoffs* (Paris: Belfond, 1989).

Cochet, François, *Les exclus de la victoire: Histoire des prisonniers de guerre, STO et déportés* (Paris: SPM, 1992).
Cochet, François 'Français retour d'Allemagne', *L'Histoire*, 179 (août 1994), pp.70–5.
Gratier de Saint-Louis, Michel, 'Histoire d'un retour: les STO du Rhône', *Lendemains*, nos. 101–2 (2001), pp.59–71.
Gratier de Saint-Louis, Michel, *Le STO dans le Rhône: histoire et mémoire (1942–1990)* (thèse de doctorat, Université de Lyon, 1990).
Harbulot, Jean-Pierre, *Le Service du Travail Obligatoire: La région de Nancy face aux exigences allemandes* (Nancy: Presses Universitaires de Nancy, 2003).
Hofnung, T. *Georges Marchais: L'inconnu du PCF* (Paris: l'Archipel, 2001).
Jouvin, Jasmyne, *Le Service du Travail Obligatoire en Ille-et-Vilaine* (mémoire de maîtrise, Université de Rennes II, 1994).
Judt, T., *Après-Guerre* [Post-War] (Paris: Robert Laffont, 2007).
Knauft, Wolfgang, *Face à la Gestapo: Travailleurs chrétiens et prêtres du STO: Berlin 1943–1945* (Paris: Le Cherche-Midi, 2007).
La main-d'œuvre française exploitée par le IIIe Reich, actes du colloque de Caen (Caen: CHRQ, 2003).
Lagrou, Pieter, *Heroes, Martyrs, Victims: A Comparative Study of the Memory of World War II in Belgium, France and the Netherlands 1945–1965* (Cambridge: Cambridge University Press, 2000).
Lamy, J.-C., *Brassens, le mécréant de Dieu* (Paris: Albin Michel, 2004).
Le Bobinnec, Chantal, *Ma drôle de guerre à 18 ans* (Paris: Les Editions de Paris, 2008).
Mémoires patriotiques et occupation nazie: Déportés, requis et déportés en Europe occidentale 1945–1965 (Bruxelles: Complexe, 2003).
Molette, C. (Mgr), *En haine de l'Evangile* (Paris: Fayard, 1993).
Pawlal, P., *Le retour des 'absents', Marseille 1945* (maîtrise, Université d'Avignon, 2001).
Ruffin, R., *La vie des Français au jour le jour: De la Libération à la victoire* (Paris: Presses de la Cité, 1986).
Simonin, A., 'Pourquoi certains crimes doivent rester impunis: Les travailleurs volontaires en Allemagne devant les chambres civiques de la Seine', in *La main-d'œuvre française exploitée par le IIIe Reich*, actes du colloque de Caen (Caen: CHRQ, 2003), pp.563–82.
Spina, Raphaël, 'French Pillar of Remembrance of Forced Labour in Germany: The Fédération Nationale des Déportés du Travail since 1945', symposium on 'Armament, War Economy and Forced Labour in the Third Reich', Munich, Deutsches Museum, 15–16 March 2007.
Tillman, Elisabeth, *Zum 'Reichseinsatz' nach Dortmund – Destination Dortmund au service du IIIe Reich: Le destin des travailleurs français du STO au camp Loh 1943–1945* (Dortmund: Katholisches Bildungswerk des Dortmunder Dekanate e. V., 1995).
Tooze, A. *The Wages of Destruction: The Making and Breaking of the Nazi Economy* (Oxford: Penguin, 2007).
Vacelet, M.-A., *Le Territoire de Belfort dans la tourmente* (Besançon: Cêtre, 2004).
Vaernewyck, Laure, *Un groupe de requis bordelais au STO* (maîtrise, Université Bordeaux-III, 2000).
Vittori, Jean-Pierre, *Eux, les STO* (Paris: Messidor-Temps Actuels, 1982).
Wieviorka, Annette, *Déportation et genocide* (Paris: Hachette, 1995).
Zambon, Walter, *Le STO dans les départements alpins: 1942–1992* (DEA, Université de Lyon-II, 1999).

NOTES

1. Quoted by R. Brune, *La Déportation du travail* (Paris: Publibook, 2001), p.302.
2. W. Zambon, *Le STO dans les départements alpins, 1942–1992* (DEA, Université de Lyon-II, 1999), p.72.
3. J.-P. Vittori, *Eux, les STO* (Paris: Messidor-Temps Actuels, 1982), p.272.
4. J.-P. Harbulot, *Le Service du Travail Obligatoire: La région de Nancy face aux exigences allemandes* (Nancy: Presses Universitaires de Nancy, 2003), p.565.
5. P. Arnaud, *Les travailleurs civils français en Allemagne pendant la Seconde guerre mondiale (1940–1945)* (thesis, Université Paris-I, 2006).
6. Records of the Fédération Nationale des Déportés du Travail (FNDT), 6 rue Saint-Marc, Paris.
7. E. Tillman, *Zum 'Reichseinsatz' nach Dortmund–Destination Dortmund au service du IIIe*

Reich: Le destin des travailleurs français du STO au camp Loh 1943–1945 (Dortmund: Katholisches Bildungswerk des Dortmunder Dekanate e. V., 1995), p.189.
8. Archives Nationales, Paris (AN), 9F3171.
9. Arnaud, *Les travailleurs civils français*, Chapter 1.
10. C. Molette (Mgr), *En haine de l'Evangile* (Paris: Fayard, 1993).
11. Interview with Claude Fèvre and her parents, 1 August 2004, about her uncle Jacques Lieber, who died of tuberculosis just after returning in June 1944.
12. Arnaud, *Les travailleurs civils français*, chapter 1.
13. In the Gau of Berlin, 30.5 per cent of *leavers* didn't return to their work by Arado-Flugzeugwerke Brandenburg, but only 17.5 per cent by AEG Wildau, 10 per cent by Auer Oranienburg, and only 4.1 per cent as far as Daimler-Benz was concerned. W. Knauft, *Face à la Gestapo: Travailleurs chrétiens et prêtres du STO: Berlin 1943–1945* (Paris: Le Cherche-Midi, 2007).
14. J.-C. Lamy, *Brassens, le mécréant de Dieu* (Paris: Albin Michel, 2004).
15. T. Hofnung, *Georges Marchais: L'inconnu du PCF* (Paris: l'Archipel, 2001).
16. Arnaud, *Les travailleurs civils français*, Chapter 3.
17. http://www.wikimanche.fr/index.php?title=STO_dans_la_Manche.
18. Tillman, *Zum 'Reichseinsatz' nach Dortmund*, p.157.
19. A. Tooze, *The Wages of Destruction: The Making and Breaking of the Nazi Economy* (Oxford: Penguin, 2007), pp.649–50.
20. Tillman, *Zum 'Reichseinsatz' nach Dortmund*.
21. Arnaud, *Les travailleurs civils français*, p.1619.
22. Ibid., p.1615. Interview with Georges Toupet, 20 January 2007.
23. Arnaud, *Les travailleurs civils français*. For confirmation, only 15,000 of the 24,500 Lorraine drafted workers were still in Germany in April 1945: Harbulot, *Le Service du Travail Obligatoire*, p.512.
24. F. Cavanna, *Les Russkoffs* (Paris: Belfond, 1989).
25. Harbulot, *Le Service du Travail Obligatoire*, p.515.
26. Interview with L. Eemans, 20 September 2004.
27. Interview with Roger Monnier, 6 October 2004.
28. Interview with Mme Courtil, 1 May 2005.
29. Knauft, p. 133.
30. P. Pawlal, *Le retour des 'absents', Marseille 1945* (maîtrise, Université d'Avignon, 2001). The first ship arrived from Odessa on 23 March 1945.
31. According to F. Cochet, *Les exclus de la victoire: Histoire des prisonniers de guerre, STO et déportés* (Paris: SPM, 1992), p.65, it took on average seventeen days to return home if freed by the Anglo-Saxons, 117 days if freed by the Soviets.
32. Arnaud, *Les travailleurs civils français*, pp.1643–51. See also A. Wieviorka, *Déportation et genocide* (Paris: Hachette, 1995), p.42 sq.
33. Wieviorka, *Déportation et genocide*, p.41 sq.
34. T. Judt, *Après-Guerre* [Post-War] (Paris: Robert Laffont, 2007), p.144.
35. L. Vaernewyck, *Un groupe de requis bordelais au STO* (maîtrise, Université Bordeaux-III, 2000), annexe S-1.
36. M. Gratier de Saint-Louis, *Le STO dans le Rhône: histoire et mémoire (1942–1990)* (thèse de doctorat, Université de Lyon, 1990), p.469.
37. C. Le Bobinnec, *Ma drôle de guerre à 18 ans* (Paris: Les Editions de Paris, 2008).
38. Harbulot, *Le Service du Travail Obligatoire*, p.566.
39. M.-A. Vacelet, *Le Territoire de Belfort dans la tourmente* (Besançon: Cêtre, 2004).
40. M. Bergere, *Une société en épuration* (Rennes: PUR, 2004).
41. Archives départementales (AD) du Rhône, 233 W 101.
42. Gratier de Saint-Louis p.550.
43. A. Simonin, 'Pourquoi certains crimes doivent rester impunis: Les travailleurs volontaires en Allemagne devant les chambres civiques de la Seine', in *La main-d'œuvre française exploitée par le IIIe Reich*, actes du colloque de Caen (Caen: CHRQ, 2003), pp.563–82.
44. J. Jouvin, *Le Service du Travail Obligatoire en Ille-et-Vilaine* (maîtrise, Université Rennes-II, 1994), p.59.
45. D. Berbiguier, *Histoire et mémoire du travail obligatoire en Allemagne à travers quelques cas héraultais* (maîtrise, Université Toulouse-Le Mirail, 2000), p.101.
46. AD Rhône, 283 W 44, report, 16 July 1945.

47. 'Le temps des restrictions en France 1939–1949', *Cahiers de l'IHTP*, no.32–33 (mai 1996), p.111.
48. Interview with Jean-Louis Forest, 2 December 2004.
49. Jouvin, *Le Service du Travail Obligatoire en Ille-et-Vilaine*, p.58.
50. R. Ruffin, *La vie des Français au jour le jour: De la Libération à la victoire* (Paris: Presses de la Cité, 1986), p.177.
51. Arnaud, *Les travailleurs civils français*, Chapter 1.
52. See Raphaël Spina: 'French Pillar of Remembrance of Forced Labour in Germany: The Fédération Nationale des Déportés du Travail since 1945', symposium on 'Armament, War Economy and Forced Labour in the Third Reich', Munich, Deutsches Museum, 15–16 March 2007.
53. AD Rhône, 283 W 46.

6

Roles and Merits of the Polish Asssociation of Ex-Political Prisoners of German Prisons and Concentration Camps: Polish Survivors in Great Britain

ALEKSANDRA LOEWENAU

BACKGROUND

The experience of Polish nationals during the Second World War is a problematic and complex theme. The policy of the Nazis towards Poles in the incorporated lands and in the General Government was extremely brutal. The first months after the invasion were characterized by terror, mass shootings and the capture of hundreds of resistance fighters, intelligentsia and clergy, who were sent for interrogation in Nazi prisons and then to concentration camps. The first incarceration of Poles in Nazi concentration camps took place on 3 September 1939, when members of the Polish resistance from Pomerania[1] were sent to the newly opened concentration camp in Stutthof, which was situated in territory of the Free City Gdańsk.[2] The majority of Polish nationals were sent to Nazi concentration camps as political prisoners, unlike Polish Jews who were imprisoned only because they were Jewish.

Although the majority of detained Poles shared a similar experience of arrest, interrogation and imprisonment as political enemies of the Nazi regime, the so-called 'crimes' they committed were numerous. Some of them were arrested for belonging to the underground movement and conspiracy, but the Nazis defined such subversive activity very broadly. For instance, listening to certain radio stations or reading forbidden newspapers counted as 'conspiracy'. Many Polish people were plucked randomly from the streets or from home and sent to concentration camps without reason, or because of their education or profession as clergymen, medical doctors, teachers, and lawyers.

At the end of the war, when the allies were advancing into the Reich and the territories occupied by Nazi Germany, they uncovered the camps that had been operated by the Nazi regime. On 24 July 1944, the Soviets marched into *KL* (*Konzentrationslager*) Majdanek, the first liberated concentration camp.[3] The last camp to be liberated, on 9 May 1945, was *KL* Stutthof. For Polish camp inmates liberated by the Soviets in Poland, their situation was straightforward – mostly they returned to where they had lived before the war. Very difficult circumstances, on the other hand, were faced by Polish nationals liberated by the western allies in Germany and Austria. By the time they were healthy enough to return to Poland, they discovered that a new Soviet regime was established in their homeland. Knowledge of the treatment meted out to members of the underground movement in Communist Poland deterred many former prisoners from returning to their native country. Despite this, many did return only to find themselves in a new reality, cut off from western Europe and aware that, forgotten and abandoned by the allies, they were now behind the Iron Curtain. Particularly disturbing was the fate of those who joined the Second Corps of General Anders's Army.[4] However, a great many Poles chose to remain abroad because of the better employment prospects and the opportunity to live in a free society, but also because there was nothing to return to, since many had lost entire families and homes during the war.

This chapter investigates the history and the activity of the Polish Association of Ex-Political Prisoners of German Prisons and Concentration Camps in Great Britain.[5] Firstly, I will discuss the beginnings of the organization, including the reason why it was established, and its status. Secondly, I will analyse the association's aims and approaches, and finally, I will look at the association's struggle for compensation from the German Federal Government.

THE POLISH ASSOCIATION OF EX-POLITICAL PRISONERS OF GERMAN PRISONS AND CONCENTRATION CAMPS IN GREAT BRITAIN: BEGINNING, BREAKTHROUGH AND STATUS

The history of the Polish Association of Ex-Political Prisoners of German Prisons and Concentration Camps in Great Britain started in 1945 when hundreds of Polish camp inmates, who were unwilling to return to Poland, joined the Polish Army in Italy. Many former Polish prisoners settled in the Barletta Polish camp. They received not only health care provided by military physicians and ex-prisoners with medical knowledge, but were also able to gain employment or continue their education at Italian universities such as Bologna. Moreover, General Anders's Army admitted various Poles who were persecuted by the Nazis, including Polish forced labour workers, who after the war were based in a number of Polish civilian camps across Europe. In addition, there were thousands of Poles in Displaced Persons (DPs) camps in the British and American zones.[6] Some continued to live in DP camps until the 1950s, waiting for the chance to emigrate.

Polish camp inmates followed the example of other nationalities in establishing their own former inmates' organization. At the end of 1945, a delegation of Polish former camp prisoners, including Władysław Gościński[7] and Marian Jagło, travelled to Hamburg where they registered the Polish Association of Ex-Political Prisoners of German Prisons and Concentration Camps in Italy.[8]

Initially it was expected that financial help and compensation might be secured, but once this expectation was known to be futile, the association focused its energies on recruiting new members. A list of eligibility criteria was drawn up which forbade former criminals from joining. Furthermore, those political prisoners who had in any way cooperated with the Nazis, for instance as *Kapos*, chiefs of the blocks or Polish inmates who signed the *Volksdeutsche List*, were also barred.[9] Another measure taken at that time was to estimate the number of Polish former political prisoners currently living outside Poland. It was reckoned that over 10,000 former Polish camp inmates lived temporarily in the British, American and French occupation zones, also including Belgium, France, Holland and Italy.[10] After a certain time, many of them returned to Poland, while others found jobs in Germany and other countries. Only a small number decided to join the Polish Second Corps. Some had no interest in joining any organization, but despite this, membership of the association rose, and by the end of July 1946 reached over 200 people.[11]

A breakthrough for the association occurred with the British government's decision to allow members of the Polish Armed Forces who had served under British command for at least a year to move from Italy to Great Britain.[12] Although in fact only a limited number of members of the Polish Ex-Political Prisoners Association were professional soldiers, all of them were permitted to enter the UK as 'dependants' of the Polish Second Corps.[13]

At the time, the British government was trying to limit the number of immigrants from Europe, so it was a particularly valuable opportunity for Polish former prisoners. By the end of the war, approximately 22,000 Polish civilians were living in the UK.[14] H.H. Prestige from the Home Office, in his letter to C.J. Edmonds, described the government's opinion on immigration of Poles to Great Britain:

> If any comparative assessment of this country's contribution towards relief of distress in Europe, we feel that it should be emphasized that we have undertaken a very large addition to our foreign population by accepting certain obligations towards former members of the Allied Forces based in this country during the war who were unwilling to return to their own countries and by accepting over 150,000 refugees from Europe between 1934–1945 exclusive of those who came as members of the Allied forces, we have largely exhausted our capacity of hospitality.[15]

This situation changed when the British government realized that it needed refugee workers. Earlier, in August 1945, the Cabinet approved the Distressed Relatives Scheme. According to the decision authorized by the home secretary on 13 November 1945, survivors of Nazi concentration camps were allowed to be admitted to Great Britain. It was stressed that younger refugees would be employed in agriculture, and that 'it will be a condition that persons admitted under the scheme shall take such employment only as is approved by the Ministry of Labour'.[16] In 1947 further groups of Polish former prisoners were brought to Great Britain as 'European Voluntary Workers' from DP camps in Germany to fill vacancies in the textiles, cotton and building industries. There was also a need for hospital workers and domestic servants.[17] Subsequently, the number of members of the Polish Association of Ex-Political Prisoners rose rapidly.[18]

Costs prohibited renting a London base, so the association took advantage of the *Stowarzyszenia Polskich Kombatantów* (Association of Polish Combatants) which offered it a room once a week for a meeting of what was now called the *Komisja Rekrutacyjna Polskiego Zwiazku Byłych Więźniów Politycznych Niemieckich Więzień i Obozów Koncentracyjnych w Wielkiej Brytanii* (Recruit Commission of the Polish Association of Ex-Political Prisoners of German Prisons and Concentration Camps).[19]

In the years that followed, several hundred more Polish former camp prisoners entered the UK from Germany, France, Italy, Sweden and Poland.[20] These newcomers were quick to seek out the association and join it – this was an important source of support and advice when setting up home in their new country. In 1947, 554 people joined – the highest number of new recruits. In the next four years, between forty and sixty-five people joined each year. In the 1950s and 1960s the intake diminished to very few indeed.[21] The main condition for becoming a member of the association was to have been held in a Nazi prison or concentration camp as a political prisoner. The need to preserve the reputation of the association was crucial, so the recruitment commission carefully vetted each applicant. If there was any doubt whatsoever as to the behaviour of the candidate at the time of imprisonment, the commission rejected the application. Thus in March 1948 nineteen applicants were refused entry on account of having served in the Wermacht.[22] In the next four years, another seven people were rejected for the same reason.

There was the difficulty, however, of discovering that an existing member had a record of shameful behaviour, such as cooperation with the Nazis inside the camp. In these cases, a special 'Colleagues' Court' was convened and several members were excluded by its decision. The most controversial was the case of Dr Władysław Dering. Dering, a Polish surgeon, was known to have been imprisoned in Auschwitz and to have eventually escaped from Poland and served with the Polish Second Corps in Italy. He arrived in the UK in August 1946, and joined the association the following June. At the end of 1947, however, Dering was arrested following allegations – made by the Polish government – of war crimes, and he was held in Brixton prison pending the 'Colleagues' Court' trial, which eventually began in March 1948. Dering was accused of four offences: signing the *Volksdeutsch List*; conducting experimental medical operations; collaborating with the Nazis to procure an early release from Auschwitz; and giving fatal phenol injections. Three former Auschwitz inmates, Dr Alina Brewda, Dr Dobroslawa Kleinowa and Dr Karl Sperber, testified against him. Their testimonies were countered by over twenty-five highly positive opinions about Dering's work in Auschwitz, and as a result he was found innocent.[23] Dering was released from Brixton on 30 August 1948 after witnesses of his 'alleged' sterilization experiments failed to recognize him.[24] In 1964 it was revealed during the libel trial, *Władysław Dering versus Leon Uris*,[25] that accusations that Dering had castrated Jewish inmates as a result of X-ray sterilization experiments[26] were true. It emerged that Dering had conducted approximately eighty such operations.[27] The evidence produced against Dering in 1948 had been based only on personal testimonies, whereas the original documents from the former Auschwitz camp hospital gave the full story.

APPROACHES AND CHALLENGES

The welfare of its members was, of course, the association's prime area of concern, and this involved assisting with accommodation and work, and also organizing health care, seeking cooperation with Poles in other countries, and funding scholarships for members who could demonstrate both talent and financial need.

London was a particularly difficult location for new immigrants. Those association members who lived in the capital were usually squashed into hostels and guest houses – often found from the association's notice board. Others, however, were based in temporary civil camps all over Great Britain, often enduring severe food shortages and a lack of hot water and privacy. For people who had experienced the trauma of the concentration camps, such conditions were disappointingly lacking and the association 'begged' American supporters to send financial aid to allow the creation of special Polish houses.[28]

Finding work could be a soul-destroying business. Polish physicians and nurses were desperately needed in the Polish military hospitals and civil clinics across the country and for them life was tolerably good. However, for those whose education had been interrupted by the war, the situation was grim.[29] Fluency in English was mandatory for many posts, and for that reason many professional soldiers and other well-educated ex-political prisoners ended up working in coal mines or factories.[30] The British government specified that any vacancy could be filled by a Polish national only when there were insufficient British candidates for a particular position.[31] The association could do little to help its members other than to provide job listings and organize courses on finding work.

The years spent in Nazi prisons and concentration camps left their mark on inmates' health. A survey among former Polish political prisoners remaining in three western occupation zones of Germany revealed that only between 5 and 10 per cent of them suffered from severe health conditions.[32] The fact is, of course, that the ill stood no chance of surviving a Nazi-run camp. The majority of camp inmates were treated by the allies for a variety of typical concentration camp diseases, such as typhus, tuberculosis (TB) or *phlegmone*. The last two of these sicknesses were particularly hard to cure. The board of the Polish Ex-Political Association was fully aware that its members could not afford to pay for health care and therefore it managed to provide treatment without charge for those who needed it the most, in two clinics which were run by Poles, *Przychodnia Lekarska Komitetu Obywatelskiego* on 5 Bulstrode Street, just behind Oxford Street, and *Przychodnia Lekarska Towarzystwa Pomocy Polakom* at 48 Wilton Crescent.[33] Despite this effort, mortality among members of the association was very high; this was partly due to age – nearly a fifth of members were at least 40 years old by the time the war was over.[34] Other reasons were the sheer stress and difficulty of adapting to life in a new country. In addition, many former Polish prisoners suffered from a recurrence of camp diseases. The most common were TB and complications after typhus. In an effort to look after not only the physical but also the psychological health of its members, the association organized support groups, poetry nights, concerts and theatre outings – the message being that the members were fighting a common cause in trying to create a normal life.

The association was doing all this at a very difficult time. Britain was in economic crisis and 'another wave of new immigrants' was not popular. Graffiti such as: 'Poles go home' or 'Less Polish, more bread' were appearing on walls with increasing regularity.[35]

The association had a different character to that of other Polish organizations established in the UK during the war. Members of the Polish Armed Forces who had served under British command were regarded as war heroes. They received better treatment, not only from ordinary people but also from the British government, who supported them in getting accommodation and jobs after the war. Although exposed to attacks from the British press – 'Polish soldiers are very expensive for British taxpayers since their only occupation is polishing their uniform bottoms'[36] – large numbers of soldiers from the Polish Army had a good education and were long familiar with British culture and customs; finding employment and generally getting on with life was easier for them. The situation of the Polish ex-political prisoners was more complicated. They were drawn from different educational backgrounds, ranging from academics to the illiterate, and embraced a huge variety of professions – ballet dancers, film directors, poets, writers, shoemakers, dressmakers, farmers, and many more. All that they had in common was to have spent horrific years in Nazi prisons and concentration camps.

To strengthen its position, the association worked on tightening cooperation with other Polish organizations in Great Britain and the rest of the world. Apart from the combatant and the Catholic organizations in the UK, the association tried to set up links with European Jews, persecuted by the Nazis, who had subsequently settled in the UK. For various reasons, such as differing programmes and aims, but also reflecting long-standing divisions, the relationship between them was rather poor. The Polish Association of Ex-Political Prisoners focused on winning allies among the other very strong Polish communities based in America, Argentina, Belgium and Sweden.[37]

Roughly half the association's members were in their twenties in the late 1940s, so had entered adult life without a full education and, as a result, without any profession or trade. As mentioned above, several former camp inmates who joined the association in Italy had a chance to start or continue their education in Italian universities, particularly Bologna University where several enrolled in the faculty of medicine. Unfortunately, these opportunities faded fast as they were transferred to the UK with the Polish Second Corps. The majority of British universities would not give academic credit for years spent in Polish universities, which meant that students had to start from the beginning. Furthermore, by the time Poles arrived in the UK, the academic year had already started, so they had to wait a year before they could apply. The biggest disadvantage, however, was the financial situation of Polish students who were studying full-time and therefore had no time for work. The ex-political prisoners' organization was determined to help its talented young members. It gathered financial resources through its connection with Polish Americans, 'older' Polish migrants to the UK, and the levy of a monthly fee. By the end of February 1948, thanks to very modest funds, the association had made around twenty-two awards of scholarships to students.[38]

'EQUAL TREATMENT FOR EQUAL SUFFERING': THE FIGHT FOR COMPENSATION

The struggle for compensation of former camp inmates who settled in Great Britain can be divided into two phases. The first was from 1947 until 1960 and was characterized by organizing cooperation with other immigrants' organizations. The second lasted from the 1960s until 1974, and during that time the first 'successful' decisions were made.

On 21 December 1945, the Paris Conference of Reparations from Germany designated three groups of victims of the Nazi persecution to be compensated. They included only those persecuted because of religion, political beliefs, and race. Poles were categorized as victims of the war who suffered merely because of their nationality, and therefore were excluded from compensation. The second conference in June 1946 did not alter this decision. It was decided that around 90 per cent of funds would be donated to Jewish victims, while the remaining 10 per cent was reserved for the non-Jewish refugees from Germany and Austria and former citizens of Germany who would like to emigrate from Germany.[39]

The reaction of the Polish Association of Ex-Political Prisoners was immediate. In April 1947, the chairman of the organization, Dr Gościński, together with its secretary, T. Łubieńska, sent a letter to the Intergovernmental Committee on Refugees pointing out the unjustness of this decision:

> The 10,500 Polish victims of Nazi concentration camps are able to prove:
> That they are nationals or former nationals of Poland, which was under German occupation during the war,
> That they were imprisoned in German concentration camps in Germany, Austria, Poland and other occupied countries,
> That they were persecuted for political/the great majority/ religious or racial reasons,
> That they were always faithful to the principles of the United Nations which they actively assisted by struggling against

> Germany and the German war effort thus incurring persecution at the hand of Germany and untold suffering,
> That almost without exemption they are living in such difficult circumstances that without help in rehabilitation and resettlement they are unable to make a new start in life,
> That they do not desire to be repatriated.[40]

Later in the document they made it very clear that they did not wish to diminish the suffering of the Jewish people, but that they wanted 'equal treatment for equal suffering':

> The Polish victims of the German concentration camps are fully aware of the terrible persecution suffered for racial reasons by their Jewish comrades and feel the deepest sympathy and compassion for these victims. They therefore greet with utmost satisfaction the decision of the United Nations to provide assistance for the Jewish victims of Nazi persecution.
>
> The Polish victims of German concentration camps associated in our organizations, desire only to submit with all emphasis that equal treatment with regard to assistance in rehabilitation and resettlement for all non-repatriable of Nazi concentration camps is fundamental exigency of equity and humanity, and moreover, corresponds to the intentions of the Final Act on Reparations of the Paris Conference which introduced no political, racial or religious discrimination.[41]

In 1950 the first memorandum was written by several members of the association and sent to representatives of the German government. Dr Jerzy Gawenda, Tadeusz Katelbach and Jerzy Panciewicz began mediations with the general consul of the German Federal Republic, Dr Schlange Schleining. The last of these conversations took place in June 1951. Despite the German government's knowledge that the issue was unresolved, its position did not change, and neither did the Polish position. The board of the Polish Association of Ex-Political Prisoners realized that a change of tactic was required and therefore in 1954 the *Komisja Prawnicza* (Legal Commission) of the association was established. Its chairman was Mieczysław Hieronim Chmielewski, a well-known consultant in international law who, most importantly, knew the German legal system, having studied in German universities. Chmielewski had escaped to Britain during the war and had not experienced the camps.[42] The first five years of his chairing of the Legal Commission were characterized by various trips to Germany and other European countries to build relationships amongst those groups persecuted by the Nazis and excluded from compensation, and other nations who had claims against the German Federal Government. Co-supporters for the cause were found among the Central Association of Foreigner Refugees, and 'the Parliament of the Persecuted' which assembled Czechs, Yugoslavs, Poles, Ukrainians and people from the Baltic States. Members of the Polish Association, particularly Aleksandra Stypułkowska, its chair for a time, made a great contribution to the success of the Parliament of the Persecuted. The organization held five meetings between 1965 and 1977. The main results of its activity were very strong protests sent to the German Federal Government against unjust treatment of non-Jews and non-Germans in the post-war period.[43] The Polish cause enjoyed support in Great Britain and other parts of the world but the German government's standpoint remained unchanged.

The second stage of the struggle for compensation of the Polish Association of Ex-Political Prisoners German Prisons and Concentration Camps in London began in 1960 with the agreement signed on 5 October between the high commissioner of the United Nations High Commission for Refugees and the representative of the German Federal Government.[44] As a result of this agreement, a person whose health was damaged by 25 per cent during the war as a result of Nazi persecution based on their nationality was given equal status with other groups. The definition of 'persecuted because of nationality' was thus accepted for the first time. In May 1965 the agreement was formally completed. Additional directives to the previous agreement towards victims persecuted because of religion, political beliefs and race were also passed. Unfortunately, however, persons persecuted because of nationality were still marginalized by the German government. The *Bundestag* stubbornly took the position that 'Poles and other people from Eastern and Central Europe weren't victims of the National Socialist doctrine but they were "victims of war", therefore the German government is not legally obligated to treat them in the same positions as groups of people who were persecuted because of religion, political beliefs or the race.'[45]

The attitude of the German government towards Poles was also stressed: 'the majority of the Eastern Germany is under Polish administration – which in total with the German Democratic

Republic is decreasing not only the economical potential of the western Germany but also the ability to compensate all the harm done by the Third Reich'.[46]

The big disadvantage of the new Act from May 1965 was that it formed a separate document for the victims persecuted because of their nationality, which was then automatically excluded from the actual Act. The positive aspect of the 'new Act' was the opportunity to reapply for compensation on behalf of those whose request had been previously rejected. The deadline for these candidates was set at 30 September 1966.[47]

Problems persisted, however. Persons persecuted because of their nationality, and who lived outside their original country, could apply for compensation from the German Federal Government only if they could demonstrate an official refugee status, according to the Geneva Convention, that had been received by 1 October 1953. Moreover, those Poles in Britain that received British nationality before 1 October 1953 were not considered for compensation.[48]

That document was ratified over twenty years after the war. A considerable number, therefore, of the Polish former concentration camp inmates had died, and although it was theoretically possible for close family members, such as spouses or children of the applicant, to receive the compensation on behalf of their dead relative, this could only happen if the victim had been medically examined by a specifically-assigned German physician. In some cases, applicants died whilst waiting for this crucial examination and their families consequently received nothing.[49]

The last conference of delegates for associations of ex-political prisoners worldwide was in Vienna on 25 June 1973. It was called following a decision to admit both the German Federal Republic and the German Democratic Republic into the United Nations. Despite a massive effort to gain the right to compensation for Poles abroad, no firm agreement was forthcoming – although a minute number of Poles in Great Britain did manage to gain some payments.[50]

Mieczysław Chmielewski devoted some time to fighting for compensation of UK-based Polish victims of Nazi medical experiments.[51] A considerable number of these applicants – victims of horrific abuse by SS doctors – were compensated.[52] The aspiration of Chmielewski to win compensation for all Polish victims of Nazi persecution in Poland and abroad, however, proved unattainable. The Polish government did not officially negotiate with Germany for such compensation until 1970 – the point at which the border agreement was finally signed by both countries.[53]

The situation of Polish victims of Nazi medical experiments who had remained in Poland was rather different.[54] In 1957 a group of Polish women, former prisoners of the Ravensbrück concentration camp, applied for compensation from the German Federal Government, invoking the Act of 26 May 1951.[55] Their applications were rejected. The German government justified its decision on the grounds that there were no formal political relations between Poland and both German Republics. A strong rebuke of this stance came from the western powers, especially the United States, and the German Federal Government subsequently modified the compensation law to include Polish victims of Nazi medical experiments.[56] In October 1960 the Polish Red Cross was authorized to deal with the individual applications of victims of Nazi medical experiments who were eligible for compensation as a result of serious damage to their health whilst in concentration camps. The first successful applicants received financial support a year later, in a single payment of up to 25,000 Deutschmark, depending on the damage to their health. Between 1961 and 1971, the German Federal Government compensated 1,357 Polish victims of Nazi medical experiments.[57] From 1973 until 1987, the Polish Ministry of Public Health Care was made responsible for dealing with compensation claims. During that period approximately 4,000 victims of Nazi medical experiments were compensated. Until the 1990s, Poles persecuted by the Nazis, other than victims of Nazi medical experiments, could not receive any compensation. Within the past decade the *Polsko-Niemiecka Fundacja Pojednanie* (the Foundation for Polish-German Reconciliation) has been responsible for compensation. They have financially supported remaining victims of Nazi medical experiments, and other persecuted Poles, such as camp survivors, and former forced labourers.[58]

The Polish Association of Ex-Political Prisoners of German Prisons and Concentration Camps was established mainly to help and support exiled Poles in rebuilding lives that had been severely shattered under Nazism. Its motto was 'Fight for Justice' and its struggle for compensation was grounded not in the uniqueness of Polish victims' suffering, but in the shared experience of all victims of Nazi mistreatment. It was not always successful in its quests, but it tried to stay true to its founding principles. At its height, the association had a membership of 1,200, but it suspended its activity about twenty years ago. Currently, only five members are still alive.

REFERENCES

Archive Sources
International Tracing Service (ITS).
National Archives: Foreign Office (FO).
Polish Institute and Sikorski Museum (PISM):
1. Collection 289, 'Kacetowcy'.
2. Collection 291, Mecenasa Mieczysława Chmielewskiego.

Published Sources
Cesarani, D., *Justice Delayed: How Britain Became a Refuge for Nazi War Criminals* (London: Phoenix Press, 2001).
Cyra, A., *Ochotnik do Auschwitz: Witold Pilecki (1901–1948)* (Oświęcim: Chrzescijańskie Stowarzyszenie Rodzin Oświęcimskich, 2000).
Kaczorowska, T., *Wyrwani z gniazd* (Ciechanów: Agencja Wydawniczo-Reklamowa 'TESS', 1997).
Ruchniewicz, K., *Polskie zabiegi o odszkodowania niemieckie w latach 1944/45–1975* (Wrocław: Wydawnictwo Uniwersytetu Wrocławskiego, 2007).
Sołtysiak, P., 'Podstawy prawne i implementacja odszkodowań niemieckich dla polskich ofiar eksperymentów pseudomedycznych w latach 1945–98', in *Problem reparacji, odszkodowań i świadczeń w stosunkach polsko-niemieckich 1944–2004* (Warszawa: Polski Instytut Spraw Międzynarodowych, 2004).
Sword, K., Davies, N. and Ciechanowski, J., *The Formation of the Polish Community in Great Britain 1939–1950: The M.B. Grabowski Polish Migration Project Report* (London: School of Slavonic and East European Studies, University of London, 1989).
Żaroń, P. and Sikorski, W., *Armia Andersa* (Toruń: Wydawnictwo Adam Marszałek, 1996).

NOTES

1. Pomerania is a land located in the north-eastern part of Poland.
2. Freie Stadt Danzig, which is the German name of the province, was established on 10 January 1920 in accordance with the Treaty of Versailles of 1919. It was placed under League of Nations 'protection', with special economic-related rights reserved for Poland.
3. It also appears in documents as the *KL* Lublin.
4. Soldiers of General Anders's Army were recruited mainly from Poles imprisoned in Soviet Russia and were therefore aware of the Soviet regime's policies. General Anders's aim was to restore freedom to Poland and therefore a communist state was not an option. As a result, he and his soldiers were seen as enemies, spies and betrayers by the newly formed temporary Polish government. The fate of Witold Pilecki proves this theory. Pilecki deliberately got himself arrested and sent to Auschwitz and managed to escape from the camp. As a result of his action the Polish Underground Movement sent to western allies information concerning the extermination of Jews in Auschwitz. After the war Pilecki was arrested and put on trial, and sentenced to death on 25 May 1948. One of his alleged offences was espionage for General Anders: see Adam Cyra, *Ochotnik do Auschwitz – Witold Pilecki 1901–1948* (Oświęcim: Chrześcijańskie Stowarzyszenie Rodzin Oświęcimskich, 2000), p.429.
5. The Polish Institute and Sikorski Museum in London holds the entire collection of documents related to the activity of the association of ex-political prisoners. Whilst investigating the collection, I have come across three different names for the organization: the Polish Political Ex-Prisoners Association; the Polish Association of Former Political Prisoners in Concentration Camps and Prisons; and the Polish Association of Ex-Political Prisoners of German Prisons and Concentration Camps. In this article I have chosen to use the last of these names.

6. On the Continent there were, overall, one million Poles, who included DPs and prisoners of war, 80,000 of them former camp prisoners: see *Historia Zwiazku*, Polish Institute and Sikorski Museum (hereafter PISM), Collection 289, 'Kacetowcy' (hereafter Col. 289), p.1.
7. Władyław Gościński was the first chairman of the organization. There were several other chairmen whose contribution to the association was important, including the lawyer Aleksandra Stypułkowska; the film-maker Teresa Łubieńska who was stabbed to death in 1957; and a journalist, Dr Stefan Benedict (see *Historia Związku*, PISM, Col. 289, pp.6–7.)
8. A number of Associations of Ex-Political Prisoners of German Prisons and Concentration Camps were established worldwide at this time, with the main branch in Hamburg: see ibid., p.1.
9. At that time 'privileged prisoners' such as *Kapos* were seen as perpetrators. There was little understanding for former prisoners who were capable of mistreating fellow inmates in order to improve their situation within a camp.
10. S. Kret, *List Zarządu Głównego Polskiego Zwiasku byłych Więźniów Politycznych Więzień i Obozów Koncentracyjnych do Społecznego Komitetu Pomocy Obywatelom Polskim w Niemczech Maczków 18 September 1946*, PISM, Col. 289, vol. 11, pp.1–2.
11. *Listy zwerbowanych członków 1–4, Barletta 14 Luty – 12 Sierpień 1946*, PISM, Col. 289, vol. 11, pp.1–3.
12. P. Żaroń, *Armia Andersa* (Toruń: Wydawnictwo Adam Marszałek, 1996), p.277.
13. K. Sword, N. Davies and J. Ciechanowski, *The Formation of the Polish Community in Great Britain 1939–1950: The M.B. Grabowski Polish Migration Project Report* (London: School of Slavonic and East European Studies, University of London, 1989), pp.334–5.
14. This number included employees of the Polish government in exile, scientists and engineers, and a number of Polish seamen of the Polish Merchant Marine: see Sword, Davies and Ciechanowski, *Formation of the Polish Community*, p.332.
15. From a letter by H.H.C. Prestige (HO Aliens Department) to C.J. Edmonds (FO), 25 September 1946, National Archives: Foreign Office (FO) 371/57833 (WR2711).
16. Sword, Davies and Ciechanowski, *Formation of the Polish Community*, p.334.
17. Ibid., p.337.
18. *Protokoły z posiedzenia Komisji Weyfikacyjnej 1–14*, PISM, Col. 289.
19. *Historia*, PISM, Col. 289, p.2.
20. Apart from members of the association who came to the UK with the Polish Second Corps, a further 30 per cent came from Italy; 20 per cent from Germany; 6 per cent from France and 4 per cent from Sweden – statistics based on personal applications from members of the association. See *Podania*, PISM, Col. 289, vols 1–8.
21. *Protokoły Komisji Weryfikacyjnej*, 1–45, PISM, Col. 289, vol. 11.
22. *Protokół z XV posiedznia Komisji Weryfikacyjnej w dniu 25 marca 1948o godz. 15 w Sekretariacie Związku*, PISM, Col. 289, vol. 11.
23. *Sprawa Władysława Deringa, Sąd koleżeński nad Władysławem Deringiem*, PISM, Col. 289, vol. 12.
24. D. Cesarani, *Justice Delayed: How Britain Became a Refuge for Nazi War Criminals* (London: Phoenix Press, 2001), p.182.
25. Leo Uris, in his book *Exodus*, claimed that Dering performed 17,000 experimental operations on inmates in Auschwitz. As a result, in 1964 Dering sued him and won the case; for more information see M. Hill, *Auschwitz in England* (London: MacGibbon & Kee, 1965), p.293.
26. Sterilization experiments on humans, using X-rays, were performed in Auschwitz-Birkenau between 1942 and 1944 by Dr Horst Schumann.
27. *Vollstädinge Ausgabe des Operationsbubuches fom 10.9.1942 23.2.1944*, International Tracing Service (ITS), p.46.
28. A. Gościński, *Memoriał w sprawie Byłych WiWięźniów Politycznych z niemieckich więzień i obozów koncentracyjnych Londyn 15 Luty 1947*, PISM, Col. 289, p.1.
29. 38 per cent of members of the association had primary education; 45 per cent secondary education; and 15 per cent higher education. Those numbers excluded thirty-two Polish Catholic priests. The percentage has been estimated based on lists of members. See *Listy członków związku*, PISM, Col. 289, vol. 11, pp.1–8.
30. T. Kaczorowska, *Wyrwani z gniazd* (Ciechanów: Agencja Wydawnicza 'TESS', 1997), pp.150–1.

31. Sword, Davies and Ciechanowski, *Formation of the Polish Community*, p.342.
32. Kret, *List Zarządu Głównego*, PISM, p.1.
33. 'Informacje', *Biuletyn Kacetowiec*, no. 2, vol. 29, PISM, pp.2–3.
34. About 35 per cent of the members in 1945 were in their 30s, and the biggest group (50 per cent) were in their 20s – statistics based on personal applications of members. See *Podania członków*, PISM, Col. 289, vols 1–8.
35. Kaczorowska, *Wyrwani z gniazd*, p.53.
36. Ibid., pp.150–1.
37. Belgium had a large Polish community who remained there after they helped in liberating this country. Apart from that, a lot of Poles liberated in Germany and Austria emigrated to countries other than Great Britain. For about 14 per cent of former camp inmates, the UK was just a stop on the way to a new homeland. Around 25 per cent of those who left Great Britain went to Argentina; 15 per cent to Canada; 10 per cent to the US – statistics based on personal application of association members. See *Podania*, PISM, Col. 289, vols 1–8.
38. *Biuletyn Kacetowiec*, no. 2, vol. 14, PISM, pp.2–3.
39. M. Chmielewski, *Niedotrzymane zobowiązaniamiedzynarodowe wobec ofiar nazizmu*, PISM, Col. 291, p.2.
40. *Letter to the Intergovernmental Committee on Refugees London 18th April 1947*, PISM, Col. 289, vol. 11, pp.1–2.
41. Ibid., p.3.
42. *Historia Związku*, PISM, Col. 289, vol. 11, p.5.
43. Ibid., pp.5–6.
44. M. Chmielewski, *Czwarty etap walki o odszkodowania niemieckie: Przed czwartym etapem*, PISM, Col. 291, p.7.
45. M. Chmielewski, *Czwarty etap walki o odszkodowania niemieckie: Uchwalenie zmiany ustawy*, PISM, Col. 291, p.3.
46. Ibid., pp.3–4.
47. M. Chmielewski, *Czwarty etap walki o odszkodowania niemieckie: Odrębne postanowienia dla narodowo-prześladowanych*, PISM, Col. 291, p.4.
48. M. Chmielewski, *Czwarty etap walki o odszkodowania niemieckie: Dalsza dyskryminacja*, PISM, Col. 291, p.6.
49. Ibid., p.7.
50. Ibid., p.9.
51. *Historia Związku*, PISM, Col. 289, vol. 11, p.8.
52. Documents related to individual claims of Polish victims of Nazi medical crimes are held in the Polish Institute and Sikorski Museum in London. Unfortunately the policy of the institute does not allow viewing of the documents.
53. During the visit of the chancellor of the German Federal Republic, Willy Brandt, to Warsaw in December 1970, the first secretary of the Polish United Worker's Party, Władysław Gomułka, engaged him in bilateral negotiation on compensation issues. See K. Ruchniewicz, *Polskie zabiegi o odszkodowania niemieckie w latach 1944/45–1975*, (Wrocław: Wydawnictwo Uniwersytetu Wrocławskiego, 2007), pp.182–95.
54. Two groups of Polish victims of Nazi medical experiments were recognized as a result of their contribution to the Nuremberg Trial: Polish Catholic priests from Dachau concentration camp who were experimented upon with malaria and *phlegmone*, and victims of hypothermia experiments. The second group were 'Rabbits', as they called themselves: seventy-four Polish women, former prisoners of Ravensbrück concentration camp, whose legs were operated on as a consequence of Karl Gebhardt's experiments with sulphadimidine. Thanks to the collaboration of the Polish victims of Gebhardt's experiments, a complete list of 'Rabbits' was lodged with the Red Cross archives at Arolsen as early as 1945.
55. According to this Act, persons from outside the German Federal Republic could apply for compensation only if they were human victims of Nazi medical experiments. See P. Sołtysiak, 'Podstawy prawne i implementacja odszkodowań niemieckich dla polskich ofiar eksperymentów pseudomedycznych w latach 1945–89', in Witold M. Góralski (ed.), *Problem reparacji,odszkodowań i świadczeń w stosunkach polsko-niemieckich 1944–2004*, vol. 1 (Warszawa: Polski Instytut Spraw Międzynarodowych: Ministerstwo Spraw Zagranicznych RP, 2004), p.275.

56. The person whose active involvement had a crucial result in the struggle by the 'Rabbits' for financial compensation was an American, Caroline Ferriday. In September 1958 she came to Warsaw to organize a visit to the US for treatment by fifty-seven female victims of Nazi medical experiments. There was press interest in their trip, with front page stories in Polish and German newspapers. See Ruchniewicz, *Polskie zabiegi o odszkodowania*, pp.116–26.
57. Information gathered from my correspondence with Elżbieta Rejf, chair of the Information and Tracing Centre of the Polish Red Cross.
58. See *Collection Eksperymenty Pseudomedyczne* (EPM), Główna Komisja Ścigania Zbrodni Niemieckich w Polsce, Instytut Pamięci Narodowej, Warszawa.

7

Surviving Behemoth's Fury Inside the Cage: Stephan Prager, Philipp Rappaport and Others in the Years Before and After 1945

KURT DÜWELL

The racism of the Nazi anti-Jewish persecution, setting aside its criminal character, was, from a perspective of national German interest, an example of self-mutilation and waste on a colossal scale. Many Jews in Germany were leaders in the fields of economy, science and technology as well as in the fine arts and literature. Most were patriotic German nationals and the majority felt a very close link to their country. Many had fought in the First World War and had been highly decorated with distinguished military service awards such as the *Eisernes Kreuz* (Iron Cross) of both Second and First Class and the *Militärverdienstorden.* One even had the highest decoration – the order *Pour le Mérite*. Among the corps of German fighter pilots were no fewer than 200 very brave and skilled airmen from Jewish families; at least fifty were killed in the war. However, in reference works and histories of the First World War this fact was rarely mentioned until recently.[1]

The Imperial War Museum is a fitting setting in which to consider the achievements of these 200 Jewish fighter pilots who actually constituted 4 per cent of the entire German air force corps. Given that Jews represented just one per cent of the German population, this was a very high proportion. So as well as celebrating the achievements of the famous hero Manfred von Richthofen, the 'Red Baron' (shot down in 1918, after sixty victories), Max Immelmann (fifteen victories), Hermann Göring and fighter aces such as

Oswald Boelcke and other non-Jewish *Pour le Mérite* holders, it is also necessary to mention the very successful Jewish German fighter-plane pilots such as W. Abramowicz, Fritz Beckhardt, Heinz Bettsak, G. Blumenthal, Arthur Chasanowicz, Hans Friedländer, Max Holzinger, Dr Walter Lissauer, Fritz Mecklenburg, Ernst Müller, Willy Rosenstein, Fritz Rosin, Jakob Wolff and Josef Zürndorfer. Wolff, 48 years old at the outbreak of war, was at first not accepted as a fighter by the German Command. But he insisted on turning up with his own personal aircraft, and was eventually admitted. After 1933, the Nazis not only concealed the relatively high proportion of Jewish air fighters who had served in the First World War, they also erased their names from the lists of the *Pour le Mérite* and other similar rolls of honour. In fact thirty Jewish fighter pilots were awarded the Iron Cross First Class. One, Max Pappenheimer (shot down in 1918), was honoured with the Golden *Kriegsverdienstkreuz*, and Wilhelm Frankl (shot down in 1917, nineteen victories) even received the *Pour le Mérite*.[2] Max Pappenheimer's captain wrote in his letter of condolence to Pappenheimer's father, after praising the young man's courage and talents: 'Find your consolation in the thought that your son fought and died as a man, convinced of our great national idea and as a hero.'[3] But what many of these young Jewish heroes wanted first and foremost was to be accepted by German society. Josef Zürndorfer wrote in his last will and testament: 'As a German I have taken the field to defend my distressed fatherland. But also as a Jew who wants to fight for the equality of rights.'[4]

The Weimar Constitution of 1919 had improved the legal and also, partly, the social conditions of Germany's Jews. But this better standing was soon attacked and finally destroyed. As in many new fields of activity, by the start of the twentieth century, German Jews had made a distinguished contribution to the science of air navigation, both civil and military. They were thrilled by advancing science and technology, arts and literature and their engagement in the new scientific and artistic fields was, statistically, stronger than average in German society. Therefore I have chosen as my focus in this chapter the field of modern urban and regional spatial planning, a new discipline for architects after the 1890s, with a strong international dimension. Here too the contributions of people from Jewish family backgrounds were very remarkable. The *International Biographical Dictionary of Central European Emigrés, 1933–1945*, though it is incomplete, gives a very impressive account of this.[5]

How did Nazi hostility affect the position and self-respect of German Jews in the field of architecture, their loyalty to the country, and their survival within Nazi Germany?

The two people I would like to introduce here, Stephan Prager (1875–1969) and Philipp Rappaport (1879–1955), had served with distinction during the First World War. They were decorated with the *Eisernes Kreuz* of both First and Second Class and one had been honoured with the *Militärverdienstorden mit Schwertern* (Order of Distinguished Military Service with Swords), a very high military award. Both were excellent architects, civil engineers and town planners, holding senior positions in the civil service and being highly esteemed by their colleagues and by many institutions. Stephan Prager came from an old Jewish family who had lived in Silesia for more than 300 years. However, he was one of the first in this family to be brought up in the Christian tradition, though possibly without a formal conversion.[6] Philipp Rappaport was from Berlin and, together with his mother and five brothers and sisters, converted in the 1890s from Judaism to Protestantism. Despite having set aside their Jewish identities and despite their courageous military service, both had to suffer ostracism and persecution under the Nazis.

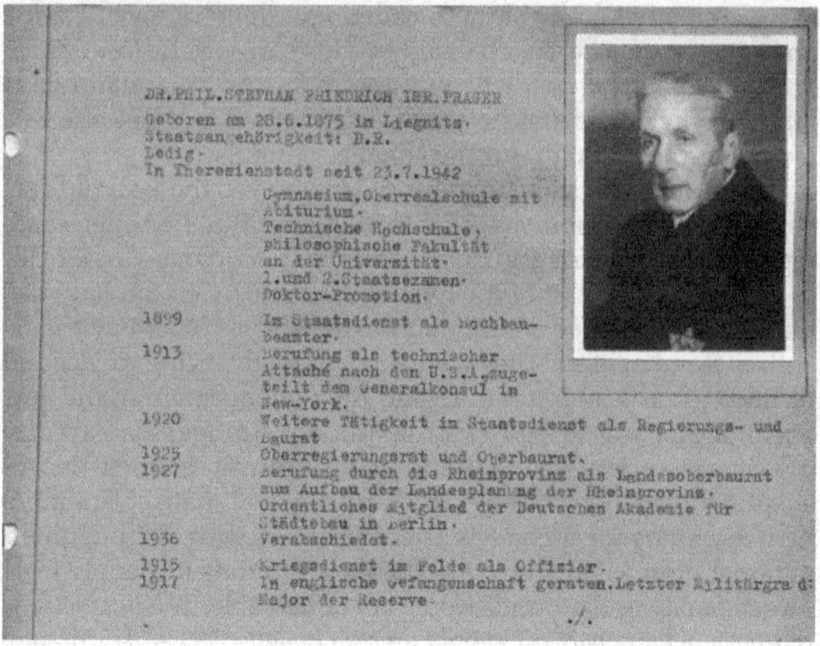

DR.PHIL.STEPHAN FRIEDRICH ISR.PRAGER

Geboren am 28.6.1875 in Liegnitz.
Staatsangehörigkeit: D.R.
Ledig.
In Theresienstadt seit 23.7.1942

Gymnasium,Oberrealschule mit Abiturium.
Technische Hochschule, philosophische Fakultät an der Universität.
1.und 2.Staatsexamen.
Doktor-Promotion.

1899 Im Staatsdienst als Hochbaubeamter.
1913 Berufung als technischer Attaché nach den U.S.A.,zugeteilt dem Generalkonsul in New-York.
1920 Weitere Tätigkeit im Staatsdienst als Regierungs- und Baurat
1925 Oberregierungsrat und Oberbaurat.
1927 Berufung durch die Rheinprovinz als Landesoberbaurat zum Aufbau der Landesplanung der Rheinprovinz.
Ordentliches Mitglied der Deutschen Akademie für Städtebau in Berlin.
1936 Verabschiedet.

1915 Kriegsdienst im Felde als Offizier.
1917 In englische Gefangenschaft geraten.Letzter Militärgrad: Major der Reserve.

./.

1. Stephan Prager: A Good but Modest Patriot.

A comparison of these two individuals' experiences of persecution, in Düsseldorf and Essen, shows that neither military service nor conversion to Christianity, neither the so-called privileges of mixed marriages, nor even special protection from officials could really help these two men avoid the *Schutzhaft* (protective arrest) or the camps. Other resources were needed and proved decisive in the survival of each.

It is not without a tragic irony to choose these two architects and city planners for this brief portrait because they had to suffer the regime of a man, Hitler, who had actually failed as an architect. As a military would-be commander-in-chief he ruined German architecture, Germany's armed forces and the German name. But Stephan Prager and Philipp Rappaport were always truly constructive people, even as forced labourers in the camps. And they proved this again after the war.

Stephan Friedrich Prager was born on 28 June 1875 in Liegnitz/Silesia.[7] He attended a secondary school there (*Oberrealschule*) and graduated with the *Abitur*. Subsequently he studied architecture at Technische Hochschule (TH) in Darmstadt and Berlin, and then remained in Berlin to study philosophy and art history at the Friedrich-Wilhelms-Universität (FWU). After passing the first and the second *Staatsexamen* as architect at the TH Berlin in 1899 he was appointed to work as civil servant in the Prussian administration of *Hochbauverwalfung* ('overground buildings'). The subject of his PhD of 1911 was 'the aesthetic foundations of architecture'.[8] By 1913 Prager's reputation in urban planning was such that he was appointed technical attaché at the German Consulate General in New York City. But in August 1914 he returned to join the German Army as a volunteer. Before he reached Germany, the British arrested and imprisoned him, releasing him in November 1914. When he finally reached Germany he became a volunteer front-line fighter on the western front from January 1915 until April 1917. Prager was made first lieutenant in the German artillery and appointed captain in 1916, commanding a battery of heavy field-guns. He was awarded the Iron Cross First and Second Class. For his courageous and patriotic defence of his battery against the British in the spring of 1917, north of Arras, he was further honoured with the *Militärverdienstorden mit Schwertern*. When the British took Vimy Ridge on 11 April, Stephan Prager was taken prisoner again. He used this period of confinement to write a research paper about housing shortages in Britain. It was published in an extended version after the war.[9]

When the British released him in November 1919 he returned to Germany and was immediately appointed councillor and surveyor of works to the district government of the Prussian province Saxony in Merseburg (his title was *Regierungs- und Baurat*). His career progressed rapidly. Having been advanced to reserve major in 1922 he was promoted to *Oberregierungsrat* in 1925. Prager was then 50 years old, yet remained unmarried. He had no close ties to the Church nor to a Jewish community and concentrated almost all his work on urban and regional spatial planning (*Städtebau und Landesplanung*), becoming a well-known expert in this new discipline. Soon he was admitted as an ordinary member of the distinguished Freie Akademie des Städtebaus (Free Academy of Urban Planning) which had been founded in Berlin in 1922 and was a forerunner of the Deutsche Akademie für Städtebau und Landesplanung, set up in 1946. Prager was well informed about international trends in modern city planning. He had seen the international exhibitions on this subject in Göteborg in 1923, in Amsterdam in 1924 and in New York in 1925. He had also learned a lot from his own experience after he was commissioned in 1923 by the district governor (*Regierungspräsident*) in Merseburg to work out a *Generalsiedlungsplan* (general land-settlement plan) for Central Germany.[10] Prager was a shrewd anticipator of future trends, working out that the brown coal resources of the region would come to an end within the next thirty or forty years. His new ideas laid the foundations for an alternative plan which, a few years later, became the foundation of the new *Landesplanungsverband* of Central Germany (founded in 1928).[11] It was Prager, fundamentally, who helped develop and promote the new notion *Landesplanung*.[12]

Prager's most important work began in 1927 when the *Landeshauptmann* (director of the provincial government) of the Prussian Rhine Province, Johannes Horion, invited him to come to Düsseldorf to found an administrative unit for urban and regional spatial planning there. In 1928 he was appointed *Landesoberbaurat* in this large Prussian province.[13] Prager's report and programme of his planning targets in the Rhineland was published some years later.[14] In 1930 he started another ambitious project when he drew up a land-settlement and development plan for the Saar area. There was a political dimension to this initiative, for since 1920 the Saar district had been under the government of Britain and France, under a League of Nations mandate, and was expected to be returned to Germany after the forthcoming plebiscite in 1935. Prager and his group's vision would be implemented in celebration of this territorial reunion. It was an imaginative scheme which won much praise. But it was implemented without Prager. What happened?

The entire political framework in Germany changed in 1933. Anti-Semitism was an official feature of Hitler's new regime. Although – according to the new *Berufsbeamtengesetz* of 7 April 1933[15] – officials of 'non Aryan descent' were explicitly exempt from dismissal if they had been front soldiers or had come to office before 1 August 1914, these 'privileges' were cancelled step by step after 1933. Stephan Prager held the *Ehrenkreuz für Frontkämpfer* (Cross of Honour for Front soldiers) and the *Verwundetenabzeichen* (Badge for the Wounded). But this did not help him in 1935 and especially not after 1938. The Saar settlement and development plan would doubtless have benefited from the continued involvement of its initiator, but Prager was forced to leave his office at the end of 1935. He was 60 years old and had no pension. Normally he would have been allowed to work until he was 65. He also was dismissed from the Freie Akademie für Städtebau. A fine career was broken and a talented man humiliated.

Prager was not without means and had no immediate dependents to consider, but he did not take steps to emigrate, preferring to stay in his home country. Curiously, until late 1941 he could rely on the protection of Heinz Haake, a member of the Nazi Party and leader of the regional and communal administration (*Landeshauptmann*) of the Prussian Rhineland.[16] When in 1941 the anti-Semitic attacks on Prager multiplied and became dangerous, Haake, in an act highly untypical of Nazis at that time, sent a letter to the *Reichsminister* of the Interior, Wilhelm Frick. In this letter Haake described Prager's merits and the appreciation he deserved from his country.[17] He called special attention to the grateful acknowledgment he himself had expressed to Dr Prager when this highly respected expert of building concerns had left his post in 1936. Haake also quoted from a farewell letter to Prager from the inspector-general of the German road and highway system, Dr Fritz Todt, thanking him for his 'unselfish cooperation of many years'.[18] So Haake suggested that Dr Prager, whom he praised as a good German patriot and also member of the former national *Stahlhelm* (steel helmet) union of former front-line soldiers, should be granted an exceptional status, and exempt from the anti-Jewish 'laws'. He proposed a status comparable, though he was unmarried, to the 'privileged' status of Jewish partners of 'mixed marriages'.[19] He even pleaded for Dr

Prager to be declared equivalent to 'persons of German blood' by a decision of the Führer. Indeed, a few months previously Hitler had personally decreed that a nephew of Prager was an 'Aryan' and could join the German Wehrmacht.[20] But the efforts of Haake were thwarted by Reinhard Heydrich, the leader of the Reichssicherheit-shauptamt (Reich Main Security Office), who refused any separate regulation. Haake's efforts led to nothing.

It may be that the Gestapo in Düsseldorf informed Heydrich about *Landeshauptmann* Heinz Haake's protection of Prager and recommended a surprise action when Haake was absent. The head of the Gestapo department of Jewish concerns in Düsseldorf, Georg Pütz, had it in mind as early as 1941 to deport Dr Prager in order to give his flat to an 'Aryan'. Prager was further denounced to the authorities for anti-Nazi remarks. The combination of denunciation from the public and the 'all pervasive' power of the Gestapo, described by Robert Gellately,[21] proved effective. In May 1942 Dr Prager had to leave his home for a '*Judenhaus*' in Düsseldorf.[22] His sister, who lived in Krefeld, had been deported to Izbica in Poland on 15 April.[23] She was not heard of again. On 17 July 1942 Dr Prager was arrested by the Gestapo. When he protested, Pütz, its department leader, replied: 'I have taken you under detention today because the *Landeshauptmann* [Haake] is on an official journey and cannot protect you when you disappear.'[24] On 21 July 1942, Dr Prager, now 67 years old, was sent to the concentration camp in Theresienstadt (Terezín). His property was confiscated and his pension cancelled. There is no indication that *Landeshauptmann* Haake tried to lighten the burden of Prager's life in Theresienstadt or have him freed. Just a year earlier, as we have seen, Haake had gone out of his way to support Prager. But he gave up on his mission. As the Gestapo leader Georg Pütz had foretold: 'The *Landeshauptmann* will become tired of protecting you.'[25]

In the camp Dr Prager's construction expertise[26] gave him the chance to become indispensable and therefore to survive. He was almost 70 years old when Theresienstadt was liberated at the end of the war. His health was weakened by hunger and illness. However, Stephan Prager was able to return to Düsseldorf on 24 August 1945 and to charge the man who had denounced both him and his sister and also another person of Jewish descent. This other victim was his neighbour in Düsseldorf, the architect Max Lennhoff, who was killed in the concentration camp of Mauthausen.[27]

Prager accused the denouncer and the Gestapo department leader before the judges. Both were sentenced to penal servitude in 1949. Prager said that he did not want vengeance on these people. He just wanted justice.

Dr Prager died on 29 May 1969 one month short of his ninety-fourth birthday. He could look back on a remarkable career. In 1946, in spite of his age, he was appointed *Ministerialdirigent* (that is, permanent head of a ministerial department) by the government of Nordrhein-Westfalen. He became leader of the *Landesplanungsbehörde*. In the post-war years he contributed to the reconstruction of the new Land Nordrhein-Westfalen, to urban and regional spatial planning and especially to the construction of roads and motorways in the Rhineland. Patriotic in an unostentatious way, he became a symbol of post-war German reconstruction. The Rheinisch-Westfälische Technische Hochschule Aachen and other universities conferred on him the title of a honorary doctor.[28] He was elected president of the Deutsche Akademie für Städtebau und Landesplanung,[29] and the Federal Republic of Germany bestowed on him the *Großes Verdienstkreuz des Verdienstordens mit Stern der Bundesrepublik Deutschland*, a late act of recognition of his accomplishments and sufferings.

This could never, of course, make up for the injustices and constant danger of death that he had experienced. With the support of a small circle, Stephan Prager had had to rely on his own self-reliance and will to survive. He was lucky, but he had to fight hard for his survival and for his post-war professional success.

I now turn to another case where the ability to withstand terrible circumstances and the victim's presence of mind proved decisive. This is the case of Dr Rappaport – in some aspects comparable to Dr Stephan Prager. Indeed the two were well acquainted.

Philipp August Rappaport was born in Berlin on 10 December 1879, the son of the merchant Adolf Rappaport and his wife Alma. Adolf Rappaport died in 1881, leaving his wife and seven children. Alma Rappaport, to provide for her children, moved to the spa town of Bad Kösen near Naumburg in the Prussian province Sachsen, and started up a guest house. The family was Jewish, but when some years later Alma Rappaport remarried – her new husband was the private tutor of her children – the entire family converted to his religion, Protestantism, allowing her to send her very talented son Philipp to the nearby famous boarding-school (*Internat*) Schulpforta. As Philipp's half-sister Gerda recalled: 'He lived in an

Evangelical-Christian neighbourhood which was, with love and a sense of duty, devoted to the German fatherland.'[30]

In 1897 Philipp Rappaport left Schulpforta with a brilliant graduation (*Abitur*) and matriculated at the Technische Hochschule in Berlin-Charlottenburg to study architecture. He passed his exam with first-class honours in 1902. Then he added a study of political economy at the University of Gießen in Hessen. In 1904 he was appointed *Regierungsbauführer* (junior architect official) in the Prussian Civil Service and in 1908 was nominated *Regierungsbaumeister* (architect official). He took his Doctorate in Engineering in 1910.[31] The subject of his research thesis – published in 1911 – was *Steigende Straßen* ('ascending streets'), a theme of interest to both architects, city planners, and engineers.[32] With this short but inspired work, Rappaport contributed to the international debate then taking place on urban planning – at that stage much influenced by the work of Raymond Unwin, whose *Townplanning in Practice* (1911) and *Roads and Streets* (1913) greatly influenced inter-war public housing in Britain, and also that of Sir Ebenezer Howard, who founded the notion of the Garden City.[33]

Following his doctorate, Rappaport returned to service in the higher state administration. His main area of interest was how to

2. Philipp Rappaport: A Patriot, not a Patrioteer.

cope with Germany's housing shortage. It is striking that both Stephan Prager and Philipp Rappaport did pioneering work on working-class housing. Both had their work interrupted, however, by the outbreak of war in 1914. Rappaport joined the army as a volunteer and served for four years as an officer. He was decorated with the *Eisernes Kreuz* of First and Second Class.

Back in civilian life, in 1920 the Prussian *Minister für Volkswohlfahrt* (minister for welfare) nominated Rappaport as state commissioner for the dwellings of miners in the Ruhr area (*Staatskommissar für Bergmannswohnungen im rheinisch-westfälischen Industriebezirk*).[34] The same year he published a lecture he had given in Berlin on the post-war housing shortage.[35] He was now widely respected as an expert in this field. In 1920, at the age of 40, he was elected deputy director of the newly-founded Siedlungsverband Ruhrkohlenbezirk (SVR – Settlement Association for the Ruhr Coal District) in Essen. In this capacity Rappaport oversaw the development of a model for traffic routes and public utilities in the highly congested zone between Duisburg and Dortmund.

In 1921 Philipp Rappaport married Gertrud Moser from Hiddesen, a village in the former principality Lippe-Detmold. By 1926 four children had been born. It was a happy union, offering some consolation to the former front-line soldier who had lost a brother and two half-brothers during the war.[36]

Rappaport's achievements provided the framework for more than a decade of urban planning in the Ruhr district. He was working on a tripartite classification system for roads and streets, and on the relatively new challenge of how best to regulate traffic within cities. The focus of much of his work was the town of Essen, the administrative hub of the SVR.[37] But there were also other parts of Germany where Philipp Rappaport successfully contributed and influenced urban planning. For instance, in the mid-1920s he submitted a special design for the reorganization of the urban area of Breslau, the capital of the Prussian province of Silesia.[38] This plan – called *Wagen und Wägen* (to weigh and to venture) – had been purchased by the city of Breslau for 10,000 Reichsmark.

Rappaport was strongly engaged in both the engineering and aesthetic aspects of architecture. He was a member of the distinguished Deutscher Werkbund, the association of German 'workmen', and from 1920 was appointed to teach at the Staatliche Kunstakademie (State Academy of Arts) in Düsseldorf. His interest in modern architecture and urban planning beyond Germany was shown in his 1927 study tour of the USA, the photographic record of which would enrich his lectures at the Kunstakademie, informing his students about new trends in modern urban architecture and city mapping. A major theme was the thinning-out of inner city areas through building garden-city clusters within a protected green belt. He developed – and here we see the economist – the idea of a modern *Wirtschaftsplan* (economic plan) for cities and regional spatial areas, in which wedge-shaped parks cut from the outside into the city centres, creating a protected green zone.[39] Such a *Wirtschaftsplan* was based on a formula '4+1' (traffic areas, industrial areas, habitation, recreation zones + free areas as reserves). This was an innovative notion, much influenced by American and British thought.[40] Another success was Rappaport's involvement in a first draft of a Prussian *Städtebaugesetz* (Statute of Town-Planning) in 1928.[41]

So it was that by the beginning of the 1930s, Rappaport had become an expert in urban, regional and resettlement planning in Germany, well known for his internationalist approach. But just when he had been elected director of the SVR in 1932 and had published a book about German resettlement programmes in 1933,[42] Rappaport became an early victim of Nazi race policy. He was dismissed from the service as early as 1933, his wartime service and town-planning achievements failing to convince the fanatical Nazi *Gauleiter* (district leader) of the *Gau* Essen that he should be given special treatment. Rappaport had to leave his official residence. For some weeks the family was able to stay in a remote part of Mecklenburg where Frau Rappaport's brother Richard Ernst Moser, a Hamburg merchant, owned an estate (Gut Vietow, near Zarrentin). This brother also helped some other Jewish people, even against the Gestapo.[43] Whenever anti-Semitic actions endangered his family in Essen, Rappaport could secure his people there and hide himself for a while.

The pension he was given was small, so he had to look for additional income to support his young family. Needing a new home, he decided to build his own, in Essen. His wife was not of 'Jewish descent', so she could invest her money and his in this new home and own it on both their behalves. Nevertheless, debts had to be repaid and Philipp Rappaport had to take private commissions, refusing no work – for every penny counted. One of his most generous sponsors was the industrialist Kurt Herberts in Wuppertal, a manufacturer of high quality varnish and lacquer, who engaged Rappaport for building projects on his large estate.[44] But after 1938 and the *Kristallnacht* pogrom, the possibility of making even a modest living became difficult and dangerous. Although their home was safe – thanks to Frau Rappaport's 'Aryan' status, the anxiety and lack of dignity oppressed Philipp Rappaport more and more. In one of his letters at the end of 1938 he wrote:

> It is striking that all circles recommend me to emigrate. They think it to be a blind necessity. Especially our parsons – our parish reverend, our youth minister and also our district minister who has been appointed expressly for such matters – they all want me to leave. The latter even wants to persuade me to an immediate departure, so serious does he consider the situation. This very thought which occurred in the beginning of this week has made Trude [Rappaport's wife] almost collapse. She looks pitifully distressed and small and so I have not pursued this plan further. I look miserable myself. The most difficult thing in this situation is the permanent insecurity: how can I do the right thing? Would the almost unthinkable big step [into exile] be right and necessary? Will it serve my family and me? The restrictions and all the things which have happened until now will still have to be endured. But can our nerves really bear it in the long run? It is hard when yesterday my friend Hans sent me a letter, saying: 'Self-preservation and a sworn obligation do not allow me to see you today.' Generally no one comes to see us. Here it is dismally lonely. We are shunned like lepers. Additionally – and this might be the worst – there is a sense of total insecurity. If somewhere in the world something momentous unexpectedly happens, and this alas is possible in all these tensions, what will happen then to ones such as we are?[45]

In a similar situation, a colleague of Stephan Prager and Philipp Rappaport, the highly esteemed architect and municipal building surveyor Gustav Oelsner (1879–1956) in Altona, born in a Jewish family and affiliated to a Christian church, had left Germany 1937 for the USA and later for Turkey. In 1939 he had the good luck to be invited by the Turkish minister of public works to be adviser to the government and professor at the Technological University, Istanbul. There he founded the first chair for town planning in Turkey. However, Gustav Oelsner, as well as the famous architect

Bruno Taut (1884–1938), who both found refuge in Turkey in the 1930s, were rare exceptions: for most German master-builders, even the most illustrious, the prospects of a career abroad were poor. Rappaport could not accept an invitation to the United States because it held no prospect of permanent employment. This, along with his complex family situation, was the reason why Rappaport was so reluctant to leave his country. Even then he felt still very strong ties to Germany. 'Vaterland', a touching poem of eight stanzas, written in 1940, describes his predicament. One stanza read:

> Nichts kann mich von Dir trennen,
> Geliebtes Vaterland,
> Ich muss Dich doch nennen,
> wenn Du dich abgewandt.
> (Nothing can separate me from thee,
> Beloved fatherland.
> I must call your name
> Though you turned away from me.)[46]

The question of whether or not to emigrate became irrelevant, in any case, in November 1941, when the Nazis forbad further emigration. From now on, Jews and those declared to be Jews by the Nazi government were trapped. It was at this point, as we have seen, that Rappaport's colleague Stephan Prager had his troubles with the Düsseldorf Gestapo. Rappaport, living in a mixed marriage, was in a different situation. But he had no confidence that this 'privileged' position would last for long. He was expecting *Unheil* (mischief), particularly when he noticed in the summer of 1942 that 'non-Aryan' partners who were divorced or lived separated, or whose the children were older than 17, had been deported.[47] But fortunately nothing happened to Rappaport during the years 1942 and 1943.

The *Unheil* came in September 1944, after the unsuccessful attempt upon Hitler's life on 20 July. In the so-called *September-Aktion* of 1944, Philipp Rappaport, like many other Jewish partners in mixed marriages, was deported by the Gestapo into a *Lager.* It was an *Arbeitslager* (forced labour camp) in a remote place named Vorwohle, close to Holzminden on the river Weser, not far from Höxter and the old Carolingian monastery of Corvey.[48] The camp was part of the German armaments industry and it was exploiting its inmates harshly. If they were no longer able to bear the tough working conditions, or fell ill, they were sent to Theresienstadt.

Some were deported, to where we do not know. One of the leading German metallurgists, Benno Strauss, 71 years old, died from exhaustion on 27 September 1944 in Vorwohle, a few days after his arrival. Rappaport, in spite of being a prisoner, was able to find work with the *Lager* architects in the board of works. This offered the 66-year-old a chance of survival. He worked as a draughtsman and played a role in the construction of barracks. So, rather like Stephan Prager in Theresienstadt, his usefulness saved his life. He learned the inner technical details of the camp ground, knowledge which helped him a lot when, in the beginning of 1945, the whole *Lager*, because of the military situation, was speedily transferred. When the labourers were put under orders to march away from the camp, Rappaport disappeared into a hidden underground installation that he knew from his work. From there he was able to creep through a tunnel deep under the electric fence and escape. No one searched for him – perhaps because the SS men overseeing this hasty retreat feared loss of time more than the loss of a prisoner.

Yet in fleeing the *Lager* Rappaport ran a great risk. He could have been seized and punished for insubordination or worse. But he was lucky. He made his way to the city of Essen where he was hidden at the home of Parson Heinrich Held, a man of the *Bekennende Kirche* (Confessing Church) in Reginenstraße 47. But Held could no longer assist once an air raid on Essen on 14 March 1945 destroyed his house. Rappaport was then sheltered in another pastor's house, that of Pastor Alfred Neuse in Essen-Haarzopf.[49] Thus he survived, finding freedom again a few months later when the war finally ended. His family also survived although more than 60 per cent of Essen – the city to which he had devoted so much of his career – was destroyed.

What could Philipp Rappaport do after the war? Valuable years had passed. Nonetheless he was rehabilitated and reinstated into his former position in the SVR in Essen. The Military Government of the British Occupation-Zone, based in Lemgo (*Zentralamt für Wirtschaft*), charged him with the special task of constructing new dwellings for miners – necessary because the reconstruction programme was focused on increasing the Ruhr's coal output, an important resource for the recovery of Europe. The need for homes for miners was acute. The former Prussian *Staatskommissar für Bergmannswohnungen im rheinisch-westfälischen Industriebezirk*, Philipp Rappaport was able to use his early experience and in spite of his age resolved the problem in a relatively short time.

Next he returned to urban reconstruction and new city and regional spatial planning. Under Stephan Prager's presidency, Rappaport was elected vice-chairman of the Deutsche Akademie für Städtebau und Landesplanung (German Academy for Urban and Regional Spatial Planning). His papers about *Wiederaufbau* (re-establishment) were highly praised.[50] On his seventieth birthday on 10 December 1949, the *Landesregierung* of Nordrhein-Westfalen bestowed on him the title of professor, and the Rheinisch-Westfälische Technische Hochschule in Aachen gave him the title of *Doktor-Ingenieur Ehrenhalber* (honorary doctor).[51]

Rappaport continued to be a very prolific author. The year before he died in 1955 he published a book which examined how city planning and the landscape could be melded together.[52] This was a new approach, bringing urban design into a wider context and linking it to spatial and regional planning. Meanwhile, the worst bomb damage in the Ruhr cities had been repaired. So far as urban planning was concerned, the SVR and its director Rappaport could then contribute to some of the pivotal post-war architectural achievements such as the Westfalenhalle in Dortmund (1952) and preparing for later the new Museum Folkwang in Essen (1959), and the plans for Mercatorhalle in Duisburg (1962).[53] However, the spatial dimension in urban and regional planning, and the desire to provide green breathing spaces in towns, became a key feature of Rappaport's favourite project – the planning of Marl, a *Landstadt* (country town), only three miles north of Gelsenkirchen. Here the very centre of the town with the *Rathaus* (council hall), the *Paracelsusklinik*, and the *Städtisches Bildungswerk*, 'Die Insel', (municipal cultural centre) are surrounded by public parkland.[54] Here Rappaport and his partners implemented their earlier ideas of a *Landstadt*. One of the streets in Marl was named after Philipp Rappaport – in recognition of his talent and dedication. It would be a just recognition of his achievements if the town of Essen also were to have one of its streets named after its former chief planner.

By the time he died, on 18 November 1955, Rappaport had paved the way towards a new city design in the Ruhrrevier. One of his characteristics was the separation between housing and the workplace. Another was the pedestrianization of streets and the creation of green zones. The latter were apparent from 1952 in the extensive parkland surrounding the new Westfalenhalle in Dortmund, where seven years later the *Bundesgartenschau* (Federal Garden Exposition) took place. A similar show was organized in

Essen 1965 on the grounds around the new Grugahalle.[55] This exhibition was prepared in the light of Rappaport's earlier evaluations of two other garden shows in Essen in 1929 and 1952, on which he had advised on behalf of the SVR.[56] Rappaport's experiences were used by his successors also in the preparation of the great *Bundesgartenschau* of 1965 which reflected his continued linkage of urban and regional spatial planning. His entire oeuvre, a bridge between the early 1930s and the post-Second World War era, was altogether very impressive. It was a blessing indeed for Germany that he and Stephan Prager survived the Nazi era.

HITLER, THE WOULD-BE ARCHITECT AS DESTROYER AND STEPHAN PRAGER AND PHILIPP RAPPAPORT, FORCED LABOURERS, BUT TRUE REBUILDERS

During the last months of the Second World War, the situation in forced-labour and concentration camps became especially desperate. Forced marches and other journeys away from the camps could spell the end for prisoners who were already dangerously ill and could not endure terrible cold, hunger and fatigue. Fortunately Stephan Prager was liberated at Theresienstadt without such a march, while Philipp Rappaport was able to escape, avoiding the perils of the death march. When he came back to Essen the war was not yet over and he had to hide from Nazi officials. Where could he go? His daughter Gerda, in a nice play on words, answered this question later, using the German word *Held* (hero) which was also the name of Philipp Rappaport's pastor, Heinrich Held, who became his saver. She wrote: 'Among the persecuted and the members of the Confessing Church it was generally known that Pastor Held of Rüttenscheid was a real hero.'[57] As we have seen, he took charge of Rappaport and hid him. When the pastor's house was bombed, Pastor Held got Rappaport to the safety of the parsonage of Pastor Neuse. Unlike emigrants who came back to Germany after 1945, and different also from Germans who had stayed in the country, people like Prager and Rappaport came neither 'from within' nor 'from without'. They came back from a strange place 'in between', from the dark world of the camps. This was a dismal *Zwischenreich* (intermediate sphere) where an oppressed *Schattenvolk* (shadow-like people) was vegetating, as the German writer Emil Barth called it ('entehrt, versklavt, verloren').[58] One may call it also 'Behemoth's terrible cage' – where they had to live together with the furious monster. Although they survived, they lost valuable years of their lives: ten for Prager, twelve for Rappaport. Theirs was a waste of outstanding talents that Germany rejected. In 1945 there were good reasons for Prager and Rappaport to emigrate, but they stayed, still considering Germany to be homeland – a country more wrong than right at that time, but with the need to be healed. They wanted to contribute to the task of recovery – physical and mental – using their talents and exploiting to the full their 'second chance'.

Last but not least, Prager and Rappaport saw themselves as experienced master-builders attracted by the massive demands of reconstruction, with all the problems it posed. This challenge attracted younger Jewish architects, too, such as Julius Posener (1904–96), a disciple of Hans Poelzig (1869–1936), and Konrad Wachsmann (1901–80) who had also studied with Poelzig. They returned from the countries to which they had fled before the war. Wachsmann brought with him his ideas about industrialized construction and building elements (*Fertighaus-System*, general-panel-system), a perfect solution for the swift repair of severely damaged cities needing quick reconstruction. Stephan Prager and Philipp Rappaport appraised the new developments that were appearing internationally in architecture and town planning, and designed and added their own solutions. Against the mounts of rubble and ashes left by the would-be architect Hitler, Stephan Prager and Philipp Rappaport, former forced labourers, now contributed as genuine 'reconstructers' to the recovery and common good of post-war Germany.

REFERENCES

Archive Sources

Landesarchiv Nordrhein-Westfalen, Abteilung Rheinland (formerly: Nordrhein-Westfälisches Hauptstaatsarchiv), Düsseldorf: NW 01 253, RW 58 – 29 013, and from the Branch in Düsseldorf-Kalkum: Rep. 372-83-85, Rep. 372-86-92, Rep. 372-104-106.

Stadtarchiv Düsseldorf: Bestand XXXII – 35.

Published Sources

A Catalogue of Camps and Prisons in Germany and German-Occupied Territories, September 1st, 1939 – May 8th, 1945, 2 vols and supplement (Arolsen: ITS, 1949–51).

Adler, H.G., *Theresienstadt 1941–1945: Das Antlitz einer Zwangsgemeinschaft*, 2nd edn (Tübingen: Wallstein, 1960).

Barth, Emil, *Lemuria: Aufzeichnungen und Meditationen* (Hamburg: Claassen & Goverts, 1947); 3rd edn (Aachen: Rimbaud Verlag, 1997).

Berger, Michael, *Eisernes Kreuz und Davidstern: Die Geschichte jüdischer Soldaten in Deutschen Armeen* (Berlin: trafo verlag, 2006).

Berghahn, Volker, *Der Erste Weltkrieg*, 2nd edn (München: Beck 2004).

Berschel, Holger, *Bürokratie und Terror: Das Judenreferat der Gestapo Düsseldorf 1935–1945* (Essen: Klartext, 2001).

Cohn, Willy, *Kein Recht, nirgends: Tagebuch von Untergang des Breslauer Judentums 1933–1941*, edited by Norbert Conrads, 2 vols (Köln/Weimar: Böhlau, 2006).

Deutsche Biographische Enzyklopädie (DBE), hrsg. Von Walther Killy, 8 vols (München: Saur, 1998).

Feuß, Axel, *Das Theresienstadt-Konvolut (Altonaer Museum)* (Hamburg/München: Verlag Dölling, 2002).

Gellately, Robert, *Die Gestapo und die deutsche Gesellschaft* (Paderborn: Schöningh, 1993).

Gellately, Robert, *Hingeschaut und weggesehen!* (Stuttgart: Deutsche Verlags-Anstalt, 2002).

GRUGA: Blumengarten an der Ruhr, bearbeitet von Heinrich Spies und Karl-Heinz Hanisch, 4th edn (Essen: Webels, 1966).

Hirschfeld, Gerhard, Krumeich, Gerd and Renz, Irina (eds), *Enzyklopädie Erster Weltkrieg* (Paderborn: Schöningh, 2003).

Institut Theresienstädter Initiative (ed.), *Theresienstädter Gedenkbuch: Die Opfer der Judentransporte aus Deutschland nach Theresienstadt 1942–1945* (Prague: Academia-Verlag, 2000).

Lekebusch, Sigrid, *Not und Verfolgung der Christen jüdischer Herkunft im Rheinland 1933–1945: Darstellung und Dokumentation* (Köln: Rheinland Verlag, 1995).

Lowenthal, Ernst G., *Juden in Preußen: Biographisches Verzeichnis*, 2nd edn (Berlin: Dietrich Reimer, 1982).

Lowinski, Heinrich, *Städtebildung in industriellen Entwicklungsräumen am Beispiel der Stadt und des Amtes Marl* (Recklinghausen: Aurel Bongers, 1964).

Marx, Christian, 'Landesplanungsverband für den engeren mitteldeutschen Industriebezirk', *Die Neue Stadt: Europäische Zeitschrift für Städtebau*, 19 Oktober 2008.

Moß, Christoph, *'Wir leben doch in Gedanken nur mit Euch': Briefe von Georg und Frieda Lindemeyer, 1937 bis 1941: Dokumente der Verfolgung von Christen jüdischer Herkunft in Düsseldorf* (Düsseldorf: Archiv der Evangelischen Kirche im Rheinland, 2002).

Obermaier, Ernst and Held, Werner, *Jagdflieger Oberst Mölders*, 3rd edn (Stuttgart: Motorbuch-Verlag, 1993).

Oppenheim, Ralph, *An der Grenze des Lebens: Theresienstädter Tagebuch* (Hamburg: Rütten & Löning, 1961).

Prager, Stephan, *Die Architektur im Lichte ästhetisch-systematischer Einteilungsprinzipien* (Erlangen: Junge und Sohn, 1911).

Prager, Stephan, *Behebung der Wohnungsnot in England* (Berlin: Verlag Ernst und Sohn, 1920).

Prager, Stephan, *Zum Entwurf eines preußischen Städtebaugesetzes* (Berlin: Deutsche Bauzeitung und Zentralblatt der Bauverwaltung, 1925).

Prager, Stephan, 'Vorarbeiten für die Aufstellung eines General-Siedlungsplans für den mitteldeutschen Industriebezirk', *Zeitschrift für Bauwesen: Hochbauteil*, Hefte 4–6 (1925).

Prager, S., *Die Bedeutung der Tätigkeit des Reichsamtes für Landesaufnahme für die Landesplanung* (Berlin: Mitteilungen des Reichsamtes für Landesaufnahme, 1927).

Prager, S., *Landesplanungsgemeinschaft Rheinland: Ein Beitrag zur Entwicklung der Landesplanung in der Rheinprovinz* (Tübingen: Wasmuth, 1929).

Prager, Stephan, *Deutsche Akademie für Städtebau und Landesplanung. Rückblick und Ausblick 1922–1955* (Tübingen: Wasmuth, 1955).

Festschrift Stephan Prager = Landesgruppe Nordrhein-Westfalen der Deutschen Akademie für Städtebau und Landesplanung (ed.), *Planen in Stadt und Land: Festschrift für Stephan Prager* (Köln/Opladen: Westdeutscher Verlag, 1961), containing a list of Prager's publications.

Rappaport, Philipp (August), *Steigende Straßen: Eine Studie zum deutschen Städtebau* (Berlin: Wasmuth, 1911).

Rappaport, Philipp, *Fürsorge und Eigensorge im Wohnungsbau* (Berlin: Ernst, 1920).

Rappaport, Philipp, *Neuzeitliche Wirtschaftspläne für Städte und Gemeinden*, manuscript of a lecture in Limburg, 29 August 1926.

Rappaport, Philipp, *Das Netz der Hauptkraftwagenstraßen in den Vereinigten Staaten von Nordamerika* (Berlin-Charlottenburg: Verlag der Studiengesellschaft für Automobilstraßenbau, 1927).

Rappaport, Philipp, *Stadtgestaltung Essen*, 2 vols (Essen: Krupp, 1929), Vol. 1: *Anhang: Baupolizeiliche Ordnung für das Stadtgebiet Essen*; Vol. 2: *Anhang: Entwurf zur Ergänzungs-Baupolizeiverordnung für den Siedlungsverband Ruhrkohlenbezirk vom 22. März 1927.*

Rappaport, Philipp, *Die innerdeutsche Umsiedlung vom Standpunkt der Wirtschaft und des Städtebaues* (Frankfurt a. M: Die Umschau, 1933).
Rappaport, Philipp, *Der Wiederaufbau der deutschen Städte*, Neuauflage (Essen-Steele: Webels, 1946).
Rappaport, Philipp, *Wünsche und Wirklichkeit des deutschen Wiederaufbaus* (Frankfurt a. M: Pippert & Morshäuser, 1949).
Rappaport, Philipp, *Leben und Landschaft im Wandel der Zeiten* (Tübingen: Wasmuth, 1954).
Rappaport, Philipp, *Die leitenden staatlichen und kommunalen Verwaltungsbeamten der Rheinprovinz 1816–1945* (Düsseldorf: Droste, 1994).
Romeyk, Horst, *Verwaltungs- und Behördengeschichte der Rheinprovinz 1914–1945* (Düsseldorf: Droste, 1985).
Romeyk, H., *Die leitenden staatlichen und kommunalen Verwaltungsbeamten der Rheinprovinz 1816–1945* (Düsseldorf: Droste, 1994).
Schäfer, Markus, 'Stadtentwicklung seit der NS-Zeit und Wiederaufbau der Städte in Nordrhein-Westfalen', report of a conference organized by the Landschaftsverband Rheinland on 22 November 2005. *AHF-Informationen*, Nr 005, 24 January 2006, pp.2–3.
Schmidt, Herbert, *Der Elendsweg der Düsseldorfer Juden: Chronologie des Schreckens 1933–1945* (Düsseldorf: Droste, 2005).
Störtkuhl, Beata, 'Wettbewerb zur Erlangung eines Bebauungsplans der Stadt Breslau und ihrer Vororte', in Jerzy Rozpedowski (ed.), *Architektura Wroclawia, T. II: Urbanistyka* (Wroclaw: Oficyna Wydawnicza Politechniki Wrocławskiej, 1996), pp.339–58.
Suchy, Barbara, *Liste der Düsseldorfer Opfer der nationalsozialistischen Judenverfolgung: Eine Dokumentation* (Düsseldorf: Stadtarchiv, 2003).
Teilhaber, Felix A., *Jüdische Flieger im Weltkrieg* (Berlin: Der Schild, 1924; Nachtrag 1932).
Theresienstädter Initiative (ed.), *Theresienstädter Gedenkbuch: Die Opfer der Judentransporte aus Deutschland nach Theresienstadt 1942–1945* (Prague: Academia-Verlag, 2000).
Victor, Adolf, *Vom Gefreitenknopf zum Pour le Mérite* (Berlin: Schild, 1922).
Weinmann, Martin (ed.), *Das nationalsozialistische Lagersystem*, 4th edn (Frankfurt a. M: Zweitausendeins, 2001).

NOTES

1. M. Berger, *Eisernes Kreuz und Davidstern: Die Geschichte Jüdischer Soldaten in Deutschen Armeen* (Berlin: trafo verlag, 2006), pp.159–67.
2. In the literature published before 1933, the fact that there were Jewish air fighters was still well known: see A. Victor, *Vom Gefreitenknopf zum Pour le Mérite* (Berlin: Schild, 1922) – Victor was the military superior to Wilhelm Frankl, whom he describes – and F.A. Teilhaber, *Jüdische Flieger im Weltkrieg* (Berlin: Schild, 1924; Nachtrag 1932). After the Second World War, this facet of the war slowly re-emerged. See Berger, Eisernes Kreuz und Davidstern, pp.138 ff., 163 ff; and, briefly, E. Obermaier and W. Held, *Jagdflieger Oberst Mölders* (Stuttgart: trafo verlag, 1993), pp.219, 221. The aspect mentioned above deserves a still stronger regard in recent literature. See V. Berghahn, *Der Erste Weltkrieg*, 2nd edn (München: Beck, 2004) and G. Hirschfeld, G. Krumeich and I. Renz (eds), *Enzyklopädie Erster Weltkrieg* (Paderborn: Schoeningh, 2003). In this very useful reference work, 'Jüdische Flieger' would be a good supplement to the articles 'Judenzählung' and 'Luftkrieg' or to the article 'Manfred von Richthofen'.
3. Berger, *Eisernes Kreuz und Davidstern*, p.167.
4. Ibid., p.169.
5. Vol. 3 (München and New York: Saur, 1983), p.167.
6. See E.G. Lowenthal, *Juden in Preußen: Biographisches Verzeichnis*, 2nd edn (Berlin: D. Reimer, 1982), p.183.
7. The following details of his life are based on files from the Nordrhein-Westfälisches Hauptstaatsarchiv Düsseldorf (HStAD) and Stadtarchiv Düsseldorf (StAD): HStAD NW 01253, RW 58-29013, HStAD-Kalkum Rep. 372-83-85, Rep. 372-86-92, Rep. 372-104-106; StAD XXXII-35. For further information, see H. Schmidt, *Der Elendsweg der Düsseldorfer Juden* (Düsseldorf: Droste, 2005), particularly pp.150–69; B. Suchy, *Liste der Düsseldorfer Opfer der nationalsozialistischen Judenverfolgung: Eine Dokumentation* (Düsseldorf: Stadtarchiv, 2003); Institut Theresienstädter Initiative (ed.), *Theresienstädter Gedenkbuch: Die Opfer der Judentransporte aus Deutschland nach Theresienstadt 1942–1945* (Prague:

Academia-Verlag, 2000), particularly p.462; A. Feuß, *Das Theresienstadt-Konvolut (Altonaer Museum)* (Hamburg/München: Verlag Dölling, 2002), p.62; see also R. Oppenheim, *An der Grenze des Lebens: Theresienstädter Tagebuch* (Hamburg: Rütten und Löning, 1961), p.202.
8. S. Prager, *Die Architektur im Lichte ästhetisch-systematischer Einteilungsprinzipien* (Erlangen: Junge und Sohn, 1911).
9. S. Prager, *Behebung der Wohnungsnot in England* (Berlin: Verlag Ernst und Sohn, 1920).
10. See S. Prager, 'Vorarbeiten für die Aufstellung eines General-Siedlungsplans für den mitteldeutschen Industriebezirk', *Zeitschrift für Bauwesen, Hochbauteil,* Hefte 4–6 (192).
11. See C. Marx, 'Landesplanungsverband für den engeren mitteldeutschen Industriebezirk', *Die neue Stadt, Europäische Zeitschrift für Städtebau*, 19 Oktober 2008.
12. S. Prager, *Die Bedeutung der Tätigkeit des Reichsamtes für Landesaufnahme für die Landesplanung* (Berlin: Mitteilungen des Reichsamtes für Landesaufnahme, 1927).
13. Lowenthal, *Juden in Preußen*, p.183. Cf. in detail H. Romeyk, *Verwaltungs- und Behördengeschichte der Rheinprovinz 1914–1945* (Düsseldorf: Droste, 1985), p.362.
14. S. Prager, *Landesplanungsgemeinschaft Rheinland: Ein Beitrag zur Entwicklung der Landesplanung in der Rheinprovinz* (Tübingen: Wasmuth, 1929).
15. *Gesetz zur Wiederherstellung des Berufsbeamtentums* ('Law for the Restauration of the Professional Civil Service').
16. H. Romeyk, *Die leitenden staatlichen und kommunalen Verwaltungsbeamten der Rheinprovinz 1816–1945* (Düsseldorf: Droste, 1994), p.490. See H. Berschel, *Bürokratie und Terror: Das Judenreferat der Gestapo Düsseldorf 1935–1945* (Essen: Klartext 2001), pp.123, 376–7.
17. The letter quoted here and also in the passages that follow is from Schmidt, *Der Elendsweg*, pp.150ff.
18. Ibid: 'Desgleichen hat ihm auch der Generalinspektor für das deutsche Straßenwesen, Dr Todt ... für 'langjährige selbstlose Mitarbeit' den aufrichtigsten Dank und gleichzeitig die besten Wünsche für einen gesegneten Ruhestand zum Ausdruck gebracht.' Cf. Berschel, *Bürokratie und Terror*, p.377.
19. Schmidt, *Der Elendsweg*, p.151.
20. Berschel, *Bürokratie und Terror*, p.377.
21. R. Gellately, *Die Gestapo und die deutsche Gesellschaft* (Paderborn: Schöningh, 1993); and R. Gellately, *Hingeschaut und weggesehen!* (Stuttgart: Deutsche Verlags-Anstalt, 2002).
22. Schmidt, *Der Elendsweg*, p.152.
23. Ibid.
24. Ibid.
25. Quoted from Berschel, *Bürokratie und Terror*, p.377: 'Der Landeshauptmann wird es müde werden, Sie zu schützen.'
26. We don't know exactly in which part of Theresienstadt concentration camp Stephan Prager had to work. Most likely it was in the *Arbeitszentrale* and in the branch *Baumaterial* (building materials) or in the branch *Reinigung und Gebäudeverwaltung* (cleaning and building management). Here, according to H.G. Adler, 266 men were put to work. But Prager's place could possibly have been also in the biggest department, *Öffentliche Betriebe und Arbeiten* (public workshops), where 1,559 forced workers had to toil. The timber-yard with additional workshops was situated in the south-west part of the old citadel of Theresienstadt. See H.G. Adler, *Theresienstadt 1941–1945: Das Antlitz einer Zwangsgemeinschaft*, 2nd edn (Tübingen: Wallstein, 1960), pp.397, 413, 422–3 and a map at the end.
27. Ibid., pp.153, 157; and Berschel, *Bürokratie und Terror*, p.203.
28. Rheinisch-Westfälische Technische Hochschule Aachen (ed.), *Personal- und Vorlesungsverzeichnis für das Sommersemester 1967*, p.8.
29. S. Prager, *Deutsche Akademie für Städtebau und Landesplanung: Rückblick und Ausblick, 1922–1955* (Tübingen: Wasmuth 1955). Also published in honour of Stephan Prager was the work edited by Landesgruppe Nordrhein-Westfalen der Deutschen Akademie für Städtebau und Landesplanung, *Planen in Stadt und Land: Festschrift für Stephan Prager* (Köln/Opladen: Westdeutscher Verlag, 1961). This book contains a selected list of his publications.
30. File in HStAD, NW 58 4245, quoted here from S. Lekebusch, *Not und Verfolgung der Christen jüdischer Herkunft im Rheinland, 1933–1945: Darstellung und Dokumentation* (Köln: Rheinland-Verlag, 1995), p.179. Cf. C. Moß (ed.), *'Wir leben doch in Gedanken nur mit Euch': Briefe von Georg und Frieda Lindemeyer, 1937 bis 1941 – Dokumente der Verfolgung von Christen jüdischer Herkunft in Düsseldorf* (Düsseldorf: Archiv der Evangelischen Kirche im Rheinland, 2002).

31. According to *Deutsche Biographische Enzyklopädie* (*DBE*), hrsg. Von Walther Killy (München: Saur, 1998), vol. 8, p.142.
32. P.A. Rappaport, *Steigende Straßen: Eine Studie zum deutschen Städtebau* (Berlin: E. Wasmuth, 1911).
33. Rappaport knew Howard's book, *Garden Cities of Tomorrow* (1902).
34. *DBE*, vol. 8, p.142.
35. P.A. Rappaport, *Fürsorge und Eigensorge im Wohnungsbau* (Berlin: Ernst, 1920).
36. Lekebusch, *Not und Verfolgung*, p.179, n.90.
37. This is shown by the list of publications of P.A. Rappaport, in: *Stadtgestaltung Essen* (Essen: Krupp, 1929) – 3 vols the titles of which are named above under References.
38. See B. Störtkuhl, 'Wettbewerb zur Erlangung eines Bebauungsplans der Stadt Breslau und ihrer Vororte', in J. Rozpedowski (ed.), *Architektura Wroclawia, T. II: Urbanistyka* (Wroclaw: Oficyna Wydawnicza Politechniki Wrocławskiej, 1996), pp.339–58. The *Bebauungsplan* (plan for erecting dwellings on a building site) had been worked out by Philipp Rappaport and his colleague Kurt Hesse.
39. P.A. Rappaport, *Neuzeitliche Wirtschaftspläne für Städte und Gemeinden*, manuscript of a lecture held in Limburg, 29 August 1926. I owe the knowledge of this manuscript to Mrs Susanne Keiter, Düsseldorf.
40. A detailed report about Rappaport's impressions of the American road and highway system is his article *Das Netz der Hauptkraftwagenstraßen in den Vereinigten Staaten von Nordamerika* (Berlin-Charlottenburg: Verlag der Studiengesellschaft für Automobilstraßenbau, 1927). Inspired by his observations of the US, Rappaport had become, as early as 1926, one of the first advocates of a German traffic census.
41. See also an early assessment by S. Prager, *Zum Entwurf eines preußischen Städtebaugesetzes* (Berlin: Deutsche Bauzeitung und Zentralblatt der Bauverwaltung, 1925).
42. *Die innerdeutsche Umsiedlung vom Standpunkt der Wirtschaft und des Städtebaues* (Frankfurt a. M: Die Umschau, 1933).
43. In 2002 Richard E. Moser was honoured by Yad Vashem with the title 'Righteous among the Nations'. Cf. *Hamburger Abendblatt*, 12 June 2002.
44. Lekebusch, *Not und Verfolgung*, p.182.
45. Quoted from ibid., p.419, trans. K.D.
46. Quoted from Lekebusch, *Not und Verfolgung*, p.186, trans. K.D.
47. Ibid., p.189.
48. *A Catalogue of Camps and Prisons in Germany and German-occupied Territories, September 1st, 1939 – May 8th, 1945*, 2 vols and supplement (Arolsen: ITS, 1949–51). See now: Martin Weinmann (ed.), *Das nationalsozialistische Lagersystem*, 4th edn (Frankfurt a. M: Zweitausendeins, 2001).
49. Lekebusch, *Not und Verfolgung*, p.192.
50. P.A. Rappaport, *Der Wiederaufbau der deutschen Städte* (Essen-Steele: Webels, 1946); and P.A. Rappaport, *Wünsche und Wirklichkeit des deutschen Wiederaufbaues* (Frankfurt a. M: Pippert & Morshäuser, 1949).
51. Lekebusch, *Not und Verfolgung*, p.194.
52. P.A. Rappaport, *Leben und Landschaft im Wandel der Zeiten* (Tübingen: Wasmuth, 1954).
53. For the public debate on these large projects, see also M. Schäfer, 'Stadtentwicklung seit der NS-Zeit und Wiederaufbau der Städte nach 1945 in Nordrhein-Westfalen', *AHF-Informationen*, Nr 005, 24 Januar 2006, pp.2–3 (report of a conference organized by the Landschaftsverband Rheinland on 22 November 2005).
54. See H. Lowinski, *Städtebildung in industriellen Entwicklungsräumen am Beispiel der Stadt und des Amtes Marl* (Recklinghausen: Aurel Bongers, 1964).
55. See *GRUGA: Blumengarten an der Ruhr*, bearbeitet von Heinrich Spies und Karl-Heinz Hanisch, 4th edn (Essen: Webels, 1966).
56. The first of these garden shows where the name GRUGA (as an acronym) came from was the 'Große Ruhrländische Gartenbau-Ausstellung' of 1929, another one has taken place in 1952, others later – the first two of them regional exhibitions which had also been promoted by Rappaport and the SVR.
57. G. Altpeter, *Dem Holocaust entkommen*, manuscript, p.64, quoted from Lekebusch, *Not und Verfolgung*, p.192.
58. E. Barth, *Lemuria: Aufzeichnungen und Meditationen* (Hamburg: Claassen & Goverts, 1947), here quoted from the 3rd edition (Aachen: Rimbaud Verlag, 1997), p.62.

PART 3
THE POST-WAR WORLDS OF WOMEN AND CHILDREN

8

Lost Homelands and Reconstructed Homes: Gender and Displacement in Post-War Germany

SILVIA SALVATICI

INTRODUCTION

D.M. and K.S. (in the documents their names are never quoted in full[1]) met in Germany immediately after Hitler's defeat. They chose to share everyday life in the camps and to plan their futures together, in ways that their status as Displaced Persons (DPs) allowed them to do. Both had been forced to leave their homes in the eastern Ukraine during the war, but they both managed to escape forced repatriation to the Soviet Union.[2] In order to stay together after their arrival in Western occupied Germany – instead of going back to their land of origin – they resorted to a twofold stratagem: they hid their nationality and at the same time they pretended to be husband and wife, although they had never actually married. In 1947 they had a baby; as a result of his parents' false claim to be married, the boy was registered as their firstborn, instead of being added to the long list of illegitimate children among DPs.

In autumn 1948, D.M. was found to have tuberculosis. His illness was not a chance diagnosis: the family had applied for the International Refugee Organization (IRO) resettlement programmes and each member had to undergo the medical screening required of all potential migrants. D.M. started his treatment in the camp's hospital, but soon realized that he could not leave Germany with his wife and son, since few countries were willing to accept tubercular immigrants. Since they did not want to abandon their migration plans, the couple decided to reveal their real status: D.M. and K.S. informed the military authorities that their wedding had never taken place, and the false husband and wife became single persons once more. From October 1949 K.S. was registered as unmarried, as a result of which she could apply for resettlement programmes reserved for unattached women.[3]

Custody of the son was granted to the father, who was classified as a so-called 'hard core' case: DPs with very low chances of being resettled because of their reduced working abilities. The formerly 'married' couple presumably hoped that this change of status would be the basis for an only temporary separation, which in the near future would be happily concluded with their reunion after resettlement to Canada, Australia or the United States.[4]

However, the story ended rather differently. The migration process was very slow, and in spring 1950, K.S. – who was officially single, but still lived under the same roof with D.M. – was pregnant once again. For unattached women pregnancy was grounds for exclusion from the resettlement programmes, while as a single mother K.S. would have no chance of being selected for resettlement once the baby was born. All hopes for migration seemed to be lost, and the Ukrainian partners eventually decided to regularize their position; in June 1951 D.M. and K.S. got married, and after a few weeks their second-born was registered as their legitimate child. The legalization of the union meant the definitive collapse of the family plan to be resettled and to leave Germany behind.

The story of D.M. and K.S. offers us one example of the difficulties presented by the resurrection of family life in the camps. Previous studies have pointed out that domesticity 'became a refuge from wartime and post-war anxiety',[5] and have shown that the new attachment to the family was very widespread in all developed countries, but was particularly evident among the DPs. Atina Grossmann offered a powerful description of the baby boom among the Holocaust survivors, and convincingly argued that for Jewish persecutees[6] 'fertility and maternity worked as a mode of re-identifying and reconstructing'; they 'offered a means of establishing a new order and a symbolic sense of "home", even and especially in the refugee camps'.[7] However – with the exception of Grossmann's studies on Jewish DPs – the trajectories of the rapid construction of new families within the assembly centres are still largely unexplored. How did the search for intimacy and domesticity within a family group coexist with the allied rule of the camps, with the policy of repatriation and the procedures for resettlement? What was the role played by the re-establishment of a 'sense of "home"' in re/constructing DPs' affiliation with the lost homeland? What difficulties did new families face in their attempts to gain a new homeland? In other words: how did the experience of displacement and the trajectories for the construction of families shape each other? This chapter attempts to address this question by focusing on the case of DPs' marriages.

SHOTGUN OR ILLEGITIMATE WEDDINGS?

In April 1945 the United Nations Relief and Rehabilitation Administration (UNRRA) welfare officer Muriel Gardner attended the opening of the Catholic church set up in the preceding weeks by Polish DPs in Hanau. Immediately after the celebration of the mass, the Polish leader approached Mrs Gardner and begged her to 'borrow' the priest from the American Army again for the following Saturday because so many women and men wanted to get married. He explained that many of these relationships had already been formed in the Nazi forced labour camps, as a result of which there were now many illegitimate children, and most of the women who lived 'illegally' with their partners were eager to 'regularize' their status. The leader also asked if the UNRRA officer was able to provide any kind of white fabric for the Polish brides. Of course Muriel Gardner (who probably had not received any instruction about 'emergency weddings' during the training course for relief workers she had attended a few weeks earlier) was in favour of the 'regularization' of the Polish couples. However, she 'couldn't see [her]self going to the American major in the middle of the war and asking him for white material for wedding dresses'. Therefore she promised only the priest; following a request by the Polish leader she then also promised to attend the ceremony. One week later, forty-five brides showed up in the church, each of them wearing a white gown. The UNRRA officer noticed that the wedding dresses had not been properly sewn and most of them were just pinned up; however, the performance was impressive and she supposed DPs had managed to obtain the cloth from the Germans living in the neighbourhood. Although the priest sped up the ceremonial as much he could, celebration of all the forty-five weddings took more than three hours. At this point Mrs Gardner decided to do her best in order to have a priest transferred to Hanau on a permanent basis.[8]

In the following months, mass celebration of weddings occurred all over occupied Germany, in churches or synagogues set up in the camps.[9] The high rate of marriages was the result not only of the couples formed during Nazi times, but also of the encounters which had taken place in assembly centres. As one DP recalled later, 'People would meet, and five minutes later would ask "Are you married?".'[10] In 1946, again in Hanau, the head of the UNRRA warehouse went through the same experience that Mrs Gardner had had one year earlier. In this case forty dark suits for the grooms were lacking, and again DPs 'cleaned out the German families in the area'[11] to find them. DPs attempted faithfully to follow traditional rituals despite the austere living conditions of the assembly centres. The literature has highlighted the role played by camp life in strengthening the identity of individual national groups,[12] and collective celebration of mass weddings probably contributed to the (re)construction of a common cultural heritage.

However, the religious rite became a public ceremony not only because of the participation of the whole national community living in the same centre, but also thanks to the attendance of the UNRRA officers. As we have seen in the story told by Muriel Gardner, the UNRRA representatives were not simply invited to the weddings, their presence was formally requested by the camps' leaders, as it conferred the needed official legitimation upon the ceremony. Usually UNRRA personnel looked favourably on DPs' weddings. On the one hand, they provided a useful exercise in the camps' community building. On the other hand, high rate of marriages 'regularized' the status of many couples 'living in concubinage' and could counteract the moral corruption of DPs: women's reduced maternal capabilities, children's 'wildness' and widespread lack of 'civilized values' were frequently denounced by both military authorities and United Nations representatives responsible for the assembly centres.[13]

The forming of new families was ratified by religion, by the approval of the national community leaders and by UNRRA's paternalism, but in most cases it lacked any legal recognition. According to the allied regulations, DPs' marriages had to be legalized by the German Marriage Registrar (*Standesbeamte*) and in conformity with local law, which required all foreigners to produce a certificate from the authorities of their native country that there were no legal impediments to their marriages.[14] Some of the military officers working in the field 'felt that [religious] marriages should be countenanced rather than people live out of wedlock';[15] however, legal advisors of both the English and the American military governments warned against 'unauthorized marriages'. In the camps hundreds of weddings 'solemnized' by religious rites were regarded by the DPs themselves as a positive regularization of their status, while the headquarters deemed them irregular acts practised on a massive scale.

From their point of view, DPs were probably not too keen to have their new family status ratified by local German authorities which, after all, represented the country they blamed for the destruction of their past lives. More important still, DPs were certainly unwilling to approach their home authorities, which could put them under pressure to repatriate. In February 1946 some provision was made for granting exemptions from fulfilling the requirements of German law; Balts – whose native countries no longer existed as independent states – were assimilated as stateless persons and could gain dispensation from submitting the 'no impediment' certificate.[16] Nevertheless, regulations issued by the military authorities and the introduction of possible exceptions did not stop the celebration of religious weddings, and three years after the end of the war occupation forces pointed out that not only were such weddings 'void, but also clergymen performing such ceremonies were commit[ting] criminal offences and were [thus] liable to prosecution'.[17]

The problem became very serious when the repatriation flows dried up and the allies gave priority to resettlement programmes. Families could emigrate only if they were recognized as such by civil law; men could qualify for resettlement as single persons, while in most cases single mothers with illegitimate children were rejected: 'unauthorized weddings' affected male and female plans for the future differently. The legalization of marriages that DPs had celebrated in front of the ministers of their faith appeared very urgent in order to reduce as much as possible the 'hard core', the 'residuum of refugees' left behind by the selection processes of receiving countries. Military authorities and the International Organization for Refugees realized that the best solution was to make the registration of civil marriages among DPs easier. According to new regulations issued in 1948, the 'no impediments' certificate could be provided by IRO officers (on the basis of information contained in old records, testimonials of camp priests, welfare committees, and so on) in cases where it was too difficult to obtain it from the representatives of DPs' native countries.[18]

However, many couples still could not get married and were therefore excluded from resettlement, as in the case of Georges Kanins and Alide Bandenieks. Georges and Alide were both Latvian; they met in Germany and had a 1-year-old baby, Juris. Georges had left his wife in Latvia when he fled the country, and had had no contact with her since. He submitted to IRO a letter he claimed to have received from a friend, stating that his wife had passed away; however, the UN officer regarded this document as insufficient for the issue of the certificate of 'no impediments' requested by German authorities. In October 1949 Georges and Alide were still counted among the unmarried couples, 'a part of the Hard Core'.[19]

Anxious to ship out as many refugees as possible, in March 1950 the Allied High Commission for Germany provided a kind of amnesty: all marriages between DPs 'solemnised between 8 May 1945 and 1 August 1948 before a minister of religion in accordance with the rites of his religion' were declared to have the same effect as if celebrated according to German law, upon their registration at the chief register office (*Hauptstandesamt*) in Hamburg.[20] The military authorities, in other words, simplified the procedures for DPs' civil marriages, under the pressures imposed by resettlement. At the same time, new couples formed among the DPs had to conform to the prescription of the law, since the ties created between women and men in the assembly centres would not be sufficient for them to be recognized as a family. The 'sense of "home"' established despite the living conditions of the camps was not sufficient for gaining a new homeland.

MIXED MARRIAGES

Not all the new couples formed within the same national communities. Although memory of camp life focused on 'endogamous weddings', mixed marriages were not unusual. In summer 1945 the Headquarters of the British 30 Corps Districts raised the issue of Soviet women married to men of another nationality, and asked for guidelines on international marriages. In this case the main problem was whether such women had to be considered 'Russian' (and therefore to be repatriated) or not.[21] Almost one year later, the issue of mixed unions was raised again, but this time it no longer concerned just Soviet nationals (whose repatriation, in any case, had already largely been carried out). Headquarters of 30 Corps Districts stated that 'frequent requests [were] received for authorization of marriages between DPs and Germans or between DPs of different nationalities'. Lieutenant General J. Kirby gave the example of a Polish man who had recently married a Balt; the service had been performed by the Polish military chaplain and the couple 'wishe[d] the marriage legalised'.[22] In the cases of mixed marriages, legalization was probably more important to the DPs themselves than was the case with all the other religious weddings celebrated in the camps. Not only could mixed unions not rely on the recognition of one national community, but the lack of official regularization could limit the immediate future options of mixed couples. British soldiers, for example, could go back home with their DP partners only if marriages had been legalized. The certificate of 'no impediments' for the bride could take a very long time to arrive and soldiers requested the headquarters of the Prisoners of War and Displaced Persons (PW & DPs) Division to sort out their position.[23] For them the best solution was to take their DP girlfriend to Great Britain and get married there; in February the Office of Deputy Military Governor of the Control Commission for Germany (CCG) informed that any male UK national could provide their partner with a letter stating that he was ready to marry her as soon as she arrived on British soil. Upon submission of this letter, alien women residing in occupied Germany could obtain a visa which would enable them to travel to the United Kingdom and remain there for two months: if they were 'not married within two months [they were] liable to be deported'.[24] This procedure allowed DP women to follow or join the British boyfriends they met in the camps; in these cases, mixed marriages, on the one hand, implied crossing the boundaries of national affiliation, and on the other they allowed displaced brides to leave Germany and gain a new homeland through the construction of a new family.

Military authorities stated clearly that the provision about marriage in the UK between alien women and British subjects didn't apply to 'women of German nationalities who [were] not permitted to enter [the] United Kingdom'.[25] Mixed weddings involving Germans were particularly complicated, from a legal perspective, and – as the statement of the headquarters of 30 Corps Districts quoted above pointed out – they happened also among DPs. Statistics are not available, but unions between DPs and German women do not seem unusual. We can assume that they were due to the higher rate of males within the camps, although they probably didn't affect all the national communities in the same way; unfortunately there is no specific information about mixed marriages among Balts, Poles or Ukrainians. However, military authorities were unhappy about the frequency of marriages between DPs and Germans and tried to counteract the consequences of this phenomenon. In July 1946 the PW & DP Division of the Office of Military Government for Germany – United States (OMGUS) raised the issue of the separation of male DPs (billeted in the assembly centres) from their German wives (prohibited from moving into assembly centres). According to the American authorities, such separation in several cases induced the DPs to abandon their families, and thereby it increased the number of single mothers and illegitimate children among the German population, already troubled by very serious economic and social problems.[26] This is probably one of the reasons why a few months later it was decided, both in the American and the British zones, that if one partner was eligible for United Nations Displaced Persons care and treatment, members of his immediate family should also be enabled to apply for assistance.[27] Through their marriage to male DPs, German women could therefore move into the camps, whose borders proved to be more permeable than the military authorities wished. Boundaries of DPs' national communities, whose reinforcement within the assembly centres has been emphasized by much literature on DPs, also proved to be porous, since they could be crossed even by women who belonged to the ex-enemy country.

Military governments found out very soon that their measures regarding German wives of United Nations DPs had several negative effects. First, their marriage to a DP entitled German women to UNRRA assistance, but did not automatically confer the husband's citizenship upon them. DPs' native countries decided on a case-by-case basis, and usually rejected applications submitted by German wives; neither did they allow them to follow their repatriated husbands. Marriages between local women and displaced men therefore turned out to be an obstacle for the repatriation programmes; according to the survey carried out by OMGUS in winter 1947, 15 per cent of the interviewed DPs declared they were not willing to go back to their place of origin because they did not want to leave their German wives[28] behind. Such negative effects of mixed marriages on repatriation seemed alarming to the military authorities, and the British were afraid that provisions taken on 'humanitarian grounds' could foster the practice of 'marriages of convenience'.

The documents do not give any detail about the advantages that husband and wife could obtain from the so-called 'marriages of convenience'. However, the CCG representatives probably referred both to the better living conditions that German women could enjoy in the camps and alluded to the fact that DPs married to Germans had an additional and indisputable reason to refuse repatriation.[29] Aiming to prevent the 'marriages of convenience', the British military government introduced a deadline. German wives could apply for UNRRA assistance only if they had married a displaced man before 17 May 1947; any wedding celebrated after this date did not entitle German women to gain DP status. Such a provision, also introduced later in the American zone, reaffirmed the borders of the camps as the limits (geographical, social and cultural) within which DPs could construct their new families.

German wives emerged to be a potential obstacle also for the resettlement of DPs, particularly during the early phase, when most of them migrated towards European countries (Great Britain, France, Belgium) which did not welcome former ex-enemy nationals.[30] From 1948, mixed couples could more easily be accepted in Australia or in the United States,[31] but IRO officers based at the Reinhardt Kaserne, in Neu-Ulm, stated that 'many DPs married German wives. Some ignored their responsibilities and left the country without caring for their children.'[32] In all these cases, families formed in Germany turned out to be only temporary, and male DPs who had left behind their children and partners were free to form new families in their new homeland.

CONCLUSION

Among the population of DPs, marriage and the formation of families had a number of distinct features. Firstly, they were built on sentiment and emotions (love and the need to overcome loneliness imposed by their refugee status, for example) more than on legal recognition. Secondly, as the story of D.M. and K.S. reminds us, unions among DPs were inherently flexible and unstable, since they were requested to adapt to the changing trajectories of displacement (repatriation and resettlement, but also transfers from camp to camp or recruitment in different employment programmes), and they were limited by the divergence between being a real family group, but one that lacked legal status. Thirdly, the constitutions of new couples and families crossed the boundaries of both camps and national communities; reconstruction of home did not necessarily go along with the reinforcement of affiliations to lost homelands. Such a complex profile of displaced marriages collided with the process of family 'regularization', which the military authorities considered a priority in the administration of the camps. This very process was also at the centre of the resettlement programmes and constituted an essential precondition for admittance to those Western countries where the 'golden age of marriage', based on lifelong unions, female domesticity and recognition of coexistence by religious authorities and state legislation, was just about to begin.[33]

REFERENCES

Archive Sources

Archives Nationales, Paris (AN): AJ43/806 Zone américaine d'Allemagne, 31/13 Conséquences sociologique de la vie de réfugiés, 1947–1951.

Imperial War Museum (IWM): Sound Archive, interview with Muriel Gardner, 18519/5.

National Archives and Records Administration Washington (NARA): OMGUS [Office of Military Government for Germany – United States], Records of the Civil Affairs Division (CAD), PW&DP Branch, 319.1 Reports, Liaison Officers, box 176 RG 260; and *Visit to Assembly Center at Bensheim*, 6 June 1945, in NARA, DPs Branch, Shaef G-5 Division, Visits-Mr Ernst, box 49 RG 331.

The National Archives, London (TNA): Legal Division of the Control Commission for Germany – British Element (CCG-BE), FO 1052/267, Administration Policy: DPs all nations, vol.2, 1945-6; *Marriage of Non-German Nationals – Position in the Civil Law*, 16 February 1946, TNA, FO 1052/267 Administration policy: DPs all nations, vol. 2, 1945–46; CCG/PCIRO (Preparatory Commission of the International Refugee Organisation) Joint Instruction n. 42, *Marriages of Displaced Persons*, TNA, FO 1052/499 PWDP/Iro instructions 1948–1949.

Published Sources

Cohen, G.D., 'Between Relief and Politics: Refugee Humanitarianism in Occupied Germany 1945–46', *Journal of Contemporary History*, 43, 3 (2008), pp.437–49.

Coontz, Stephanie, *Marriage, a History: From Obedience to Intimacy, or How Love Conquered Marriage* (New York: Viking, 2005).

Danys, Milda, *DP Lithuanian Immigration to Canada after the Second World War* (Toronto: Multicultural History Society of Ontario, 1986).

Dyczok, Marta, *The Grand Alliance and Ukrainian Refugees* (New York: St Martin Press, 2000).

Elliott, Mark R., *Pawns of Yalta: Soviet Refugees and America's Role in their Repatriation* (Urbana, IL, University of Illinois Press, 1982).

Grossmann, Atina, 'Victims, Villains, and Survivors: Gendered Perceptions and Self-Perceptions of Jewish Displaced Persons in Occupied Postwar Germany', *Journal of the History of Sexuality*, 11, 1 and 2 (2002), pp.291–318.

Grossmann, Atina, *Jews, Germans, and Allies: Close Encounters in Occupied Germany* (Princeton, NJ, and Oxford: Princeton University Press, 2007).

Harzig, Christiane, 'McNamara's DP Domestics: Immigration Policy Makers Negotiate Class, Race and Gender in the Aftermath of World War II', *Social Politics*, 10, 1 (2003), pp.23–48.

Holborn, Louise W., *L'Organisation Internationale pour les Réfugiés: Agence spécialisée des Nations Unies 1946–1952* (Paris: Presses Universitaires de France, 1955).
International Refugee Organization, *Statistical Report: With 43 Months Summary* (Geneva: Office of Statistics and Operational Reports HQ, April 1950).
Isajiw, Wsevolod W., Boshyk, Yury and Senkus, Roman (eds), *The Refugee Experience: Ukrainian Displaced Persons After World War II* (Edmonton: Canadian Institute of Ukrainian Studies, University of Alberta, 1992).
Jacobmeyer, Wolfgang, *Vom Zwangsarbeiter zum Heimatlosen Ausländer: Die Displaced Persons in Westdeutschland, 1945–1951* (Göttingen: Vandenhoeck und Reprecht, 1985).
Jaroszyńska-Kirchmann, Anna D., *The Exile Mission: The Polish Political Diaspora and Polish Americans, 1939–1956* (Athens, OH: Ohio University Press, 2004).
Kay, Diana and Miles, Robert, *Refugees or Migrant Workers? European Volunteer Workers in Britain (1946–1951)* (London: Routledge, 1992).
Königseder, Angelika and Wetzel, Juliane, *Waiting for Hope: Jewish Displaced Persons in Post-World War II Germany* (Evanston, IL: Northwestern University Press, 2001).
Mazower, Mark, *Dark Continent: Europe's Twentieth Century* (London: Penguin Books, 1999; 1st edn 1998).
McDowell, Linda, *Hard Labour: The Forgotten Voices of Latvian Migrant Volunteer Workers* (London: UCL Press, 2005).
Office of Public Information, *International Refugee Organization: The Hard Core: Selection of Typical Histories* (Geneva: Office of Public Information, October 1949).
Proudfoot, Malcolm J., *European Refugees: 1939–52: A Study in Forced Population Movement* (London: Faber & Faber, 1956).
Salvatici, Silvia, 'Le Gouvernement anglais et les femmes réfugiées d'Europe après la Deuxième guerre mondiale', *Le Mouvement Social*, 225, 4 (2008), pp.53–64.
Therborn, Goran, *Between Sex and Power: Family in the World 1900–2000* (London and New York: Routledge, 2004).
Wyman, Mark, *DPs: Europe's Displaced Persons, 1945–1951* (Ithaca, NY, and London: Cornell University Press, 1998; 1st edn 1989).
Zahra, Tara, 'Lost Children: Displacement, Family, and Nation in Postwar Europe', *Journal of Modern History*, 81, 1 (2009), pp.45–86.

NOTES

1. The story of D.M. and K.S. is summarized by the International Refugee Organization in the document *Effect of Resettlement Plans on Family Life*, Archives Nationales, Paris [AN], AJ43/806 Zone américaine d'Allemagne, 31/13 Conséquences sociologique de la vie de réfugiés, 1947–1951.
2. According to the Yalta Agreement, 'All former prisoners of war and citizens of the USSR liberated by the Allied Forces and all former prisoners of war and citizens of Allied Nations liberated by Red Army will be delivered through the Army lines to the corresponding Army Command of each side'; Malcom J. Proudfoot, *European Refugees: 1939–52: A Study in Forced Population Movement* (London: Faber & Faber, 1956), p.208. On the interpretation of the Yalta Agreement which led to forced repatriation of Soviet civilians, see Mark R. Elliott, *Pawns of Yalta: Soviet Refugees and America's Role in their Repatriation* (Urbana, IL: University of Illinois Press, 1982), and Wolfgang Jacobmeyer, *Vom Zwangsarbeiter zum Heimatlosen Ausländer: Die Displaced Persons in Westdeutschland, 1945–1951* (Göttingen: Vandenhoeck und Reprecht, 1985) pp.123–52.
3. See, in particular, the resettlement schemes implemented by the United Kingdom and Canada: Linda McDowell, *Hard Labour: The Forgotten Voices of Latvian Migrant Volunteer Workers* (London: UCL Press, 2005); Diana Kay and Robert Miles, *Refugees or Migrant Workers? European Volunteer Workers in Britain (1946–1951)* (London: Routledge, 1992); Christiane Harzig, 'McNamara's DP Domestics: Immigration Policy Makers Negotiate Class, Race and Gender in the Aftermath of World War II', *Social Politics*, 10, 1 (2003), pp.23–48; Silvia Salvatici, 'Le Gouvernement anglais et les femmes réfugiées d'Europe après la Deuxième guerre mondiale', in *Le Mouvement Social*, 225, 4 (2008), pp.53–64.
4. The United States, Australia and Canada held the first three positions in the list of countries of destination for resettled European displaced persons; see Proudfoot, *European Refugees: 1939–52*, p.425.

5. Mark Mazower, *Dark Continent: Europe's Twentieth Century* (London: Penguin Books, 1999; 1st edn 1998), p.227.
6. 'Persecutees' was a particular category of DPs, which contained 'persons persecuted by the enemy because of their race, religion, or activities in favour of the United Nations': Proudfoot, *European Refugees: 1939–52*, p.243.
7. Atina Grossmann, 'Victims, Villains, and Survivors: Gendered Perceptions and Self-Perceptions of Jewish Displaced Persons in Occupied Postwar Germany', *Journal of the History of Sexuality*, 11, 1 and 2 (2002), pp.308–9; by the same author see also *Jews, Germans, and Allies: Close Encounters in Occupied Germany* (Princeton, NJ, and Oxford: Princeton University Press, 2007), pp.184–236. On marriages among Jewish displaced persons, see also Angelika Königseder and Juliane Wetzel, *Waiting for Hope: Jewish Displaced Persons in Post-World War II Germany* (Evanston, IL: Northwestern University Press, 2001), pp.196–7.
8. Imperial War Museum [IWM], Sound Archive, interview with Muriel Gardner, 18519/5.
9. See, for example, *Report on Displaced Persons Installation*, 30 June 1945, NARA [National Archives and Records Administration], OMGUS [Office of Military Government for Germany – United States], Records of the CAD, PW&DP Branch, 319.1 Reports, Liaison Officers, box 176 RG 260; and *Visit to Assembly Center at Bensheim*, 6 June 1945, in NARA, DPs Branch, Shaef G-5 Division, Visits-Mr Ernst, box 49 RG 331.
10. Mark Wyman, *DPs: Europe's Displaced Persons, 1945–1951* (Ithaca, NY, and London: Cornell University Press, 1998; 1st ed. 1998), p.111.
11. Ibid.
12. See Milda Danys, *DP Lithuanian Immigration to Canada after the Second World War* (Toronto: Multicultural History Society of Ontario, 1986); Marta Dyczok, *The Grand Alliance and Ukrainian Refugees* (New York: St Martin's Press, 2000); Anna D. Jaroszyńska-Kirchmann, *The Exile Mission: The Polish Political Diaspora and Polish Americans, 1939–1956* (Athens, OH: Ohio University Press, 2004); Wsevolod W. Isajiw, Yury Boshyk and Roman Senkus (eds), *The Refugee Experience: Ukrainian Displaced Persons after World War II* (Edmonton: Canadian Institute of Ukrainian Studies, University of Alberta, 1992). As Atina Grossmann has pointed out, the historiography has presented the DP experience as part of the history of Zionism and emphasized the role of Holocaust survivors in the founding of Israel; see Grossmann, *Jews, Germans, and Allies*, pp.6–7.
13. See Tara Zahra, 'Lost Children: Displacement, Family, and Nation in Postwar Europe', *Journal of Modern History*, 81, 1 (2009), pp.45–86.
14. For the British zone see the paragraph on *Marriages* of the *Working Paper Number One for the History of IRO*, AN, AJ43/439, History of the British Zone of Germany; for the American zone see the *Memorandum* issued by the Office of Military Government for Germany – United States (OMGUS) in September 1947; NARA, OMGUS, Records of the CAD, PW&DP Branch, 319.1 Reports Congressional Committee, box 176 RG 260. In the British zone, the certificate requested by the German law could be produced by the liaison officers of DPs' native countries; see the correspondence of the field officers with the Legal Division of the Control Commission for Germany – British Element (CCG-BE) in The National Archives, London (TNA), FO 1052/267, Administration policy: DPs all nations, vol. 2, 1945–46.
15. HQ 30 Corps District, *DP Marriage*, 5 Jan 1946, TNA, FO 1052/267 Administration policy: DPs all nations, vol. 2, 1945–46.
16. Legal Division, Main HQ, CCG-BE, *Marriage of Non-German Nationals – Position in the Civil Law*, 16 February 1946, TNA, FO 1052/267 Administration policy: DPs all nations, vol. 2, 1945–46.
17. CCG/PCIRO (Preparatory Commission of the International Refugee Organisation) Joint Instruction n. 42, *Marriages of Displaced Persons*, TNA, FO 1052/499 PWDP/Iro instructions 1948–1949.
18. See the memorandum on *Marriage and Divorce* in AN, AJ43/822 Zone américaine d'Allemagne 34/2 Documents concernant les camps de la zone américaine 37 Archives de la Reinhardt Kaserne à Neu Ulm, 1947–1951, and the paragraph on *Marriages* of the *Working Paper Number One for the History of IRO*, AN, AJ43/439, History of the British Zone of Germany.
19. Office of Public Information, *International Refugee Organization: The Hard Core: Selection of Typical Histories* (Geneva, October 1949), p.19.
20. Allied High Commission for Germany, *Law on Legal Position of Displaced and Refugees,*

part 2, article 6, AN, AJ43/795 Zone britannique d'Allemagne, vol. 3, chapitres 44 à 46; Louise W. Holborn, *L'Organisation Internationale pour les Réfugiés: Agence spécialisée des Nations Unies 1946–1952* (Paris: Presses Universitaires de France, 1955), pp.225–6.

21 . The *Guide to Soviet Repatriation Problems*, issued by the Prisoners of War & Displaced Persons (PW&DPs) Division of the CCG (Be) stated that all the cases of Russian women who had married men of other nationality had to be referred to the headquarters, which was supposed to solve the problems according to the law of husband's native country: TNA, FO 1052/260, Repatriation Policy Russians I 1945–46.
22. HQ 30 Corps District, *DP Marriages*, 9 April 1946, in TNA, FO 1052/267 Administration policy: DPs all nations, vol. 2, 1945–46.
23. See, for example, the case of Sergeant J. Williams and Marta Bialkowska in TNA, FO 1052/267 Administration policy: DPs all nations, vol. 2, 1945–46.
24. Office of the Deputy Military Governor, *Marriage in the UK between Alien Women and British Subjects*, 22 February 1946, TNA, FO 1052/267 Administration policy: DPs all nations, vol. 2, 1945–46.
25. Ibid.
26. Office of Military Government for Germany (US), PW&DP Division, *Marriages of Displaced Persons with Germans*, 24 July 1946, in NARA, OMGUS, Records of the CAD, PW&DP Branch, 383.7 Displaced Persons (General), box 167 RG 260.
27. Material for *Weekly Information Bulletin*, 16 August 1946, NARA, OMGUS, Records of the CAD, PW&DP Branch, 383–7 DP General, box 168 RG 260.
28. NARA, OMGUS, Records of the CAD, PW&DP Branch, 061.2 Survey, UNDP, box 149 RG 260.
29. See the correspondence between the Legal Division, the PW&DP Division and the Headquarters of the CCG in TNA, FO 1052/462, DPs: legal, 1946–48.
30. In 1947 around 100,000 DPs were resettled in Great Britain, France and Belgium; see International Refugee Organization, *Statistical Report: With 43 Months Summary* (Geneva: Office of Statistics and Operational Reports HQ, April 1950), p.28.
31. In 1948 more than 40 per cent of resettled DPs migrated to Australia, the United States and Canada, ibid.
32. *Illegitimate children of DPs & Germans*, AN, AJ43/822 Zone américaine d'Allemagne 34/2 Documents concernant les camps de la zone américaine 37 Archives de la Reinhardt Kaserne à Neu Ulm, 1947–1951.
33. See Goran Therborn, *Between Sex and Power: Family in the World 1900–2000* (London and New York: Routledge, 2004), pp.162–6, and Stephanie Coontz, *Marriage, a History: From Obedience to Intimacy, or How Love Conquered Marriage* (New York: Viking, 2005), pp.225–8.

9

German Women from the Pinzgau (Salzburg) as Victims of Nazi Racial Politics

ALOIS NUSSBAUMER

This chapter looks at an area that has so far only rarely been touched upon, the so-called 'sexual intercourse crimes' (*GV-Verbrechen*).[1] It is based on the research project 'Forced Labour in Agriculture in Pinzgau (Salzburg)'. Of interest is how and why German women apparently became victims of Nazi racial ideology. The research focuses on local women in Pinzgau in the district of Salzburg, who were sentenced to prison in extra court trials (*Sondergerichte*) due to suspected sexual relations with forced labourers and prisoners of war. But who had denounced these women and what motives had led to the charges? A further set of questions which this chapter investigates deal with the arrests and the hearing of evidence concerning the offences, as well as the extra court trials at the regional court in Salzburg. Finally, the chapter assesses the significance of the victims' relief documents (*Opferfürsorgeakten*), which allow insights into the fate of those women in the post-war years and the reaction of the Austrian authorities to their experiences.

FORCED LABOUR AND RACIAL POLITICS

The Pinzgau is an Austrian mountainous region in the district of Salzburg. Due to the construction of electric power plants by the National Socialists, this region made use of a comparatively large number of civilian forced labourers and prisoners of war during the Second World War. Out of the 6,974 foreigners registered in September 1944,[2] more than half were so-called *Ostarbeiter* (workers from eastern Europe), particularly people from Poland and Ukrainians from Galicia; a high percentage of them are likely to have been women.[3] The remainder of the foreign workers were Belgians, Frenchmen, Italians, and Croatians.[4]

Besides the Alpine construction sites, forced labourers were also used in the agriculture of Pinzgau. While those foreigners who were housed in barracks and prisoners of war camps faced control by the National Socialists, those civilian forced labourers and prisoners of war who lived and worked directly on the farms could partially escape the regime's clutches. This lack of control greatly troubled the officers in charge of the employment and supervision of foreigners, as they saw the 'purity of the race', as imagined in the Nazi racial ideology, endangered by sexual contacts between local people and foreign workers.[5]

In a 1939 report about pastoral care (*Seelsorgebericht*), the priest of Niedernsill decried the moral life of the youth in his congregation. He blamed the local situation, the 'massive concentration in larger farms'.[6] What to the Catholic priest was objectionable from a moral perspective appeared to the National Socialists in terms of race politics. In response they attempted to safeguard the German Volk (or '*Deutsche Volkskörper*') through a range of measures, such as the installation of brothels and the even distribution of women and men among Polish forced labourers.[7] From 25 November 1939 a decree for the protection of the military forces (*Wehrkrafschutzverordnung*) was enacted, paragraph 4/1 of which specified: 'persons who deliberately break one of the regulations enacted to govern the contact with prisoners of war or otherwise maintain contact with prisoners of war in a way that severely hurts the "decent national feeling" (*gesunde Volksempfinden*) will be sentenced to imprisonment'.[8] The German people could read in any newspaper that every contact with prisoners of war beyond the level required by their employment was going to be severely punished.[9] At one end of the scale this 'unlawful interaction' comprised such little things as passing on letters and the receipt or dispensation of gifts (tips, cigarettes, drinks, and so on); at the other it included sexual contact.[10] At the end of 1941 the Criminal Law Edict Concerning Polish People (*Polenstrafrechtsverordnung*) extended those regulations to Poles and Jews, and in 1942 it was further extended to forced labourers from eastern Europe, the *Ostarbeiter*.[11]

The RHSA (Reichssicherheitshauptamt, Institute of National

Security) generally aimed at a prohibition of sexual contact of Germans with foreigners of any other nation, but the regulations and fines differed according to the race or nationality of the person involved.[12]

For example, Jews, Sinti or Romas, *Ostarbeiter*, Poles and Russian prisoners of war convicted of sexual intercourse with a German partner in most cases received the death penalty or confinement in a concentration camp.[13] Prisoners of war from other states were sentenced to jail.[14] Dutch, Danes and Norwegians were not prosecuted at all, given their racial affiliation to the Germanic people.[15] Civilian workers from Italy, France and Belgium, and also members of the allied states, Slovakia, Croatia, Romania, Bulgaria and Hungary, were basically allowed sexual relationships with Germans, even if close contact was to be limited, both by the police and the population at large.[16] The National Socialists constantly had to juggle between their own racial ideology on the one hand and the political requirements of the war on the other.

DENUNCIATION AND ARREST

In the execution of the delict, the Nazi regime relied on the support of the villagers – that is, on denunciation and informants. This can be seen as a form of society's self-control, which the Nazi security apparatus knew how to make use of.[17] Considering that in the light of the policemen's conscription into the army, many police offices were understaffed, and that communities with a German population between 1,096 and 2,492 people[18] often did not have more than two policemen, the importance and extent of denunciation quickly becomes evident.[19] In addition, the area of Pinzgau lies at a very high altitude and is accessible only on bad roads or mere dirt tracks, which additionally hampered police control of the locals, the prisoners of war and the civilian forced labourers. Thus, the regime waited for tip-offs from the villagers, followed these cases up, arrested the respective persons and took legal action. Why did locals willingly become informants? Reasons for denunciation may, on the one hand, be explained by a sense of duty to the Nazi State; on the other hand, by such emotions as jealousy, greed, hate and revenge. In addition, informants at times had personal motives for discrediting enemies, and with the help of the National Socialist let them 'disappear'.[20]

One particular victim's file (*Opferfürsorgeakte*) illustrates how the process worked. A widow was reported by her daughter for having had 'illegal contact with prisoners of war. The police reported to the Gestapo in Salzburg, the woman was brought to Salzburg and treated in such an inhuman way in the police custody that she, in order not to be exposed to any further imprisonment[,] admitted contact with prisoners of war'.[21] In the subsequent extra trial the judge sentenced the accused to three years of jail (*Zuchthaus*) on the basis that she had sexual contact with three different French prisoners of war between 1940 and 1942.[22] The case raises a further question: why did this daughter denounce her mother as late as 1943, if she was accused of sexual relationships between 1940 and 1942? The explanation must lie in the fact that individuals' knowledge about such contacts were used in personal conflicts or at particular tactical moments.

Even more dangerous for the women involved was the general village gossip, which was harmless only until the information reached the wrong person. Simple suspicion and gossip about 'illegal contacts' could quickly turn into detailed detective work to satisfy private nosiness. This was the case with the wife of a farmer, for example, where two farmhands drilled a hole into the ceiling of a house in order to watch the woman's sexual activities with a prisoner of war. The 'story' was told to a colleague, who reported it to the authorities.[23] Some trial documents suggest that even employers were responsible for denunciations.[24] It is not clear from the documents whether it was routine to use forced confessions of prisoners or accused people, but it does seem clear that the police officers put women under great psychological pressure and that 'assertion of deliberately wrong facts' accelerated confession.

NUMBERS OF WOMEN

The Salzburg regional archive (*Landesarchiv Salzburg*) has twelve documents on extra trials which took place between 7 May 1941 and 26 May 1943 at the Salzburg regional court. They testify to the fact that German women[25] from Pinzgau[26] were put into jail for periods between three months and three years because of 'illegal contact with prisoners of war'.[27] With the exception of two cases, those women were accused of sexual intercourse with prisoners of war. Four women were sentenced to three years of jail, four others to two years, one farmer's lady to fifteen month and the daughter of a farmer to thirteen months of jail. A female farmhand was put into prison for ten months and the wife of a soldier for three months because the trial concluded that this case was not a serious crime but only a 'delict of illegitimate contact with a prisoner of war'.[28] In the trials, seven women were accused of sexual intercourse with French prisoners of war; one female farmer was accused only of sexual contact. One woman was sentenced for sexual relationships with three different French prisoners of war. For two women it was believed that they had had sexual intercourse with Serbian prisoners of war. At the moment of sentencing the women were between 18 and 52 years old. The majority of those women came from agricultural backgrounds, working as wives of farmers, farmhands and agricultural labourers, or as helpers, waitresses or home helps. More difficult for the regime was the fact that one of the sentenced women had also been a party member, a block chief (*Blockleiterin*) of a Nazi women's organization as well as a head of the local female farmers' group (*Ortsbäuerin*). Eight out of twelve women were mothers; six were unmarried; four were married and two widowed.

Local police chronicles and reports make clear that more women were arrested and sentenced than are preserved in the available extra trial documents. For example, the chronicle of one village shows that in September 1941 three women were deported to the police jail in Salzburg because of contact with French prisoners of war, and handed over to the Gestapo.[29] In October two more women were arrested in the same village and taken to Salzburg. A policeman remarked that the other two women were also imprisoned.[30] However, out of these five women only the names of two are mentioned in the extra trial documents. Similarly, the police chronicle of Saalfelden lists the execution of two Polish forced labourers in January 1942 and in September 1943[31] because of their sexual relationships with local women.[32] These women are also not in the extra trial documents. The same chronicle mentions that in 1942 two females were sent to a concentration camp for the duration of the war because of their sexual relationships with prisoners of war.[33]

Other details from the case files can shed further light on the nature of these convictions and the available archival record. For example, the police chronicle of Lofer states that in 1942 an 18-year-old Polish forced labourer was arrested and sent to Salzburg because of repeated offences against public morality and refusal to work.[34] The Gestapo returned the man to Lofer and ordered that two other forced labourers were to hang him, while all other Polish and Russian forced labourers in the villages of Lofer and Unken had to watch.[35] It is not clear whether a local woman was sentenced, but none is mentioned either in the police chronicle or the village chronicle of Lofer.[36]

In another case, a policeman in the village of Piesendorf informed the administrative authority (*Landrat*) in Zell am See in a letter of 5 November 1943 that a 19-year-old Polish farmhand had been arrested and taken to Salzburg, as ordered by the Gestapo. The policeman considered it a fact that the man and a German female worker of the same age and working on the same farm had maintained a sexual relationship for more than a year.[37] At the time of his letter the woman was six months pregnant.[38] The documents contain hardly any further information about the fate of the Polish forced labourer and the woman. The parish register of Piesendorf states that the woman gave birth in the local hospital in 1944 and that her child managed to survive the war.[39]

Another case concerned the village Leogang, where a local woman was pregnant by a Polish forced labourer. After the birth of her child in summer 1942, she was imprisoned in the women's concentration camp at Ravensbrück.[40] Another woman in Leogang was arrested by the Gestapo in early December 1944 following her own testimony, because of illegal listening to the radio, and was then accused of a relationship with a French forced labourer. She was imprisoned in Aichach in Upper Bavaria, Germany.[41]

In another case, the police from the mountain office in Kaprun reported in late April 1942 to the office in Zell am See that a woman from Niederdonau, working as a cleaner with the firm Union Baustelle Zefret, had been arrested for illegal contact with a French prisoner of war.[42] These three women from Leogang and Kaprun are also mentioned in the extra trial documents in the Salzburg regional archive.[43]

Overall, the available sources do not allow a conclusive statement about how many women from Pinzgau had been sentenced for their contact with prisoners of war and forced labourers. It is possible, as a newspaper article from towards the end of the war suggests, that extra trials were conducted in various villages across the region.[44] However, no documents to support this assumption could be traced. It is to be assumed that documents relating to these situation were destroyed in the post-war period.

THE LEGAL PROCESS

The extra trial documents show extraordinary humiliation of the women by the judges and the hearing officials. The crimes of which the women were accused were reconstructed in a painstakingly detailed and degrading manner. For example, the courts took notes on whether or not the women assisted the prisoner of war in their sexual contact by taking off their clothes, as well as detailed sexual information. It was recorded in which locality the liaison took place, in which sexual position and how often, and whether or not it resulted in ejaculation. For any of the women accused, the trials must have seemed endless.

The trial documents concerning the woman from Oberpinzgau, mentioned above, state the following:

> In that room in which the prisoner of war slept she had kept her clothes and for this had to enter the room every now and then to get clothes. On Sundays the man usually slept longer. As she entered the room on Sunday, April, 26, 1942 again the prisoner of war was awake on the bed and asked her about the weather. She then, without thinking about anything, sat down on the bed of the Frenchmen, took back the curtain besides the window near the bed to look outside. The man had then immediately taken her hand and said that it was so hard as he never had a woman and had put her hand to his erected phallus. She had rubbed against it until ejaculation. The prisoner of war had neither kissed nor touch her ...[45]

This document also contains the statement of the two witnesses, a farmhand and a milker, who watched the bed of the French prisoner of war through a hole. The farmhand said that he had seen the accused lying in bed. He had only seen part of the body, from her chin to her breasts. She had worn a frock, and she had made coitus-like movements. He had not seen the prisoner of war, because the hole had been too small.[46] The milker supported this statement. He had not seen any further parts of her body, but from the movements he had witnessed was able to conclude that it must have been a complete coitus.[47] The farmhands also accused their farmer's wife of having fed the prisoner of war better than the local workers. The milker said that he himself had seen four times how she had given the Frenchman a tart. He was also often given coffee while they, the other farmhands, were only given skimmed milk.[48] This document clearly shows the social tensions on the farm, particularly the jealousy towards the French prisoner of war. Despite the National Socialist regime the farmhands did not experience any improvement in their personal living situation, and saw what they perceived to be a more favourable treatment of an enemy of the German people. What must have enforced their anger even more was that the woman was an official of the National Socialist Party (Nationalsozialistische Deutsche Arbeiterpartei, NSDAP). The woman managed to reject the claim of unequal treatment, but was sentenced to fifteen months of imprisonment for her sexual deeds.[49]

The procedures to collect proofs for these liaisons contained two tiers. On the one hand, the confessions of the women (however they may have been obtained) were frequently used against them. In some cases the sexual partners, the prisoners of war, were also questioned.[50] On the other hand, information was obtained from a series of witnesses. Policeman and Gestapo officers were asked as witnesses at trials; their statements were 'proofs' for the influence of officials on the women. Other witnesses also included former lovers, employees, inspectors of prisoners of war, and so on.

It also becomes evident in the documents that the *gesunde Volksempfinden* (sense of public decency) was considered in the trials. Policemen collected information about the women from the village community to weaken their reputation.[51] In the case of a 20-year-old waitress, the local police officer found that she was considered a loose woman, addicted to sex. This was confirmed by her former boss of two months, who testified that she had received many male visitors in her room and for this reason had been dismissed.[52] The documents also show that the police arranged for house searches to secure material, such as letters that could be used in trials against the women.[53]

The judges' pronouncements considered a series of aggravating and mitigating factors in the women's cases, both sets of which directly drew upon the Nazi ideal of the 'German mother and wife'. Her responsibilities encompassed, on the one hand, the role of the *Gefährtin und Geliebte* (companion and lover) and, on the other hand, her function as a *Gebährmaschine* (reproduction machine), for the German people. In the files, evidence that sexual intercourse had taken place 'more than once' was considered as aggravating the accused woman's case. Other issues specifically highlighted by the judges which offended the Nazi ideal of women included the fact that 'a mother of seven children had caused public uproar';[54] that the sexual intercourse 'did not remain without consequences';[55] that 'the woman was married and lived in a good relationship';[56] that 'the woman betrayed a lover who wanted to marry her and with whom she had also maintained a sexual relationship';[57] as well as 'the extreme neglect of duty of the accused towards her husband at the front';[58] the 'extremely reckless breach of faithfulness towards her husband'; and the 'severe neglect of her honour as a German mother in giving herself away'.[59]

These statements demonstrate the extent to which the state ideology seeped into the private arena and the lives of individual women and punished them for their offences against the purity of the race.[60] Similarly, mitigating factors often included the accused women's caring duties for children or grandchildren, which moved the judges to place weight on the importance of the roles as a 'German mother'. The judges' identification of these factors demonstrates the extent to which their analyses were grounded in Nazi ideology, but neither mitigating nor aggravating circumstances ultimately seemed to have had much influence on the length of imprisonment.[61] By contrast, the court's assumption that the woman was seduced by the prisoner of war tended to influence the sentence positively.[62]

AFTER 1945

After the Second World War, the so-called *Opferfürsorgegesetz* (*OFG*, Victim Relief Act) was enacted in order to compensate victims of the Austro-fascistic state and the Nazi regime for damages and disadvantages through persecution between 6 March 1933 and 1 May 1945. Compensation was to take place in the form of social justice acts.[63] Although a first OFG version was passed in 1945, it was only the 1947 amendments which for the first time provided benefits, relief and compensation not only for so-called 'active victims' – that is, victims who had actively fought for a free and democratic Austria – but also for those 'passive victims' who had suffered political persecution.[64] The fourth OFG amendment of July 1949 now provided for 'passive victims' who were seriously impaired in the state of their health following imprisonment or maltreatment. The condition for receiving the benefits of the OFG was the possession of an 'official attestation' (*Amtsbescheinigung*) or of a 'victim certificate' (*Opferausweis*), which confirmed the victim status of a given individual.[65]

The regional archive in Salzburg contains files of two women from Pinzgau who had been sentenced for their illegal sexual liaisons. The first concerns the case of the woman who had been reported by her own daughter and imprisoned from February 1943 until shortly before the end of the war. In mid-1949 she applied for an official attestation based on the fourth amendment of the OFG. As reasons for the application the woman cited 'illegal contact with prisoners of war', as well as 'disreputable comments about National Socialism'.[66] The local government of Salzburg turned down the application on the basis that 'this friendly contact with a prisoner of war can in no case be considered as a struggle for the reconstruction of a free and democratic Austria'. And further, it stated: 'no doubt that the imprisonment was a very hard experience, nevertheless it can not be seen as a political reprimand along the provisions of OFG/47'.[67] The woman appealed to the federal Ministry for Social Administration against the order of the regional administration in Salzburg, and explained that she considered herself a political victim of the Nazi regime. The appeal was rejected by the Ministry in a letter of 12 July 1950, because the woman had missed the deadline in September 1949 by two days.

Two-and a-half years later the woman appealed again, and in December 1952 asked the *Landesamtsdirektor* in Salzburg for the issuance of a victim certificate or similar document as well as for the reopening of the proceedings, using the extra trial documents in Salzburg.[68] She referred to her conservative political attitude, which was, she claimed, the reason for the fact that, in her words, the punishment by the judges had been so severe. Furthermore, the woman remarked that in the concentration camp she had been treated with exceptional severity, having been accused in one document of being a die-hard conservative.[69] The local government requested the relevant extra court documents from the legal court in Salzburg. The legal court reported to the government that the file *act Kls 20/43* had been destroyed upon notice of the Public Prosecution Service before the invasion of the allied troops.[70] (This, according to today's knowledge, does not comply with the facts.) Thereupon the Salzburg regional government asked the prison institute in Aichach, in a letter of March 1953, for the remittance of an arrest certificate and, if existing, the imprisonment documents of the woman.[71] A letter of late March 1943 from Aichbach confirmed her imprisonment and that 'the woman was released early on April, 12, 1945 on probation. The illegal contact with prisoners of war in her situation was not on the basis of political reasons, she rather maintained sexual relationship with some French prisoners of war.'[72]

Almost eight years after the end of the war, the director of the Aichbach prison used the same code as is to be found in the police and court documents of the war years. The letter does not show any understanding of the fact that her liaison with the prisoner of war had been unlawful, nor does it display any sympathy with her case; whenever the official referred to the woman it was by using the former convict's family name only. In mid-July 1953 the woman's application for the issuance of a victim certificate was irrevocably rejected by the Salzburg regional government (Amt der Salzburger Landesregierung), arguing that no further new evidence allowing a different decision could be produced.[73]

In the second case, in November 1952 a housemaid (let us call her Notburga M.), who had been imprisoned between 1941 and 1943,[74] applied for an official attestation on the basis of paragraph 4 of the OFG.[75] In her letter the woman argued that for those two years of imprisonment she had had to work in terrible conditions outside in the forest, in severe cold and without appropriate clothing, and therefore had suffered severe health damages.[76] The local administration ordered the police of the home village to check the reasons behind the imprisonment of the woman, and asked them to find out if she had been a member of the NSDAP or an affiliated organization.[77] Furthermore, the woman was examined by a medical authority to find out the degree and timing of her inability to work. According to the OFG of 1945, 'victims in the struggle for a free and democratic Austria' – that is, active victims – could in the case of severe physical damages caused by battle injuries or contracted disease, or through imprisonment or maltreatment, receive an official attestation and then apply for a subsidy to secure their subsistence. These regulations were continued in the OFG of 1947.[78] The doctor was also asked to find out whether there had been a connection between the purported health damage and the imprisonment. The doctor certified damage to vessels due to frostbite on both feet.[79] The medical examination could not state when the frostbite had happened, and a direct link with imprisonment could not be proven.[80]

The regional administration passed on the findings to the authorities in Salzburg and stated that no legal claims existed, as an active commitment to a free and democratic Austria could not be proven.[81] The authorities in Salzburg supported this assessment and rejected the application in March 1953. Notburga M. had also applied for prison compensation. This was also rejected by the Salzburg authorities as the applicant neither had an official attestation nor a victim certificate.[82] The application for an official attestation, which had been rejected in March 1953, would have been a precondition for the grant of a prison compensation.[83] The appeal at the federal ministry for social administration was rejected in February 1954. The concluding remarks stated that a forbearance for grace in case of a missing document stating victim status was not provided by law and could therefore not be granted.[84]

Four and a half years later, Notburga M. appealed again for prison relief. She was told that her application would only be successful if she could prove that her contact with the prisoners of war was on the basis of political reasons, and if she had helped them to flee. Notburga M. could not prove this but argued that she had been accused of contributing to the demoralization of the German army. She further referred to the decree of the Salzburg regional court of 20 December 1957, which stated that after a hearing with the public attorney, Notburga M.'s conviction was not valid for the realm of the Austrian Republic. Notburga M. considered this as the proof of the unlawfulness of her conviction.

However, the regional authorities in Zell am See did not accept this argument; they referred to the regulations of the OFG and suggested to Notburga M. that she could nevertheless apply for the issue of a victim certificate or the granting of prison compensation. In October 1958 Notburga M. applied again to the regional authorities in Salzburg for both an official attestation and a victim certificate. The application was submitted to the local authorities, who demanded further information from the local police office, inquiring whether Notburga M. had been a member of the NSDAP or an affiliated organization and whether she had had any close links to the NSDAP. The local authorities also required a notification from the penal records. Again no membership of or close relation to the NSDAP could be discovered. The Salzburg offices declined the application in January 1959 because of the previous decision, and argued that the actions of Notburga M. had been of an entirely private nature and not political.[85] The woman tried again with a letter to the Austrian prime minister, but received a negative reply from the Ministry of Social Administration.

In some ways her case was not unique. In other victim files, too, the 'illegal contact' with foreigners was not accepted as 'political' according to the provisions of the OFG of 1945.[86] A large number of the applications for victim status analysed by the Austrian Historic Commission (Österreichische Historikerkommission) were rejected because of the suspicion that mere private motivation had been the basis of the sentences.[87] The verdicts of the judges were accepted by the offices enacting the OFG, no matter how reliable they were, and also used in the assessment of the applications.[88]

The files, therefore, document serious shortcomings in the legal process. In addition, questions arise concerning the lives of those women after imprisonment and after the end of the Nazi regime. Into what kind of psychological and physical conditions did those women return after their imprisonment?[89] Did the community – where, after all, everyone knew everybody – accept them? Were they isolated in everyday life or did they isolate themselves? Or were people indifferent after the war and concerned with themselves? Did the villagers think that those women had got their just penalty and had suffered for their actions, or was there also some sympathy or willingness to help? Why did ultimately only so few women apply for victim status?

The account of a woman from Leogang may be seen as representative of many women:

> Then I returned to Leogang and was very disappointed because the people in the village let me feel it, they talked about me, did not believe me that I was not guilty, even today they would not believe that Clement (the French prisoner of war) had been totally unblamable and I, too. My husband wherever he was had not taken it too seriously with fidelity, when he returned from captivity did not believe me either. So I wanted to get divorced so that it all would come to an end.[90]

The extra court documents show that six out of twelve women involved were around 20 years of age when they were sentenced. Going by their age we can assume that those women were looked after by their parents after their return from prison, just like Notburga M., who had lived with her parents before her imprisonment and went back to her parents' house after her release. She still lived there, unmarried and with her two children, in 1958.

The exchange of letters between Notburga M. and the local administration in Zell am See shows the injustice experienced by these women. The local administration let the woman know upon her second application in 1958 that her demand would only be successful if she could prove that she had helped some prisoners of war to flee, supporting her case by naming relevant witnesses.[91] Notburga M. replied to the authorities: 'how could I possibly name witnesses, those people who denounced me and had brought so much sorrow and despair for me I could not ask and those people that knew about the proceedings of those days are no longer alive'.[92] It becomes clear how much the experiences of the war burdened the social relationships within the village, especially if one considers that this village had less than 700 inhabitants.[93]

From the home village of Notburga M., five women had been arrested almost at the same time and then sentenced to prison for 'illegal contact'. If those women returned to that village again, what was life in the village like? Was it dictated by the same fate? Or coined by mutual hate? Shortly before Notburga M. was arrested the police also arrested three women in this village and brought them to Salzburg.[94] The village chronicle reports that a week later Notburga M. was arrested; this could indicate that one or more of the arrested women charged her in the course of their trial.[95] Two weeks after the arrest of Notburga M., one more woman from this village was brought to Salzburg.[96] In the extra court trials Notburga M. said that the 'wenches' (*Weiber*) in the police prison had urged her to say exactly the same as to the police.[97] A woman who was among those first arrested sided with Notburga M., and confirmed that the women sharing the cell with her had put pressure on her to say 'yes' to everything, and that this would be far better. She thus had agreed to everything at the police office and had admitted things that were not true.[98] It is surprising to see that those two women, aged 25 and 18, were sentenced to two years and thirteen months of prison respectively, while the other women only received prison sentences of six months and one week of juvenile imprisonment respectively.[99] It seems as if the women had tried to burden the co-defendants with their own guilt in order to escape long-term imprisonment.[100]

The woman who had been denounced by her daughter no longer lived in the same village when applying for victim relief in 1949; the mayor's letter shows that she had moved into a neighbouring village. The negative response by the regional government in Salzburg, dated July 1953, shows that the woman yet again had moved and stayed at a farm in a village further away.

The collective memory of the people in Pinzgau does not include these women. A coming to terms with those experiences is not evident – the subsequent life of the victims, the perpetrators and all other villagers seem to be strongly shaped by a mentality of neglect and repression. The files speak a clear language of neglect and misunderstanding, and the same can, on a non-official level, be assumed for the post-war society. If one considers that the returning German soldiers felt humiliated in their male honour by the GIs and the betrayal by the local girls and women who had relationships with the 'American enemies,'[101] then it becomes obvious that no social and especially no male sympathy with the fate of those women sentenced to jail during the war could be possible. Today, in 2009, only a few people in Pinzgau know about those cases. To quote a woman from Leogang: 'I did not think that one would ever speak about this drama again, yet, the truth has to be told.'[102]

REFERENCES

Archive Sources

Archive of the Catholic Church in Salzburg (AES): R-Registratur 9/28 Niedernsill; Piesendorf Taufbuch 8.

International Tracing Service (ITS), Bad Arolsen, Germany: ITS/ARCH/Landkreis Zell am See, Ordner 64, p.22.

Municipal Archives: Chronik der Marktgemeinde Lofer 1900.

Police Chronicles: Gendarmeriepostenkommando Bez. Zell a. S. Ld. Salzburg Postenchronik; Chronik des k. k. Gendarmeriepostens Bruck im Pinzgau;

Posten-Chronik Kaprun 1 August 1929 – 18 October 1950 (first part); Chronik des Gendarmeriepostens Lofer 1855–1960; Chronik des GP Maria Alm; Chronik des Gendarmeriepostens Saalfelden; Chronik des k. k. Gendarmeriepostens Taxenbach.

Salzburg Regional Archives (SLA): BH-Akten Zell a.S.,Ld. Opferfürsorgeakten; Sondergerichtsakten.

Printed Primary Sources

Amtliches Gemeindeverzeichnis für das Deutsche Reich auf Grund der Volkszählung 1939, Herausgegeben vom Statistischen Reichsamt, 1st edn (Berlin, 1940).

Rassenpolitik: Schriftenreihe für die weltanschauliche Schulung der Ordnungspolizei, nos. 4–6 (1943).

Salzburger Landeszeitung, Amtliches Blatt der NSDAP: Gau Salzburg und der Staats- und Gemeinde-Behörden, vol.5, no.62 (14/15 März 1942), p.4.

Salzburger Zeitung, vol.58, no.4 (Freitag 9 März 1945), p.2.

Published Sources

Bauer, Ingrid, '"Die Amis, die Ausländer und wir": Zur Erfahrung und Produktion von Eigenem und Fremdem im Jahrzehnt nach dem Zweiten Weltkrieg', in Ingrid Bauer, Josef Ehmer and Sylvia Hahn (eds), *Walz – Migration – Besatzung: Historische Szenarien des Eigenen und des Fremden* (Klagenfurt: Drava Verlags- und Druckges, 2002), pp. 197–276.

Berger, Karin, et al., *Vollzugspraxis des 'Opferfürsorgegesetzes': Analyse der praktischen Vollziehung des einschlägigen Sozialrechts* (Klagenfurt: Drava Verlags- und Druckges, 2002).

Dohle, Oskar and Slupetzky, Nicole, *Arbeiter für den Endsieg: Zwangsarbeit im Reichsgau Salzburg 1939–1945* (Wien/München: Oldenbourg Verlag, 2004).

Freitag, Gabriele, *Zwangsarbeiter im Lipper Land: Der Einsatz von Arbeitskräften aus Osteuropa in der Landwirtschaft Lippes 1939–1945* (Winckler: Bochum, 1996).

Garscha, Winfried R. and Scharf, Franz, *Justiz in Oberdonau* (Linz: Oberösterreichisches Landsarchiv, 2007).

Hauch, Gabriella, '" ... das gesunde Volksempfinden gröblich verletzt": Verbotener Geschlechtsverkehr mit "Anderen" während des Nationalsozialismus', in Gabriella Hauch (ed.), *Frauen im Reichsgau Oberdonau: Geschlechtsspezifische Bruchlinien im Nationalsozialismus* (Linz: Oberösterreichisches Landsarchiv, 2006), pp.245–69.

Herbert, Ulrich, *Fremdarbeiter, Politik und Praxis des 'Ausländer-Einsatzes' in der Kriegswirtschaft des Dritten Reiches*, 2nd edn (Berlin/Bonn: Dietz, 1986).

Hornung, Ela, Langthaler, Ernst and Schweitzer, Sabine, *Zwangsarbeit in der Landwirtschaft in Niederösterreich und dem Burgenland* (Wien/München: Oldenbourg, 2004).

Nussbaumer, Alois, 'Osteuropäische Frauen als Zwangsarbeiterinnen in der Landwirtschaft des Pinzgaus', in Evelyn Steinthaler (ed.), *Frauen 1938: Verfolgte – Widerständige – Mitläuferinnen* (Wien: Milena Verlag, 2008), pp.118–28.

Schernthaner, Peter, 'Pinzgauer NS-Bürgermeister im Spiegel lokalhistorischer Darstellungen', *Mitteilungen der Gesellschaft für Salzburger Landeskunde* (2007), pp.323–66.

Schwaiger, Alois, *Leogang 1938–1945, Zeitzeugen berichten* (Leogang: Leoganger Bergbau-Museumsverein, 1998).

NOTES

1. '" ... das gesunde Volksempfinden gröblich verletzt": Verbotener Geschlechtsverkehr mit "Anderen" während des Nationalsozialismus', in Gabriella Hauch (ed.), *Frauen im Reichsgau Oberdonau: Geschlechtsspezifische Bruchlinien im Nationalsozialismus* (Linz: Oberösterreichisches Landsarchiv, 2006), pp.246f.
2. By contrast, in 1939, shortly before the outbreak of the Second World War, 45,584 people lived in this area. See SLA, *Amtliches Gemeindeverzeichnis für das Deutsche Reich auf Grund der Volkszählung 1939, Herausgegeben vom Statistischen Reichsamt*, 1st edn (Berlin, 1940).
3. Prisoners of War and Volksdeutsche (ethnic Germans) are not included here. See Alois Nussbaumer, 'Osteuropäische Frauen als Zwangsarbeiterinnen in der Landwirtschaft des Pinzgaus', in Evelyn Steinthaler (ed.), *Frauen 1938: Verfolgte – Widerständige – Mitläuferinnen* (Wien: Milena Verlag, 2008), p.119. See also Oskar Dohle and Nicole Slupetzky, *Arbeiter für den Endsieg: Zwangsarbeit im Reichsgau Salzburg 1939–1945* (Wien/München: Oldenbourg Verlag, 2004), pp.65f.
4. Nussbaumer, 'Osteuropäische Frauen', p.119.
5. *Rassenpolitik: Schriftenreihe für die weltanschauliche Schulung der Ordnungspolizei*, nos. 4–6 (1943), p.50; Gabriele Freitag, *Zwangsarbeiter im Lipper Land: Der Einsatz von Arbeitskräften aus Osteuropa in der Landwirtschaft Lippes 1939–1945* (Winckler: Bochum, 1996), p.59.
6. AES, R-Registratur 9/28 Niedernsill.
7. Ulrich Herbert, *Fremdarbeiter: Politik und Praxis des 'Ausländer-Einsatzes' in der Kriegswirtschaft des Dritten Reiches*, 2nd edn (Berlin/Bonn: Dietz, 1986), pp.76ff., 127; Freitag, *Zwangsarbeiter im Lipper Land*, p.59. Also, for Kaprun there is some evidence that brothel barracks were planned; the existing building documents do not testify if they had ever been built. See Nussbaumer, 'Osteuropäische Frauen', p.123.
8. Hauch, '" ... das gesunde Volksempfinden gröblich verletzt"', p.248.
9. *Salzburger Landeszeitung, Amtliches Blatt der NSDAP: Gau Salzburg und der Staats- und Gemeinde-Behörden*, 5, 62, Samstag, den 14. März/Sonntag, den 15. März 1942, p.4.
10. Ibid.
11. Winifred R. Garscha and Franz Scharf, *Justiz in Oberdonau* (Linz: Oberösterreichisches Landsarchiv, 2007), p.452f.
12. Freitag, *Zwangsarbeiter im Lipper Land*, p.60.
13. Hauch, '" ... das gesunde Volksempfinden gröblich verletzt"', p.250.
14. Ibid.
15. Freitag, *Zwangsarbeiter im Lipper Land*, p.60.
16. Hauch, '" ... das gesunde Volksempfinden gröblich verletzt"', p.250.
17. Ela Hornung, Ernst Langthaler and Sabine Schweitzer, *Zwangsarbeit in der Landwirtschaft in Niederösterreich und dem Burgenland* (Wien/München: Oldenbourg, 2004), p.382.
18. It also has to be considered that many German men were at war. The figure is for

residents on 17 May 1939. Cf. Peter Schernthaner, 'Pinzgauer NS-Bürgermeister im Spiegel lokalhistorischer Darstellungen', *Mitteilungen der Gesellschaft für Salzburger Landeskunde* (2007), pp.329, 331, 334, 351.

19. Chronik des GP Maria Alm; Posten-Chronik Kaprun 1 August 1929 – 18 October 1950, 1.Teil; Chronik des k. k. Gendarmeriepostens Bruck im Pinzgau; Chronik des k. k. Gendarmeriepostens Taxenbach.
20. Hornung, Langthaler and Schweitzer, *Zwangsarbeit in der Landwirtschaft*, p.383.
21. SLA, Sondergericht Sbg., Kls-1939–43 Urteilsblätter 11, KLs 20/43; SLA, Landesregierung Abt. III OF-Akten A-Z.
22. Ibid.
23. SLA, Sondergericht Sbg., Kls-1939–43 Urteilsblätter 11, KLs 58/42.
24. SLA, Sondergericht Sbg., Kls-1939–43 Urteilsblätter 11, KLs 34/43; KLs 104/42; KLs 1/43; KLs 94/42.
25. Neither the documents of extra trials nor the municipal chronicles of the Pinzgau contain a case where a local male was arrested or sentenced for a sexual relationship with a female forced labourer. 'GV'crimes primarily referred to sexual relationships between local females and male foreigners. See also: Hauch, '" ... das gesunde Volksempfinden gröblich verletzt"', pp.250f., 263.
26. One woman was born in Pinzgau, grew up there and then got married in the neighbouring district, the Pongau. Due to the fact that there is a file (*Opferfürsorgeakte*) on her, her experience has been included here.
27. SLA, Sondergericht Sbg., Kls-1939–43 Urteilsblätter 11.
28. SLA, Sondergericht Sbg., Kls-1939–43 Urteilsblätter 11, KLs 21/41.
29. Gendarmeriepostenkommando Bez. Zell a. S. Ld. Salzburg Postenchronik! (Author's note: in this specific case and due to reasons of data protection the name of the municipality can not be quoted.)
30. Ibid.
31. A forced labourer from Wienic was executed on 8 January 1942, only one month before his twenty-second birthday; on 20 September 1943 the Gestapo hanged a forced labourer from Ksiaznice, one month before his twenty-sixth birthday. Further: ITS/ARCH/Landkreis Zell a. See, Ordner 64, p.22; Chronik des Gendarmeriepostens Saalfelden, pp.83, 90f.
32. Chronik des Gendarmeriepostens Saalfelden, pp.83, 90f.
33. Ibid, p.87.
34. Chronik des Gendarmeriepostens Lofer 1855–1960.
35. Ibid.
36. Chronik der Marktgemeinde Lofer 1900.
37. SLA, Zell/See HB-Akte 1943, 302-1943.
38. Ibid.
39. AES, Piesendorf Taufbuch 8, p.205.
40. Alois Schwaiger, *Leogang 1938–1945: Zeitzeugen berichten* (Leogang: Leoganger Bergbau-Museumsverein, 1998), p.221.
41. Ibid p.228f.
42. SLA, Zell/See HB-Akte 1942, 213-21-42.
43. SLA, Sondergericht Sbg., Kls-1939–43 Urteilsblätter 11.
44. *Salzburger Zeitung*, nr 58, 4, Jahrgang, Freitag, 9. März 1945, p.2.
45. SLA, Sondergericht Sbg., Kls-1939–43 Urteilsblätter 11, KLs 58/42.
46. Ibid.
47. Ibid.
48. Ibid.
49. Ibid.
50. SLA, Sondergericht Sbg., Kls-1939–43 Urteilsblätter 11, KLs 63/41; KLs 45/41.
51. SLA, Sondergericht Sbg., Kls-1939–43 Urteilsblätter 11, KLs 37/41.
52. Ibid.
53. SLA, Sondergericht Sbg., Kls-1939–43 Urteilsblätter 11, KLs 62/41.
54. SLA, Sondergericht Sbg., Kls-1939–43 Urteilsblätter 11, KLs 34/43.
55. According to the documents this woman was pregnant by a French prisoner of war. The baby died after birth. See SLA, Sondergericht Sbg., Kls-1939–43 Urteilsblätter 11, KLs 1/43.

56. SLA, Sondergericht Sbg., Kls-1939–43 Urteilsblätter 11, KLs 58/42.
57. SLA, Sondergericht Sbg., Kls-1939–43 Urteilsblätter 11, KLs 37/41.
58. SLA, Sondergericht Sbg., Kls-1939–43 Urteilsblätter 11, KLs 45/41.
59. SLA, Sondergericht Sbg., Kls-1939–43 Urteilsblätter 11, KLs 34/43.
60. Freitag, *Zwangsarbeiter im Lipper Land*, p.59.
61. SLA, Sondergericht Sbg., Kls-1939–43 Urteilsblätter 11, KLs 45/41; KLs 34/43; KLs 20/43; KLs 63/41.
62. Following her testimony, one woman was raped by a prisoner of war, yet the court did not believe her. As a mitigating factor the court accepted 'seduction by a prisoner of war'. See SLA, Sondergericht Sbg., Kls-1939–43 Urteilsblätter 11, KLs 62/41; SL A, Sondergericht Sbg., Kls-1939–43 Urteilsblätter 11, KLs 62/41; KLs 58/42; KLs 104/42.
63. Karin Berger et al., *Vollzugspraxis des 'Opferfürsorgegesetzes': Analyse der praktischen Vollziehung des einschlägigen Sozialrechts* (Klagenfurt: Drava Verlags- und Druckges, 2002), p.13.
64. Ibid.
65. Ibid, p.15.
66. SLA, Landesregierung Abt. III OF-Akten A-Z.
67. Ibid.
68. Ibid.
69. Ibid.
70. Ibid.
71. Ibid.
72. Ibid.
73. Ibid.
74. At the end of her indemnity, Notburga M. was in Bernau/Chiemsee.
75. SLA, Landesregierung Abt. III OF-Akten A-Z.
76. Ibid.
77. For neither this woman nor the woman in the previous case could NSDAP membership be verified. See SLA, Landesregierung Abt. III OF-Akten A-Z.
78. Physical damage was considered severe by the BMsV (Bundesministerium für soziale Verwaltung – Federal Ministry for Social Administration) when there was evidence of a minimum of 50 per cent reduction of an individual's earning capacity for at least half a year. An official attestation and possibly a subsidy could be applied for. Concerning health damage, a considerable amount was granted when the damage through persecution following the regulations for war victims in injury category 3 applied. In 1950, instead of the injury category, a reduction of earning capacity of 70 per cent was fixed. In this case a victim certificate was granted which, in contrast to the prior official attestation, did not entitle to a subsidy. See Berger *et al.*, *Vollzugspraxis des 'Opferfürsorgegesetzes'*, p.183f.
79. Ibid. The diagnosis certified that the reduction in earning capacity was lower in colder than in warmer seasons, and that on average it comes to between 20 and 30 per cent.
80. Ibid.
81. Ibid.
82. Ibid.
83. Berger *et al.*, *Vollzugspraxis des 'Opferfürsorgegesetzes'*, p.15.
84. SLA, Landesregierung Abt. III OF-Akten A-Z.
85. Ibid.
86. Berger *et al.*, *Vollzugspraxis des 'Opferfürsorgegesetzes'*, p.243.
87. SLA, Landesregierung Abt. III OF-Akten A-Z.
88. Ibid.
89. Alois Schwaiger writes about a woman from Leogang who had been imprisoned in the Ravensbrück concentration camp, who returned severely damaged, physically and mentally, but who could, with the help and understanding of her family, overcome the agony imposed on her. See Schwaiger, *Leogang 1938–1945*, p.221.
90. Quote from Schwaiger, *Leogang 1938–1945*, p.231.
91. LA, Landesregierung Abt. III OF-Akten A-Z.
92. Ibid.
93. Resident population per 17 May 1939. Schernthaner, 'Pinzgauer NS-Bürgermeister'.
94. Gendarmeriepostenkommando Bez. Zell a. S. Ld. Salzburg Postenchronik!
95. A letter from Notburga M. to the local government testifies that not one but more than one person denounced her.

96. Gendarmeriepostenkommando Bez. Zell a. S. Ld. Salzburg Postenchronik!
97. SLA, Sondergericht Sbg., Kls-1939–43 Urteilsblätter 11, KLs 63/41.
98. SLA, Sondergericht Sbg., Kls-1939–43 Urteilsblätter 11, KLs 62/41.
99. Gendarmeriepostenkommando Bez. Zell a. S. Ld. Salzburg Postenchronik!
100. The file of the extra trials of Notburga M. shows that the woman who had been sentenced to thirteen months of jail was accused by Notburga M. of having forced her during pre-trial custody to admit to sexual intercourse with the French prisoner of war.
101. Ingrid Bauer, '"Die Amis, die Ausländer und wir": Zur Erfahrung und Produktion von Eigenem und Fremdem im Jahrzehnt nach dem Zweiten Weltkrieg', in Ingrid Bauer, Josef Ehmer, and Sylvia Hahn (eds), *Walz – Migration – Besatzung: Historische Szenarien des Eigenen und des Fremden* (Klagenfurt: Drava Verlags- und Druckges, 2002), pp.237ff.
102. See Schwaiger, *Leogang 1938–1945*, p.232.

10

Dealing with Survivor Youth in West European Jewish Communities After the War

DAVID WEINBERG

The study of survival in the Holocaust has been marked by an ongoing controversy concerning its meaning and significance for contemporary society. In seeking to counter the commonly-held view of survival as largely a matter of luck and circumstance, some scholars – and many individuals who have written memoirs of their experiences – have chosen to frame the stories of Jews who escaped the Final Solution as paradigms of the courage and resilience of human beings in the face of extreme trauma and devastating loss. Increasingly, screenwriters and novelists who see its dramatic and commercial potential have adopted this perspective as well. Other researchers and survivors have rejected this tendency to typologize victims of the Holocaust. Instead, they argue, survivors should be seen as representing nothing other than themselves. To suggest that there are lessons to be learned from their attitudes and behaviour during the war is both absurd and obscene.[1]

Such concerns found little resonance in post-war discourse about survivors of the Holocaust. In the first decade-and-a-half after 1945, European communal leaders and American relief workers generally did not theorize about the lessons that could be learned from those who had escaped the Nazi genocide. Instead, it was the immediate issue of what to do with them that consumed most of their time and energy. Hundreds of thousands of survivors would eventually find their way to Palestine and to the United States. The plight of those who chose to remain on the Continent presented more pressing problems, however. In addition to providing for the survivor's physical and material needs, local and American officials had to deal with two complex challenges that threatened the very future of European Jewry. How would survivors be reintegrated into the larger society, which during the war had stood by or had actively collaborated with the Nazis as they carried out their murderous policies against Jews in occupied Europe? And how could survivors be convinced to play a constructive role in the reconstitution and maintenance of Jewish communal life now that the war was over?

THE DISTINCTIVE PROBLEMS FACING SURVIVOR YOUTH

The problem of reintegration into general and Jewish society was most acute among survivor youth in western Europe. In contrast to American and Israeli Jewry, which welcomed tens of thousands of survivors of the Holocaust but which drew much of their sustenance from native-born and settled immigrant populations, and to communities in eastern Europe, whose religious, cultural, and educational life would be largely suppressed in the late 1940s and early 1950s by newly emerging communist regimes, the Jews of France, Belgium and the Netherlands could not hope to revitalize their communal life without the active involvement of young men and women who returned from camps, who emerged from hiding, and who had migrated westward from DP camps. Once they had readapted or had become socialized to their native or adopted country, they would be called upon to become the membership core of western Europe's reconstituted communities. Local leaders also counted on their most committed elements to ultimately take the place of the hundreds of religious and community leaders murdered during the Holocaust.[2]

The first encounters with returning deportees and refuges, however, convinced local leaders and American relief officials in western Europe that the assimilation of adolescent survivors into general and Jewish society would be a daunting task. On the most basic level, there was the fact that the experience of the war had alienated survivor youth from the conventions and responsibilities of social and communal life. Living underground or in camps where they were forced to steal to survive, divorced from their families and friends, and constantly fearful of being discovered by Nazi and collaborationist soldiers and guards, they were distrustful of all forms of authority. Used to relying upon themselves, they did not adapt easily to social settings.

The result was that, too often, young Jews emerged from the

war undisciplined, violent, cynical and hard. In the immediate post-war period, Jewish educators in France, Belgium, and Holland talked openly about the anti-social behaviour of Jewish 'juvenile delinquents' and the plight of so-called 'feral children' who were said to join gangs, engage in random sex, traffic in and consume drugs, and drink to excess out of a sense of deep alienation, anger and loneliness. As the director of relief and rehabilitation at the World Jewish Congress (WJC), Aryeh Tartakower, wrote in an article in the *Journal of Educational Psychology* at the beginning of 1945, a young person who has seen the passive indifference of the surrounding population, and in many cases their active participation in terror and murder, could easily believe that 'all humanity is corrupt and foul'.[3] A decade later, officials of American relief organizations, always distrustful of ideology, continued to express fears that young Jews without a sense of belonging could easily fall prey to what they described as the allure of the 'anti-democratic ideals' of philosophies such as existentialism.[4] Religious leaders in the post-war period detected a similar rebelliousness in the tendency of adolescents to desert the melodies of the synagogue for swing music and jazz. Leaders of established Jewish organizations debated whether estranged Jewish youths endangered the survival of the community by refusing to socialize with one another and to marry. A report on France presented to the American Jewish Joint Distribution Committee (JDC – or the 'Joint', as it was known in Europe) in 1953 warned that unless something was done to integrate the younger generation, 'one can envision a period, close at hand, in which all Jewish efforts, in whatever sphere, will have lost all possibility to survive'.[5]

One of the most troubling outcomes of this alienation was that adolescent survivors faced serious difficulties in securing employment. During the war, their daily activity had alternated between struggling to meet basic needs and sitting around doing nothing. The result was that those who had grown to adolescence during the period of Nazi occupation lacked vocational skills and could not easily adjust to a normal work routine. In the period of chronic unemployment that followed immediately after the cessation of hostilities, employers generally favoured 'trustworthy' individuals who had remained in the country during wartime over 'sullen' and 'suspect' returning deportees or foreigners for jobs. The young survivors' negative response to attempts to discipline them also meant that they had difficulties holding on to jobs. In some cases, they preferred the 'easy money' of the black market to steady employment.

International organizations like ORT (Organization for Rehabilitation and Training) and local relief agencies responded by instituting vocational training programmes both in the cities and in the various children's homes that were established throughout western Europe in the immediate post-war period. Aside from learning work skills, young men and women were taught the virtues of saving, of hard work and of proper appearance. Efforts were made to steer young men and women away from 'unproductive' trades in commerce and trade toward artisanal and industrial jobs. In engaging in 'productive' labour, social workers argued, young survivors would prove to be more marketable and their economic activity less 'offensive' in a recovering society.

Within the west European communities themselves, officials worried about the negative or apathetic attitude of survivor youth toward Judaism and Jewish life. The asocial and at times antisocial nature of their daily life during the war, and the fact that most young men and women had had no connection with formal Jewish communities, meant that they often evinced little interest in relating to other Jews after 1945. In some cases, they had been forced to convert in order to escape deportation and death. In other cases, surviving parents after the war refused to raise their children as Jews or to have them publicly identified with the Jewish community, a phenomenon that one writer called 'the Marrano complex'.[6]

Then there were the distinctive and agonizing problems associated with so-called 'hidden' children. The situation was especially tragic in the Netherlands, where it was estimated that some 5,000 Jewish children had been placed in Christian homes by their parents during the war to prevent their deportation. Hundreds had been converted by their foster parents, either out of religious zeal or because of the fear that the children might be discovered. After the war, many of these children, now in their teens, did not want to leave their adoptive homes and had no desire to return to the Jewish fold. Government and Church officials were often unsympathetic to the Jewish community's efforts to recover them, arguing that it was in the child's best interest to remain with their adoptive parents. Jewish social service agencies were of two minds. While desirous of returning the children to Judaism, they were fearful of the repercussions on the individual child's mental health and of the potential backlash in the larger society toward what it might perceive as an 'ungrateful' community. It was not until the mid-1950s, and in some cases even later, that the issue was finally put to rest.[7]

RELIGIOUS OUTREACH

Cognizant of the alienation of young survivors from Judaism, religious institutions in Belgium, Holland and France attempted to adapt their rituals and activities to make them more attractive and relevant. In major cities such as Paris and Brussels, synagogues conducted youth and family services, and introduced prayers in the vernacular. In place of calls for devotion to God and country, rabbis increasingly used their sermons to preach what one British Jewish observer called 'living Judaism', the application of traditional beliefs to contemporary issues and problems.[8] In Paris and elsewhere, attempts were made to supplement religious training taught by clergy with informal Bible sessions and study circles led by lay members.

Rabbis looked for hopeful signs in the increasing number of bar mitzvah ceremonies, as young men who had not been able to celebrate their coming to Jewish adulthood during the war were now formally recognized as members of the community. At the services, administrators of the community often took the place of parents who had been deported. As the growing number of advertisements for social-hall and orchestra rentals in the Jewish press attest, religious leaders in Belgium, France and Holland encouraged the celebration of bar mitzvahs as social events, in imitation of American Jewish community practices, as a means of drawing young people closer to Judaism. By the early 1950s, at least some rabbis had acceded to the demands of young women to participate in a variation of the ceremony.[9] Rabbis also struggled to find ways to ease the readmission of converted Jews back into the community.

A NEW APPROACH TO JEWISH EDUCATION

In response to the young survivor's lack of both Jewish education and social skills, plans were also implemented to institute a new approach to adolescent learning. The work of Isaac Pougatch, a pedagogue and community activist in France, was especially significant. Soon after liberation, Pougatch founded a teacher-training school in a suburb east of Paris to minister to the needs of Jewish war orphans. He was firmly convinced that traditional methods of Jewish pedagogy, with their emphasis upon rote memorization and mastery of traditional texts, were of little use in educating young survivors. An amalgam of his own experiences growing up in a left-wing east European Jewish milieu and later as a leader in the French scouting organization, the Eclaireurs israélites, Pougatch's programme consisted of a series of informal learning sessions led by 'mentors', who were often young survivors themselves, which stressed collective living and experiential learning within an intensively Jewish environment. In an atmosphere of mutual support and camaraderie, both 'mentors' and students would put aside, at least temporarily, their sense of alienation and loneliness. The hope was that in this way they would learn about Judaism and Jewish culture in a non-threatening atmosphere. The programme soon attracted the attention of the Joint. Pougatch was given an office in the JDC's building in Paris, which he used as a resource centre for teachers and community leaders. Throughout the late 1940s and early 1950s, Pougatch's mobile van filled with educational manuals and audiovisual aids was a familiar sight throughout France and Belgium.

While relatively successful in metropolitan areas, Pougatch's approach could not be easily applied to smaller communities that lacked a cadre of committed young men and women to serve as 'mentors'. Nor did the programme have much success in non-French-speaking communities such as Holland, Denmark and Sweden, which had special language needs that could not be met with general educational materials. Despite the eventual demise of the programme, largely as a result of the lack of funds and Pougatch's insistence upon making all decisions by himself, his basic approach to education continued to shape the perspectives of Jewish educators in western Europe into the 1950s and 1960s. Drawing upon Pougatch's perspective and influenced by the general ethos of post-war western Europe, that stressed the importance of national unity and reconstruction, Jewish educators in Belgium, France and the Netherlands insisted on the importance of incorporating both religious and secular components into their curricula and of underscoring the centrality of community in the Jewish consciousness of young men and women.

THE JEWISH COMMUNITY CENTER

By the 1950s, local leaders in western Europe were becoming aware that there was a need to facilitate the interaction of adolescent boys and girls outside the traditional framework of religious and educational institutions. Amidst the many competing institutions and programmes, educators and social service workers talked increasingly about the importance of creating a neutral and attractive environment where individuals of different backgrounds and orientations – or of little background and commitment – could meet to interact in a Jewish milieu.

The push to develop new communal facilities for young men and women was fuelled as much by continuing fears over the failure of established institutions to attract youth as by pedagogical theory. For the truth was that despite intensive efforts, children – and their parents – generally shied away from involvement in the new religious services and rituals that were created after the war to appeal to disaffected Jews. In Paris in the mid-1950s, for example, it was estimated that despite intensive efforts by the Consistoire, the central religious organization of French Jewry, only a quarter of eligible Jewish boys were being prepared for their bar mitzvah.[10] Nor was there a significant return of converted youth to the Jewish fold.

The onset of the Cold War in the late 1940s and early 1950s also raised concerns about the active recruitment of young boys and girls into Jewish communist youth groups. Left-wing youth movements had been a major force in the communities of Belgium, France and the Netherlands in the 1920s and 1930s. Though diminished in numbers as a result of wartime deportations and the slow but steady embourgeoisement of their pre-war working-class and artisan constituency, Jewish communist organizations found new adherents in the post-war period among both young survivors and recent immigrants from eastern Europe. Indeed, for reasons that often had little to do with their ideology or programmes, and despite the efforts of the national party to dissolve or at least diminish the role of distinctively Jewish groups, Jewish communists seemed to gain new respectability in western Europe after the Second World War. The activity of communists during the war profoundly affected both immigrant youth newly-arrived from Displaced Persons' (DPs) camps, the Soviet Union and Poland, and the children of native-born Jews who were troubled by what they believed was the passivity of local Jewish leadership under Nazi occupation. In communist organizations, young Jews who had struggled to escape the German vice during the war could avoid the awkward and painful confrontation with average Frenchmen, Belgians and Dutchmen, many of whom had collaborated with the German invader, and find comfort and security among militants who had fought against Nazi occupation. Throughout the late 1940s, the image of the noble communist resistance fighter willing to sacrifice his life for the Jewish people remained a powerful symbol in left-wing propaganda addressed to Belgian, French and Dutch youth.[11] After 1945, the communists' call to continue the struggle against fascism resonated with young men and women seeking revenge for lost relatives and friends.

Communist movements targeted recently-arrived young Jewish immigrants and refugees in particular. Recruiting actively in night schools, factories and social clubs, militant youth groups in western Europe attracted thousands of young Polish Jews by providing them with practical assistance in learning the local language, gaining new work skills, finding lodging, and absorbing the national culture. The highly structured environment of such groups, their strong leadership, rigid discipline and clearly defined goals, proved extremely attractive to many disoriented and disillusioned young survivors. After 1945, communist organizations also played a crucial role in immigrant cultural and recreational activities geared to young boys and girls, running libraries, staging plays, organizing sports clubs and sponsoring concerts.

It was the search for an alternative to left-wing youth activity in western Europe, which became a particular obsession of American relief officials in their discussions with local leaders in western Europe, that led in the late 1940s and early 1950s to the development and expansion of the Jewish Community Center (JCC) movement. Modelled after the American JCC and YMHA (Young Men's Hebrew Association), as well as social centres in western Europe that had been established by Catholic and Protestant churches before the war, the purpose of the community centre was to break down the differences in socio-economic status, ideology, religious faith, gender, age and cultural heritage that existed within each community. The centre was envisioned as an educational institution in the broad sense of the term, inculcating youth who had grown up during the war with the rudiments of Jewish history and culture, a regular regimen of physical exercise and hygiene, and fundamental social skills. Following in the footsteps of Pougatch's early efforts, the centre would create a friendly and warm environment outside established communal institutions such as synagogues and religious schools, thereby reinforcing the notion of Judaism as a communal way of life rather than merely a belief system. Instead of formal classes, the centres would emphasize 'peripheral' activities that had become central in the lives of young men and women in the post-war era, including sports, cinema clubs and dances. As Pougatch – who himself had been an early proponent of a community centre in Paris – remarked, 'the young person will be led to consider the centre in its entirety – from its movie theatre to its library, from its gymnasium to its course offerings – as a profound unity, in which Judaism constitutes the central element'.[12]

The idea of building a community centre on the Continent had been first raised in 1945 among members of the so-called Jewish Relief Units (JRU), who had been sent by the British Jewish organizations to administer aid on the Continent, including most especially Italy and the Netherlands. (A few recreational and social centres had existed in Europe in the 1930s, but they were generally ad hoc institutions established by local communities.) As young survivors emerged from death and labour camps and settled in DP camps or drifted westward, the idea seemed to acquire a special urgency. Charles Zarback, a British volunteer in Rome, echoed the general sentiments of communal leaders and outside observers when he commented in his report sent to British relief agencies in March 1945 that survivor youth on the Continent were in need of 'a great deal of instruction in "the art of living" ' so that they could 'return to a dignified way of living'. A Jewish community centre, Zarback maintained, would steer young people away from 'their lives of paupery and petty black market transactions' by offering them a wholesome place to congregate and opportunities for housing and employment. JRU volunteers also felt that a community centre would provide a secure environment where young boys and girls, many of whom had lost their entire families, could meet and share their concerns and hopes.[13]

In 1946, members of the JRU in Holland created a Jewish community centre in Amsterdam complete with an assembly hall, library and reading room. The concept was soon adopted by the Joint, which beginning in late 1945 took over Continental relief efforts from British Jewish agencies. The Joint focused much of its energy and attention on creating centres in France. Under the leadership of the local Joint representative in France, Laura Margolis, the French community initiated several projects in the first two years after the war to attend to the needs of youth. All Jewish delinquents were referred to the community's Service Social des jeunes (SSJ – Youth Social Services), where they were given maintenance funds if necessary, placed in apprenticeship programmes and sent to vocational training schools. In an effort to prevent recidivism, both JDC and local officials began to look more seriously at the possibility of establishing a centre for youth activities. They also hoped to create an open environment and common meeting place to break down the deeply-rooted divisions that had plagued French Jewry in the pre-war years and that threatened to weaken its efforts to reconstruct a vibrant post-war community.

In early 1952, the Joint requested a $50,000 grant from the Ford Foundation to build a centre in Paris. French Jewish leaders also envisioned constructing centres in smaller communities, whose only formal Jewish institution was the sparsely attended local consistorial synagogue. In 1954, the French community submitted a series of proposals to establish Jewish community centres of its own to the Conference on Material Claims against Germany, which allocated reparations money for cultural and educational work to surviving communities in Europe. With the beginnings of the influx of Jews from north Africa in the mid-1950s, French community leaders created a master plan in 1955 to establish centres throughout the country. In the same year, the majority of French requests for German Material Claims money and two-thirds of Joint and Central Claims allocations to French Jewry were for establishing community centres. Eventually, centres would be built throughout the country, first in Paris, then in Belfort, Roanne, Lens, Metz, Grenoble, Lyon, Marseilles, Nancy and Strasbourg.

The community centre concept soon spread to other countries in western Europe. The idea was especially popular in Belgium, where there was a noticeable gap between rich and poor, and a not insignificant Jewish communist presence, and where there was little contact between the large population of post-war refugees and the established community. By 1957, 70 per cent of external Jewish funding for capital investments in Europe was being allocated for the construction and maintenance of community and youth centres.[14] The American YMHA movement fostered the development of centres in smaller European communities where religious affiliation was generally weak and leadership lacking, such as Oslo and Trondheim in Norway, Bossum and the Hague in Holland, and Liège in Belgium. In a few cases, such as Le Lilas in suburban Paris, centres also housed synagogues. In addition, several centres sponsored summer-camp and scouting programmes to ensure that young people were exposed to Jewish culture throughout the year.[15]

Though the community centres made some strides in establishing a modicum of unity in several communities, they generally could not override the deep-seated divisions among competing ideological factions and cultural groups. In Paris, for example, community leaders originally thought of creating three separate centres – one apiece for the native French, immigrant and Sephardic communities. In many cases, JCC activities were co-opted by influential political and religious youth groups in the community, a development that went against the original hopes of its founders. In Brussels, Zionist groups, which had developed their own network of youth groups, considered the local centre as 'enemy territory' and actively worked to prevent their members from participating in its activities.[16] With the exception of a few larger cities, the JCC's programmes of cultural enrichment and adult education had limited appeal to Jewish youth. Increasingly, the JCC in Europe took on the role of a cultural centre that was geared as much to adults as to young men and women. It was far more successful in smaller cities, where there was little public communal space, than in more populated urban areas where Jewish life was scattered over a large area. Rising construction and equipment costs and the chronic shortage of skilled builders proved to be serious obstacles. Community leaders also found it difficult to find skilled individuals who could deal with the legal, technical, and financial challenges associated with the construction and maintenance of centres.

The chequered experience of Jewish community centres in western Europe in the 1950s demonstrated how difficult it was to transform a specialized American Jewish institution, which was one of many social service organizations in a community with significant financial support from individual donors and fundraising campaigns, into an all-purpose agency in communities such as those in France, Belgium and Holland that had limited funds and lukewarm community support. In a larger sense, it reflected the fact that despite the decline in religious affiliation and observance after the war, the Jewish identity of the newer generation of west

European youth – to the extent that it existed – remained traditional and did not mesh easily with the openly ethnic and pluralistic perspective that was emerging across the Atlantic.

THE APPEAL OF ISRAEL

Zionist movements in western Europe in the immediate post-war period sought to provide an alternative for alienated youth by running programs connected with the *yishuv* or pre-state Jewish settlement in mandatory Palestine. At meetings and rallies, Zionist youth groups in Paris, Brussels and Amsterdam disseminated news of the struggle of Jewish pioneers to build settlements and to defend themselves against Arab attacks. Youth-oriented papers eagerly followed the efforts by DPs to run the British blockade and to gain entry into Palestine.

The fate of the *Exodus* ship, which sailed from the port of Sète near Marseilles in July 1947, had a particularly riveting effect on young Jews in western Europe. In the space of a week, over 4,000 men, women, and children from DP camps had been brought to France to board the boat. Designated for the scrapheap in the United States, *The President Warfield* had been bought by members of the Mossad l'Aliya Bet, the Palestinian Jewish agency responsible for illegal immigration from Europe. Once the boat left France and entered international waters, the passengers renamed it the *Exodus 1947*. British soldiers boarded the ship near the coast of Palestine and, after a bloody battle, it was forced to return to France. Upon its arrival in Port du Bouc, French officials refused to forcibly offload the passengers. The situation remained in limbo until September, when the ship was ordered to sail to the port of Hamburg, where passengers were forced to disembark and sent back to DP camps.[17]

Throughout the summer of 1947, the plight of the *Exodus* was the major topic of conversation within the Jewish communities of the major capitals of western Europe. Young and old flocked to news-stands to read the daily updates on the condition of the passengers. They cheered the activities of the hundreds of local functionaries, policemen, engineers, dockworkers, customs inspectors, truck drivers, maritime agents and owners of small boats who aided in the transport of Jews across France to waiting ships. They were thrilled when after the *Exodus* incident, French officials continued to allow other illegal ships bound for Palestine to leave from

Marseilles and other ports along the Mediterranean and the Atlantic.[18]

Incidents like the *Exodus* led hundreds of young Jews in France, Belgium and the Netherlands to participate in the active defence of the *yishuv* and then later to serve in the Israeli army. In 1947, the Haganah, or military wing of the Palestinian Jewish settlement, began to actively recruit youth throughout central and western Europe. Though the bulk of the 40,000 volunteers were conscripted from DP camps in Germany and Austria, the Jewish force ran successful campaigns in several cities in western Europe, including Paris and Brussels. The recent interactions with members of the Jewish Brigade, which shortly after the liberation had been a highly visible presence in aid work to Jews in the Netherlands and in Italy in particular, undoubtedly had a profound effect. Government authorities and political parties eager to rid their countries of 'dangerous' immigrants and refugees seemed to have aided in the campaign. According to the historian Katy Hazan, members of the French Secret Police assisted a leader of the Eclaireurs israélites in the recruitment of volunteers to join the Haganah.[19] For its part, the Parti communiste belge (Belgian Communist Party), strongly pressured by the Soviet Union, which undoubtedly saw migration as a means of emptying the ranks of its local parties of fractious 'foreigners', urged Jewish youth in the Union socialiste de la jeunesse juive (USJJ) to go and fight. Communist leaders in western Europe also saw support of the volunteer effort as a means of gaining adherents within the local Jewish community and to reinforce a communist presence in the *yishuv.*[20] Supporters of the effort who remained at home supplied the young volunteers with food, clothing, and books.[21]

While community leaders urged young men and women in western Europe to follow the struggle for independence in Palestine, they were ambivalent about organized efforts to encourage aliyah or immigration to the Land of Israel. The efforts by Zionist activists to recruit potential *olim* (immigrants) in the immediate post-war period clashed with the efforts of local Jewish leaders in France, Belgium and the Netherlands to induce young survivors to remain to help build their local communities. The issue of the transportation of orphaned Jewish children to Palestine in the years before the creation of the State of Israel was a topic of particularly intense discussion in the pages of community newspapers and at organizational meetings. In each community, Zionists, left-wing elements, and religious leaders attacked each other and fought to gain control over Joint funding of the children's education and of their ultimate place of settlement.[22]

European governments were generally opposed to allowing the children to leave for Palestine. In the case of France, for example, officials claimed that they had a responsibility toward the children's parents whose fate was still unknown. While awaiting their parents' return, 'orphaned' children were to be regarded as 'pupils of the nation', young boys and girls under the care of the authorities who were obliged to inculcate them with the values and ideals of a renascent nation. The pressures from Zionist elements and external organizations such as the World Jewish Congress were intense, however. After much discussion, the children were allowed to leave, with the proviso that officials of Zionist organizations would bring back any children whose parents returned from Germany.[23]

After the establishment of Israel in 1948, Zionist movements continued to try to convince young men and women in France, Belgium, and Holland to make aliyah. While voicing doubts about the logic of sending adolescent survivors into a war zone and fearful of weakening their own communities, local leaders in western Europe nevertheless sought to connect young men and women who remained in France, Belgium and Holland with the new State. Religious and educational officials urged youth to participate in Independence Day celebrations, to learn Hebrew and Israeli folk dances, and to write to pen pals in Israel. Community organizations also organized trips to the Jewish State and arranged for student exchange programmes. Teachers imported by the Jewish Agency in Jerusalem to teach in France, Belgium and the Netherlands trumpeted the virtues of the young country. In injecting the lives of adolescents in western Europe with a sense of adventure and purpose, it was argued, pro-Israel activity would infuse them with a commitment to Jewish collective survival. The fact that some of the best and brightest of Jewish youth eventually emigrated to Israel in the 1960s, especially after the Six-Day War, demonstrated the tensions and contradictions in such efforts.

CONCLUSION

Many of the religious and educational reforms and projects initiated in the years after 1945 in France, Belgium and Holland to address the needs of survivor youth proved to be of only limited success, suggesting that the three communities and their young adults could not easily overcome the legacy of the pre-war period and of their recent tragic past. The fact that by the early 1960s, most communities in western Europe had stabilized themselves, however, demonstrates that they were ultimately able to draw upon a pool of interested and talented young people to support and administer their institutions and activities. In devising plans and programs to socialize and integrate young boys and girls who had survived the Holocaust in the first decade-and-a-half after the war, local leaders in France, Belgium and Holland thus laid the groundwork for a viable Jewish life in western Europe. In so doing, they were also signalling their readiness to rejoin other diaspora communities in the west in their ongoing efforts to maintain Jewish identity and commitment in an open society.

REFERENCES

Archive Sources
American Jewish Archives – Cincinnati.
American Joint Distribution Archives – New York.
Archives of the Central British Fund for World Jewish Relief – on microfilm.
Central Archives of the History of the Jewish People – Jerusalem.
Central Zionist Archives – Jerusalem.
University of Southampton Archives – Southampton, UK.
YIVO Archives – New York.

Published Sources
Berg, Roger, 'La Pratique du Judaïsme en France', *Yod*, 21(1985), pp.81–97.
Brasz, F.C., 'After the Second World War: From "Jewish Church" to Cultural Minority', in J.C.H. Blom, R.G. Fuks-Mansfeld and I. Schöfer (eds), *The History of the Jews in the Netherlands* (Oxford: Lippman Library of Jewish Civilization, 2002), pp.336–92.
Cesarani, David, *The Jewish Chronicle and Anglo-Jewry, 1841–1991* (Cambridge: Cambridge University Press, 1994).
Des Pres, Terrence, *The Survivor: An Anatomy of Life in the Death Camps* (New York: Oxford University Press, 1976).
Fishman, Joel, 'Jewish War Orphans in the Netherlands, The Guardian Issue', *Wiener Library Bulletin*, 27, 1 (1973), pp.31–6.
Hazan, Katy, *Les orphelins de la Shoah: les maisons de l'espoir (1944–1960)* (Paris: Les Belles Lettres, 2000).
Kapel, Samuel René, *Au lendemain de la Shoa: temoignage sur la renaissance du Judaîsme de France et d'Afrique du Nord, 1945–1954* (Jerusalem: S.R. Kapel, 1991).
Kochavi, Arieh J., *Post-Holocaust Politics: Britain, The United States, and Jewish Refugees, 1945–1948* (Chapel Hill, NC: University of North Carolina Press, 2001).
Langer, Lawrence, *Admitting the Holocaust: Collected Essays* (New York: Oxford University Press, 1965).
Lapowier, Alain, *Libres enfants du ghetto: 1944–1978* (Bruxelles: Points Critiques, 1989).
Lapowier, Alain, 'Hertz Jospa et le mileu juif progressiste, une légende vivante?', in Jean-Philippe Schreiber (ed.), *Hertz Jospa: Juif, resistant, Communiste* (Bruxelles: EVO, 1997), pp.112–22.
Mandel, Maude S., 'Philanthropy or Cultural Imperialism? The Impact of American Jewish Aid in Post-Holocaust France', *Jewish Social Studies*, 9, 1 (Fall 2002), pp.53–94.

Pougatch, Isaac, *Se ressaisir ou disparaître* (Paris: Les Editions de Minuit, 1955).
Tartakower, Aryeh, 'Problems in Jewish Cultural Reconstruction in Europe', *Journal of Educational Sociology: The Jew in the Postwar World*, 18, 5 (January 1945), pp.271–7.

NOTES

1. For an example of the tendency of scholars to view the survivor as a reflection of the resilience of the individual in the face of physical brutalization and psychological dehumanization, see T. Des Pres, *The Survivor: An Anatomy of Life in the Death Camps* (New York: Oxford University Press, 1976). For a sharply opposing view, see L. Langer's *Admitting the Holocaust: Collected Essays* (New York: Oxford University Press, 1965).
2. Of the sixty rabbis in France who were members of the Consistoire central, the quasi-official religious body in the country, in 1939, for example, twenty-three were deported to death camps and two were shot. Four other non-affiliated rabbis and twenty-five *ministres officiants* had also been murdered. In the Netherlands, only three of the twelve pre-war consistorial rabbis (*Operrabbijnen*) survived the war. In Belgium, in the mid-1950s, there were only two formally ordained rabbis – one in Brussels and one in Antwerp. Of all the communities in western Europe, only Switzerland was said to have an adequate number of religious leaders. Information taken from R. Berg, 'La Pratique du Judaïsme en France', *Yod*, 21 (1985), p.83; F.C. Brasz, 'After the Second World War: From "Jewish Church" to Cultural Minority', in J.C.H. Blom, R.G. Fuks-Mansfeld and I. Schöfer (eds), *The History of the Jews in the Netherlands* (Oxford: Lippman Library of Jewish Civilization, 2002), p.360; Report on 'Religion, Education and Culture in Western Europe', prepared for the meeting of the Consultative Conference of Jewish Organizations held in London in June 1955, p.2, in the University of Southampton Archives, MS147/AJ86; 'Possibilités de cooperation entre les communautés juives – Domaine religieux, culturel et educatif', issued jointly by the Alliance israélite universelle, the American Jewish Committee and the Anglo-Jewish Association, 15, in the American Jewish Archives MS361 B68.
3. Aryeh Tartakower, 'Problems in Jewish Cultural Reconstruction in Europe', *Journal of Educational Sociology: The Jew in the Postwar World*, 18, 5 (January 1945), p.272.
4. Memo by an unnamed author (possibly Zachariah Shuster) on 'The Community Program', stamped as received by the American Jewish Committee on 11 July 1958, in the YIVO Archives, FAD-2, Box 2, 'Community Program Europe 42–62' folder. See also the report by Tartakower to the WJC after a trip through Europe in November/December 1955, held in the University of Southampton Archives, IJA16 MS237 1/336. On the danger of juvenile delinquency among Jewish youth, see, for example, the application for funds to aid in the creation of a Jewish community centre in Brussels presented to the Conference on Material Claims against Germany by the Centrale d'oeuvres sociales juives, 1 October 1953, in the American Jewish Archives, MS361 H58/15.
5. Report on 'Cultural and Educational Activity in France, 1953', prepared for the American Jewish Joint Distribution Committee, April 1953, in Joint Distribution Committee Archives/New York 45/54 #357.
6. 'Report on Jews of France in 1945', in the Central Zionist Archives, C2/1927.
7. For a discussion of the problem of 'hidden' children in the Netherlands, see J. Fishman, 'Jewish War Orphans in the Netherlands, The Guardian Issue', *Wiener Library Bulletin*, 27, 1 (1973), pp.31–6; on the problem in France, see Katy Hazan, *Les orphelins de la Shoah: les maisons de l'espoir (1944–1960)* (Paris: Les Belles Lettres, 2000), passim.
8. Cited in David Cesarani, *The Jewish Chronicle and Anglo-Jewry, 1841–1991* (Cambridge: Cambridge University Press, 1994), p.214.
9. Report on 'Religion, Education and Culture in Western Europe', prepared for Consultative Council of Jewish Organizations (CCJO) meeting in London, June 1955, p.3, in University of Southampton Archives, MS147/A86.
10. Ibid.
11. A statement addressed to Jewish youth in *Appel des jeunes* (Appeal of Youth), a Belgian Jewish communist journal, in September 1946 was typical:

    > It is to you, my young Jew, that I address my comments, and I would ask you: 'What will you be doing with your life, this most precious of possessions. When your

> brother Mordechai [Morcechai Anielewicz], the leader of the Warsaw Ghetto revolt, cried out: 'The Jewish people lives', it was you he was thinking of. You are 15 years old. You will eventually be 18 like Henri Dobrzynski, when he heroically resisted Nazi torture, or maybe 24 like Mala [Mala Zimetbaum], whose last act in this world was to slap the face of an evil SS man. You should know that it was for you that they died. They perished, Henri, Mala, and so many others, because they loved life so much, theirs and yours! And they have charged you to make your life worthy of them. They wanted you to be young, courageous, honest, and happy.'

Cited in A. Lapowier, *Libres enfants du ghetto: 1944–1978* (Bruxelles: Points Critiques, 1989), p.29.

12. Isaac Pougatch, *Se ressaisir ou disparaître* (Paris: Les Editions de Minuit, 1955), p.81.
13. Charles Zarback, 'Report on Conditions in Jewish Ghetto', March 1945, in the Archives of the Central British Fund for World Jewish Relief, File 124; Erica Lunzer, 'Report on Activities of Jewish Relief Unit in Amsterdam from August 1945 – April 1946', in the Archives of the Central British Fund for World Jewish Relief, File 75.
14. 'Report for the Year 1957 of the American Jewish Joint Distribution Committee to the Conference on Jewish Material Claims against Germany', in the Central Archives of the History of the Jewish People, CC 19001b, p.30.
15. M.S. Mandel, 'Philanthropy or Cultural Imperialism? The Impact of American Jewish Aid in Post-Holocaust France', *Jewish Social Studies*, 9, 1 (Fall 2002), pp.80, 82–3; R. Berg, 'La Pratique du Judaisme en France', *Yod*, 21 (1985), p.91; L. Kraft, 'Report on Jewish Center Developments in Europe, June 1955, from the World Federation of YMHAs and Jewish Community Centers', statement made at the London Conference of Jewish Organizations, in YIVO Archives RG347.7.41–46, FAD 41–46, Box 70.
16. Minutes of the meeting of the Fonds social juif unifié (FSJU), the Jewish Federation of France, 14 novembre 1960, in the Joint Distribution Committee Archives/New York 45–54 #357.
17. For details on the *Exodus* incident, see A.J. Kochavi, *Post-Holocaust Politics: Britain, The United States, and Jewish Refugees, 1945–1948* (Chapel Hill, NC: University of North Carolina Press, 2001), pp.266–72.
18. See, for example, the article in *Nieuw israëlietisch weekblad*, 1 August 1947, p.1.
19. Hazan, *Les orphelins de la Shoah*, p.172.
20. A. Lapiower, 'Hertz Jospa et le mileu juif progressiste, une légende vivante?', in Jean-Philippe Schreiber (ed.), *Hertz Jospa: Juif, resistant, Communiste* (Bruxelles: EVO, 1997), p.116; Lapiower, *Libres enfants du ghetto*, pp.56–8.
21. See, for example, the discussion of the activities of the organization 'Pour nos soldats' (For Our Soldiers) in the minutes of the Comité central of the Consistoire de Paris, 17 janvier 1949, in the Archives of the Consistoire israélite de Paris.
22. See, for example, the letter from Major Bernard Homa of the British Army to Dr Munk of the Central British Fund for Relief and Rehabilitation, 26 November 1944, in the Archives of the Central British Fund for World Jewish Relief, File 57.
23. S.R. Kapel, *Au lendemain de la Shoa: temoignage sur la renaissance du Judaîsme de France et d'Afrique du Nord, 1945–1954* (Jerusalem: S.R. Kapel, 1991), p.32.

11

Between Worlds: The Submerged Narratives of Soviet Child Survivors of the Holocaust

SVETLANA SHKLAROV

> But an invisible force was crushing him. He could feel its weight, its hypnotic power; it was forcing him to think as it wanted, to write as it dictated. This force was inside him; it could dissolve his will and cause his heart to stop beating ... Only people who have never felt such a force themselves can be surprised that others submit to it. Those who have felt it, on the other hand, feel astonished that a man can rebel against it even for a moment – with one sudden word of anger, one timid gesture of protest.
>
> Vasily Grossman, *Life and Fate*[1]

A large part of the *she'erit hapleta*, remnants of the European Jewish population after the Holocaust, stayed in the Soviet Union at the end of the war. According to the Claims Conference, today there are approximately 114,000 Jewish Holocaust survivors residing in the Former Soviet Union.[2] Roughly one third of these survivors were children during the time of their persecution. Most of the children encountered extreme life-threatening events, severe hardships, and deprivation – factors that had potential to cause significant psychic trauma and lifelong post-traumatic consequences. We know little about the Soviet child survivors' post-Holocaust coping and adjustment.

In the Soviet Union, the history of the Nazi persecution of Jews was intentionally silenced for over four decades.[3] Although after perestroika and the fall of the Soviet Union the historical knowledge slowly began to be recovered both in public and academic discourses, the psychological and sociological dimensions of individual trauma and resilience of Soviet Holocaust survivors still remain under-analysed.[4] Virtually no studies of post-traumatic sequelae in Holocaust survivors have been initiated in the former Soviet Union. Likewise, in the west, the group of Soviet survivors – recent immigrants – did not receive much attention from the public or academia. The arrival of aging Soviet Jewish émigrés in western countries has not opened for them an opportunity to voice their experiences. Ironically, in the societies where the history of the Holocaust has long been a significant part of public consciousness, Soviet child survivors continue to be a profoundly silent group.

This study is based on the analysis of life stories of nine Soviet Jewish child survivors of the Holocaust. I collected the stories in a series of unstructured interview conversations with each participant, in the Russian language. The analysis employed a combination of two qualitative research approaches: narrative analysis and the classical grounded theory method.[5] In this chapter, I focus on the parts of the participants' narratives that reflect on their early post-traumatic recovery in the environment of post-war Soviet Union. I introduce several social and historical factors of that time and analyse the impact of those factors on the processes of individual working through trauma.

THE POST-WAR ENVIRONMENT: HOMECOMING AND NARRATIVES OF OPPRESSION

The issues of memory, recounting, silence and suppressed recollection are central in many studies of trauma sequelae, recovery and resilience.[6] The ability to construct and voice individual narratives about distressing events, together with the availability of communal acknowledgement of personal and collective trauma,[7] can impact the individual prospects of recovery. It has been shown in research that suppression of open recounting and lack of societal acknowledgement may affect the process of post-traumatic healing.[8]

The process of voicing traumatic experiences is often inhibited by multiple barriers associated with both internal psychological defences and external, social factors of rejection and disbelief. Such factors were studied widely and described, for example, by Fogelman[9] and Krell[10] in the west, and by Cohen[11] in Israel. In the Soviet

Union, in addition to emotional, psychological and interpersonal factors, Jewish child survivors experienced fierce political oppression under the dominance of the totalitarian regime that rendered them and their communities voiceless.

There was another important factor in the Soviet post-war environment that distinguished the Soviet survivors' experiences from those who emigrated to the west. In the west, Holocaust survivors were introduced, as new immigrants, into established Jewish communities whose members did not have any war experiences. In the Soviet Union, there was practically no Jewish non-survivor establishment. Practically all Jewish families shared one universal, indisputable collective memory of destruction and survival. Therefore, the painful divider of silence did not split the Jewish communities, and there was no rejection of Jews by Jews. The remnants of Soviet Jewry, as a whole, resisted the totalitarian oppression and silence. In defiance of the mainstream majority, the Jews became virtually united through maintaining the collective memories that did not comply with the official history revisions.

THE HOMECOMING: SOVIET CHILD SURVIVORS IMMEDIATELY AFTER LIBERATION

Jewish children had gone through unspeakable hardships under the Nazi occupation. Some were saved in hiding, some survived ghettos, death marches or labour camps, and some witnessed and avoided mass killings. Others spent the war years in evacuation – having fled from the Nazi persecution to remote areas, where they often experienced severe hunger, losses, separation from their parents, and hard labour.

At the end of the war, Soviet Jewish children returned from hiding, imprisonment or exile. At the time of their homecoming, they fully realized the extent of the global tragedy. Entire communities were destroyed by the Nazi occupation; the remnants of other communities consisted of small, scattered groups or just a few surviving friends or families. There were no formal Jewish institutions; remaining Jewish schools and synagogues were closed by the Soviet government, and religious practices were only rarely maintained in private, because they were formally prohibited.

Upon liberation, survivors also realized their inferior status as Jews in the Soviet country. Many survivors recall that before the war, anti-Semitism did not affect them, but they began feeling its impact immediately after the war. They faced hostility and discrimination at school, in their pursuit of higher education, and in the work place.

THE DUAL COLLECTIVE TRAUMA

In their war-torn country, Jewish survivors of the Nazi persecution shared with the entire Soviet population a broad range of collective, universal traumatic experiences. Individual stories varied widely, but many factors of severe stress affected practically all Soviet citizens, on a larger or smaller scale. The commonality of this collective trauma was twofold. First, the entire Soviet people experienced the enormity of wartime and post-war suffering. The Soviet Union lost over 26.6 million lives during the war.[12] Almost every family, regardless of their ethnicity, had suffered losses and hardships. Across the country and among all its citizens, the consequences of the war were massive; every aspect of life was affected by post-war devastation, poverty, and distress.

Second, in addition to the inevitable war hardships, the entire population suffered from fears and repressions of the totalitarian regime. Nearly every family had a story about imprisonment or execution of an acquaintance, friend, or loved one by Stalin's secret police. Most citizens lived with the silent, often suppressed awareness of the threat of being arrested with no explanations.

Many Soviet soldiers who had been prisoners of war were arrested upon their return by the authorities of their own state. They were charged with treason, exiled to Soviet labour camps, or executed.[13] Survivors recall that a history of staying under occupation or being taken prisoner was often falsely equated with cowardice and betrayal. Lydia, who survived in Nazi-occupied Odessa as a Jewish child under a false identity, says that both Jewish and non-Jewish victims of Nazism became vulnerable to Soviet persecution after the war, '[In our country], those who had been prisoners there, and were fortunate to return home, once again were put into their own, domestic concentration camps.'

The shock of wartime suffering and post-war devastation, on the one hand, and totalitarian repression, on the other, created a dual collective trauma that impacted on virtually every Soviet citizen.

THE IMPOSED SILENCE AND REPLACEMENT MYTHS

Within the dual trauma, one component was widely socially acknowledged, but another was entirely silenced. The first cluster of historical factors, namely, the impact of the war, was legitimately recognized in the public discourse. However, the facts of suffering due to political abuse were eliminated from the legitimate public knowledge. The majority of the country's population was forced into either a paradoxical sincere oblivion, or forced silence regarding the countrywide arrests, executions and mass incarcerations. The knowledge about these facts became illegitimate, or socially *undiscussable* – a term coined by Bar-On[14] in reference to facts that are intentionally eliminated, within 'totalitarian logic', from all spheres of social consciousness.

As a replacement for undiscussable facts of political abuse, the Soviet regime constructed powerful narratives about the Soviet people's righteous suffering and heroism during the war. Narratives of pure righteousness also served to guarantee the bright future under the socialist leadership. Along with pride in the victory and the grandiose dreams for the communist future, Soviet public consciousness was permeated by artificially-fuelled, oversized collective vigilance towards the alleged 'enemies of the people'.

The narratives of Soviet victorious heroism during the war, together with the post-war enthusiastic call for selfless work towards the communist future, fitted effectively into the entire people's natural desire for a rational and positive explanation of the past, validation of their present suffering, and confirmation of their hopes for the future. Therefore, the dominant totalitarian narratives were readily accepted by the majority of the Soviet people, and irresistibly impacted the beliefs and values of virtually every citizen. These narratives were omnipresent in the Soviet post-war culture.

SILENCING THE HOLOCAUST MEMORY: A PART OF REALITY RECONSTRUCTION

Together with other citizens, Jewish survivors of the Nazi persecution experienced the pervasive traumata, both induced by the war and imposed by the domestic regime. In that, they were at one with their non-Jewish compatriots. However, Jewish children also faced specific, unparalleled adversities. During the war, they were specifically targeted by the Nazis, and were aware of the threat of total annihilation. Many of them survived unspeakable atrocities, about which there was no knowledge among the mainstream population. Upon liberation, Jewish children were confronted with anti-Semitism and discrimination, due to which they often became singled out among their peers.

Neither past nor present Jewish experiences fit into the legitimate public discourse. Along with the other events and conditions of totalitarian tyranny, the Jewish condition in the Soviet society became utterly undiscussable.

The complex causes and patterns of suppression of the Holocaust memory in the Soviet Union have not been comprehensively analyzed by historians.[15] For the purposes of this chapter, which is not a historical analysis, but rather an exploration of personal and communal experiences of Soviet child survivors, I present several key factors that were indicated in the narratives of the survivors whom I interviewed.

The facts of the Nazi persecution of Jews fell under the category of the undiscussable because they had the potential for contradicting the dominating totalitarian narratives. First and foremost, these facts were inevitably intertwined with the stories about Soviet citizens' active collaboration with the Nazis, as well as the frequent incidents of anti-Semitism in the army and partisan movement.[16] The memory of these events did not match the myth about the flawless righteousness of the Soviet military effort, and therefore were threatening to the regime.

Second, exposing the true history of the Holocaust in the Soviet Union could result in the disclosure of the Soviet government's cruel betrayal of its Jewish citizens. In the early days of the war, the Soviet government failed or purposefully refused to inform the Jewish population about the immediate threat of annihilation by the Nazis. Prior to the German occupation of their land, Soviet Jewish communities had received only scarce, unconfirmed information about mass killings, ghettos and death camps in Europe. Many Jews did not believe the rumours and did not flee in time (almost all survivors whom I interviewed mentioned this fact). The authorities failed to protect the Jews, although millions of deaths could have been prevented by communicating the right information and providing support for evacuation.

Finally, uncovering the truth about the Jewish resistance and the sizable Jewish contribution to the Soviet war effort could catalyse the revival of Jewish identity and the rising of collective consciousness. This could empower the Jews towards opposing the growing domestic anti-Semitism.

These and many other factors contributed to the silencing of the events of the Holocaust by Soviet authorities. Information about the Jewish contribution to the victory was also purposefully concealed. The goal of annihilating illegitimate knowledge was often achieved through devaluing, denunciation, or physical annihilation of its bearers who dared to speak out.

THE STRATEGIES OF PERPETRATION: SILENCING THE KNOWLEDGE AND ANNIHILATING ITS BEARERS

The best-known and most destructive totalitarian act of post-war suppression was the notorious arrest and execution of the members of the Soviet Jewish Antifascist Committee (JAC).[17] The JAC was established by the Soviet authorities in 1942 to mobilize the support of western Jewry for the Soviet struggle against Nazi Germany. The committee included the most visible Soviet Jewish artists, writers, musicians and scientists. One of the significant projects of the JAC was *The Black Book*[18] that contained eyewitness testimony and documents about the tragedy of Eastern European Jewry. In 1947, the work on *The Black Book* was banned, and it was denounced as an example of 'bourgeois nationalism' and 'rootless cosmopolitism'. The committee was dismissed, its chair Solomon Michoels was covertly murdered, and its most active members were arrested in 1948/49. After long imprisonment and torture, twenty-five of them were executed in 1952.

The patterns of perpetration involved in the JAC trial were re-enacted in many repressive campaigns in the early 1950s, such as the notorious Doctors' Trial and the persecution of artists and scholars that routinely affected large numbers of Jews. Likewise, the mass arrests of former prisoners of war and inmates of Nazi camps served the ideological mechanism of suppressing the undesired witness accounts that these people could bear.

THE FACETS OF SILENCING IN CHILDREN'S IMMEDIATE ENVIRONMENTS

Most Soviet citizens had no means to fully comprehend the extent or roots of political oppression at that time. The oppression reached people indirectly, through the influence of their everyday world, in which their individual voices were muffled. Jewish child survivors often became subjects of the dominant myth indoctrination through absorbing the omnipresent Soviet narratives, beliefs and doublespeak language. The dominant stories that surrounded the children conflicted with their live, silent memories. This conflict interfered with their efforts to make sense of the past trauma.

INDIVIDUAL EXPERIENCES OF FORCED SILENCE

The high-level political executions, such as the JAC trial, were re-enacted countless times in private, individual events that had similar meaning and followed similar patterns. Each of the life histories recounted now by Jewish child survivors includes moments akin to having their virtual personal 'black books' arrested, when their individual and family stories of persecution were banned from being told. The memories about these events were forced into secrecy and hiding, as if underground.

Many survivors whom I interviewed recall that they felt a strong impulse to tell about their experiences, but their desire to have their memories validated was met with cold rejection. Esfir, a survivor of the Minsk ghetto, remembers that she, then a 7-year-old girl, was ridiculed by her teacher in front of the class when she told her story of hiding with partisans together with her mother. She was mockingly nicknamed 'a partisan' (*partisanka*), and this was so painful that she stopped sharing her story with anyone. For long years she felt stigmatized and vulnerable.

Fira has similar memories. She was 11 when her family was forced into a horrible journey through death marches, ghettoes, and camps in Bukovina. She remembers that her father considered their vital desire to tell a major force of survival:

> We survived to tell people ... so they would believe it in the future! ... because we [Jews] had not believed that this could happen in the twentieth century, that they would kill people like this, we had not believed! ... I tell you, in all my life in Russia nobody ever asked me what I had gone through, except my own [people] of course.

In Fira's close environment, the knowledge about the past events was secretly shared among family and close Jewish friends. Other survivors recall that such discussions rarely happened even among their families. Leib, who survived as a 7-year-old boy together with his family in evacuation, recalls that he knew little about his extended family members murdered by the Nazis. His knowledge was limited to scattered stories he overheard in the first instances of sharing, shortly after liberation. Despite the missing recollection of open conversations, Leib maintains that as long as he remembers himself, he carried the knowledge about the Holocaust 'in brains, in bones'. Together with their families, in the hostile environment of social silence, the children struggled to make sense of their memories.

Beyond their peers' rejection and the parents' prohibition of sharing their stories in public, there was another, more tangible factor that silenced the children. Survival under the Nazi occupation became a dangerous stigma after the war. Liza escaped from a mass execution in a ghetto where her parents were murdered. In concurrence with the accounts of many other survivors, she recalls:

> The thing is that when after the war I started to work, then – God forbid – nobody knew that I was in the ghetto and all that had happened, because at that time nobody disclosed it ... because at once, if you were looking for a job ... the first question used to be, 'How come you were in a ghetto under the Germans, in the occupied territory – how come you – a Jewish girl – stayed alive?' It was all a secret.

According to many survivors, disclosing their past could make them vulnerable, threaten their freedom or jeopardize their options for work, education and social adjustment.

THE ABSENCE OF A FRAME OF REFERENCE IN THE PUBLIC KNOWLEDGE

The children's environment provided many hints that made them acutely aware of the undiscussability of the facts which they carried in their memory or received from their parents. The history of the war was broadly reflected in literature and the media, and taught at school. However, the events of the Nazi persecution of Jews were omitted from school curricula, historical works, the media and public discussions. Jewish names were rarely mentioned in the lists of war heroes, and if prominent fighters happened to be Jewish, any hint of their ethnicity was carefully concealed.

Within the public knowledge, there was no frame of reference available for the survivors' memories. The history of the Holocaust seemed to have ceased to exist in the public discourse. Jewish children's public worlds were saturated with the proud Soviet victorious narratives, but there was no space within these narratives for their own stories. The silent knowledge they carried inside felt uncommon, different and awkward, and so felt the children among their non-Jewish peers.

Many survivors remember that they craved validation so much that any random sign or public mention of the familiar facts in the Soviet outside world felt precious to them. Fira recalls that in her vital need for validation of her memories she kept searching for scarce literary stories related to her experiences, scanning through the Soviet censored publications. She remembers: 'Oh! [you ask] if I wanted to read! I was interested in anything that was written about the war and about the Jews – I read everything that came my way ... Yes! I wanted it very much – but there was not much written about what we went through.' Searching for familiar facts or names that were acknowledged in the legitimate discourse was an expression of the children's desire for validation, which was vital to their adjustment in the big world outside of their home communities.

THE OPPRESSIVE POWER OF LANGUAGE: DOUBLESPEAK

In their struggle to make sense of their experiences and voice their feelings, the children often did not have words or conceptual constructs available to describe the facts of their past suffering and present oppression. The word 'Holocaust', or *katastropha* in Russian, did not appear in the public language in connection to the events of the war until the late 1980s.[19] Monuments in the places of mass killings (where allowed by the authorities) routinely bore a standard, legitimate sign: 'Peaceful Soviet civilians murdered by German fascists'. The very word 'Jews' was omitted, and Hebrew inscriptions often were banned.

The mainstream ethnicity discourse and the corresponding language did not allow for expressing one's Jewish identity, or even for verbally defining the oppression itself. The word 'Jew' was virtually absent from the common, everyday language. Within the dominant picture of the ideal Soviet society, there was no place for racism, therefore no relevant words were pronounced, and no references to the existing anti-Semitism or discrimination could be made within the legitimate vocabulary. Political campaigns routinely used the words 'rootless cosmopolitan' as Soviet doublespeak for 'Jew'. Leib relates to his voiceless struggle and powerlessness against the abuse, in which the facts of oppression could not be named unless the word was explicitly pronounced by the oppressor:

> In general, as it is related to ethnicity, in the Soviet country, you probably know, there was only one idea – a 'Soviet man'. A Soviet man: it was considered unseemly to even talk about different ethnicities, and we were usually brought up in this key. So I used to think about my Jewish identity only when they told me, well, that Jews are bad, and then I used to say, you fool, you don't understand anything; let's compare what is a Jew and what is a non-Jew.

The myth of the Soviet people as an ethnically-faceless entity eliminated the language that could support any reference to the Jewish condition, thus making all related knowledge unpronounceable, and any definition of it 'unseemly' – undiscussable. Leib recalls that when his application to the university was rejected, he understood that his Jewish identity was the reason, but not a word was said by the university committee; no explanation was offered. Many survivors whom I interviewed referred to stunningly similar events of unspoken persecution, for which there was no legitimate name.

THE UNDERCURRENT NARRATIVES BETWEEN WORLDS: FACTORS OF RESILIENCE

In parallel with the large countrywide social processes, silence was imposed within the survivors' individual local settings through rejection, indoctrination, threats, and persecution. From their routine communications at home and in the big world, the children received clear indications that any Jewish knowledge was illegitimate, awkward or dangerous. This knowledge was maintained in the underground, and expressed in powerful, as if *undercurrent*, stories that defiantly coexisted with the dominant narratives. These alternative stories were invisible from the mainstream surface, but vital for the individual and communal existence. The children's memories of trauma and survival belonged to this undercurrent world.

BETWEEN WORLDS

The child survivors' early healing and adjustment upon liberation was defined by the two worlds to which they belonged. On the one hand, in order to establish themselves and build their future in their given environment, Jewish children had to blend in and identify with the mainstream collective, accept this world and become at one with the common narratives of Soviet post-war struggle. On the other hand, their identities were defined by the world of their marginalized Jewish communities, their values and traditions. The knowledge of the latter world was closely intertwined with the grave memories of persecution and loss.

After liberation, child survivors' priorities were to return to regular life, adjust at school, pursue higher education, and build their future. They could not afford to let the past trauma define their present lives because they were determined to succeed. In general, Jewish children could often feel at one with their non-Jewish peers, because the common everyday hopes and challenges, together with the dual collective trauma of the Soviet people, were still a large part of their personal past and present. They could identify with many mainstream stories.

However, the trauma of the Nazi persecution was vivid in their memories. Many recall persistent post-traumatic signs, such as anxiety, sleep disturbances and flashbacks. Their healing had only begun, and their ability to communicate their feelings and receive acknowledgement was often vital for their recovery. Some children had a strong desire to talk about their experiences. Others say that they were 'too busy' to think of sharing their stories or that it was too painful. Regardless of the wide range of personal attitudes towards sharing their stories, the children often had experiences of rejection, hiding their identities, and feeling profoundly different among their non-Jewish peers.

The children had to learn how to make sense of the two worlds of their memories; they also had to learn how to adjust and grow between the two worlds of their immediate social environments.

THE JOURNEY INTO ASSIMILATION AND BACK: PERFECT STORIES BETWEEN WORLDS

Liza's story is particularly illustrative of the children's resilience and ability to adjust between worlds. Liza was 16 when her parents were murdered, just months before liberation, in a ghetto in Ukraine, where they were together. At liberation, she discovered that her only surviving older brother lived in the Russian Far East, and set out to reunite with him. She recalls being in a desperate condition, ridden with anxiety, fear and a profound sense of desperation: 'a lost soul' alone in the entire world. During her journey of more than a month-and-a-half, she struggled with uncertainty, hunger and dependence on strangers for food and shelter.

It was then, in the early days after liberation, that Liza learned her first lessons of living between worlds. To survive and be accepted by compassionate strangers, she began telling the legitimate part of her story and filtering out the other, Jewish content. Her story resonated with the stories of her random non-Jewish listeners:

> Oh, it happened so many times ... they [the Soviet militia] used to catch children in every train station. There were very many orphans ... those who did not have documents were sent to orphanages ... but I had good documents that I was going to my brother ... It happened so many times ... The train stops, and there is a village nearby ... and a woman comes up and begins talking to me, 'What, are you travelling alone?' – 'Alone' – 'Where are you going?' – 'To my brother' – and I begin to cry, the same moment ... And she, 'I have a lunch left over today, take it, eat the sandwich.' And the bread was [precious] by cards only – the card system ... *You know, everything assimilated in me during this journey of nearly a month and a half* [italics added]. So many people gave me their kindness and cared about me, even militia men – you know who usually go to work in the militia – but even they, oh, they felt so sorry for me – of course, I showed them the documents that I had ... Nothing Jewish was on my mind ...

As Liza describes herself at that time, she was too small for her age, a beautiful child with frequent tears in her dark expressive eyes, emaciated and exhausted. The story that she was telling reached her listeners as a story of a lost orphan, a perfect story of innocent suffering (she had 'good documents' that made her story well legitimized). There was also a strong appeal of happy resolution that the listeners must have craved to hear: Liza was travelling to be reunited with her older brother, her only living relative, and once she arrived she would be finally protected and safe. Liza was feeding, in the spiritual and emotional sense, on the compassion of people, regardless of their language or identity; in the same way that the bread given by strangers kept her physically alive, their expressed sympathy was a vital source of strength for her wounded soul. She could filter out the Jewish part of her narrative because it was irrelevant to the resonance of validation that her story caused, or, rather, she intuitively felt that it could likely interfere with this resonance.

In order to adjust and fit in, child survivors had to create legitimate and perfect, *outside* stories, from which their Jewish experiences had to be filtered out. These stories were intended for the stranger's ear, and had to fit into the standard, dominant Soviet narrative. Identifying with these narratives gave the children the sense of belonging to the big world, and led them through the obstacles and threats of the system towards their goals of acceptance and social achievements. The filtering helped them play by the socially-imposed rules and blend in, at least marginally, with their environments.

The accounts of specifically Jewish suffering, such as incarceration in ghettos or escaping from death marches or mass killings, were untellable to outsiders in the atmosphere of Soviet marginalization of the Jews. In Liza's story, her memories emerged after a long silence when she reunited with her brother and met her future husband. I asked Liza what happened with her 'assimilation' at that time, and she responded:

> And then I got into this family ... I came to meet [my husband's] parents ... They spoke Yiddish and looked at me like this ... my mother-in-law, she was so kind ... When we first met, I came in, and she embraced me, and we wept together for half a day, we could not say a word, and then she says, 'You are my daughter, [long lost and] found' [crying, pause]. She had a girl like me [killed by the Nazis]. She loved me so much ... so I cannot blame my fate; as I say, people in my life did so many kind, good things for me.

This moment of sudden shared tears and the feeling of complete emotional unity marked the outburst of forcibly suppressed memories that finally and unexpectedly became safe to express. This episode was a turning point in Liza's journey. Now, Liza recalls her connection with her newly found family as a beginning of her difficult healing; she notes: 'They helped me out of where I came from', out of her pain of trauma and loss.

THE UNDERGROUND ACKNOWLEDGEMENT

Soviet children's belonging to the Jewish world often made them feel different and exposed. They had to learn to maintain the distinction between the two worlds of their everyday life, and master the secrecy that enveloped their home knowledge. Making sense of this parallel existence was a hard task for someone who struggled with the unresolved consequences of severe trauma, and thus was particularly sensitive to rejection and silencing.

At times, the burden of belonging to a marginalized group made the children vulnerable. However, their unity with the Jewish world also presented a salutary factor for the children's post-traumatic healing. Endorsed by their tiny, informal communities, the children found safe refuge from the silence of the outside world. In this space, the hidden parts of their personal stories were accepted and acknowledged. This *underground communal acknowledgement* of the children's memories created the most valuable protective environment for their recovery, development, and personal fulfilment.

In addition to the validation of the children's memories of suffering during the Holocaust, the communal acknowledgement also supported the precious, positive stories about their pre-war memories, traditions, significant events of the past, and their parents' teachings and values. Because of their specific Jewish content, these positive narratives of hope, love, and fulfilment could only be voiced in the safe environment of the children's underground communal refuge. Preserving these narratives was essential for the children's ability to make sense of their world after the immense trauma that they had experienced.

Acknowledgement and validation did not necessarily involve explicit verbalization of the memories. Jewish communal groups, as small as they were, provided the survivors not only with fellow listeners to their recounting, but also with understanding healers to their silent suffering, akin to Liza's mother-in-law in the story of their first meeting. When children were unable to verbalize their memories of suffering, their internal knowledge could resonate with the stories that they were hearing from others. A child's story could seamlessly fit into the indestructible communal 'in brains, in bones' (using Leib's expression) narratives. Solidarity was often expressed through simple acts of kindness, affection, or mere presence, as in this recollection by Liza:

> It was all a secret ... Well, of course my husband knew and his parents knew and all those who survived in the ghetto knew too. We never talked about it ... But we used to – *you know – kind of on the sly, on the sly* [italics added] ... My family was better off than the family that took me in [in the ghetto, after my parents were killed]. We helped them always, all my life.

Many survivors whom I interviewed cherish similar memories of validation until today. Jewish communal protection often defined the stability of children's identities and helped them make sense of their experiences.

THE SALUTARY POWER: COMMUNAL RESILIENCE

The patterns of silencing the victims in the Soviet Union are reminiscent of similar strategies employed by perpetrators of many other forms of abuse. The voiceless state of a victim is particularly harmful for individual processes of healing, as described by Herman: 'When the victim is ... devalued (a woman, a child), she may find that the most traumatic events of her life take place outside the realm of socially validated reality. Her experience becomes unspeakable. The study of psychological trauma must constantly contend with this tendency to discredit the victim or to render her invisible.'[20]

In the Soviet Union, the study of psychological trauma was never represented in academic or public discourses on such a scale that it could contribute to the contending action advocated by Herman. Professional treatment was never available to the survivors. Neither could any other legitimized discourses or institutional social powers provide protection or give a voice to Jewish child survivors of the Holocaust.

Instead, the salutary factors of resilient healing were developed informally and spontaneously within Jewish groups, evolving from age-old practices of maintaining communal unity. In the absence of formal liberating support groups or outspoken grassroots social movements, Soviet Jewry formed hidden but powerful protective environments. In these environments, the victims of persecution provided each other with a healing shield of communally constructed 'realm of socially validated reality,' the lack of which Herman considered profoundly damaging for a person recovering from trauma.

Lydia, a child survivor who became a prominent child psychiatrist, maintains that Jewish spontaneous communal support was a potent antidote against the ideologically imposed taboo of the Holocaust in the Soviet Union. I asked for her thoughts about the impact of social silence on individual survivors, and she theorized:

> But to me it seems that there is no such great dependence, well ... in fact, it is not so at all. To me it seems that *there is no such thing in the Jews – such great dependence on what is happening around them; it is also one of their characteristic features that they are somehow ... by their inner essence they are protected from all this. The very awareness that he is supported by his own* [italics added] ... this feeling of certain exceptionality – being *the chosen* – there is such thing, and it protects the person ... Well, I don't give a damn [laughs] ... I am chosen by God [laughs] ... [The Jews] did not give a damn; they knew everything about their own troubles, so to say, and they were surrounded by people ... who were close to them and with whom they shared their views, and this, I think it was quite enough for a Jew that he always had support from his own people.

In Lydia's interpretation, the meaning of being 'the chosen,' one of the narrative motifs shared within the Jewish groups, is rooted in the very essence of being at one with the community. The exceptionality of mutual acknowledgement presented an important factor of communal resilience that protected the victims of totalitarian abuse and enhanced their post-traumatic healing.

CONCLUSION

The environment of Soviet child survivors at the end of the war was defined by pervasive repression of the historical memory of the Holocaust and indoctrination of fabricated historical myths. The power and omnipresence of these discourses deprived Jewish survivors of legitimate social validation of their suffering. Under the oppression of silence, the children did not have the privilege of openly voicing their memories, nor were they granted the benefit of societal acknowledgement. These social and psychological processes impacted the children in the most formative stages of their development and during the most critical time of their early post-traumatic healing.

The excerpt from *Life and Fate* by Grossman, quoted as an epigraph to this article, refers to the powerful impact of the totalitarian mode of thinking on the individual ability to form decisions, create meanings or make sense of life experiences. How did this 'invisible force', which can find its way 'inside' a person, interfere with the processes of working through trauma and forming individual pathways to adjustment in young Holocaust survivors in the Soviet Union? The environment of forced silence, together with the dominance of totalitarian discourses that enforced an inferior status of the Jews and the Jewish culture, strongly impacted on trauma recovery processes in child survivors. The prevalence of history revisions and narratives of oppression influenced the ability of individual survivors and their small local communities to tell and interpret their stories of persecution and survival during the war.

However, the survivors' stories also reveal the evidence of rebellion against the oppressive totalitarian force: the acts that Grossman characterized as 'astonishing'. The rebellion expressed itself in the individual and communal ability to create, preserve and secretly share hidden, undercurrent narratives of collective memories, traditions and values. These alternative interpretations of social and historical reality were indestructible within Jewish groups, and their persistence alleviated the harmful effects of ideological suppression on individual survivors. Belonging to the communal unity became a powerful salutary factor that supported resilient post-traumatic recovery of young Jewish survivors of the Holocaust.

REFERENCES

Altman, I., 'Мемориализация Холокоста в России: история, современность, перспективы [Memorializing the Holocaust in Russia: History, modern times, perspectives],' *Неприкосновенный запас* [Emergency Ration], 2–3 (40–41) (2005), pp.2–3.

Bar-On, D., *The Indescribable and Undiscussable: Reconstructing Human Discourse after Trauma* (Budapest: Central European University Press, 1999).

Cohen, S.K., *Child Survivors of the Holocaust in Israel: 'Finding their Voice': Social Dynamics and Post-War Experiences* (Portland, OR: Sussex Academic Press, 2005).

Danieli, Y., 'Healing components: The Right to Reparation for Victims of Gross Violations of Human Rights and Humanitarian Law', in D. Pollefeyt, G.J. Colijn and M.S. Littell (eds), *Hearing the Voices: Teaching the Holocaust to Future Generations* (Merion Station, PA: Merion Westfield Press International, 2000), pp.219–33.

de Young, M., 'Collective Trauma: Insights from a Research Errand', (1998) in The American Academy of Experts in Traumatic Stress: http://www.aaets.org/article55.htm.

Dodik, S., *Судьба и жизнь мальчика из расстрелянного гетто* [Life and Fate of a Boy from the Executed Ghetto] (Москва: Калейдоскоп, 2004).

Ehrenburg, I. and Grossman, V., *The Complete Black Book of Russian Jewry*, trans. D. Patterson (Piscataway, NJ: Transaction Publishers, 2003).

Fogelman, E., 'Exploding Psychological Myths about Generations of the Holocaust in Israel and North America', in J.K. Roth and E. Maxwell (eds), *Remembering for the Future: The Holocaust in an Age of Genocide*, vol. 3 (New York: Palgrave, 2001), pp.93–107.

Gitelman, Z., 'Internationalism, Patriotism and Disillusion: Soviet Jewish Veterans Remember World War II and the Holocaust', in J.K. Roth and E. Maxwell (eds), *Remembering For the Future: The Holocaust in an Age of Genocide*, vol. 3 (New York: Palgrave, 2001), pp.296–308.

Glaser, B.G. and Strauss, A.L., *The Discovery of Grounded Theory: Strategies for Qualitative Research* (Chicago, IL: Aldine, 1967).

Grossman, V., *Life and Fate*, trans. R. Chandler (New York: New York Review Books, 1980; original work published 1959).

Herman, J.L., *Trauma and Recovery* (New York: Basic Books, 1992).

Jewish Black Book Committee, *The Black Book: The Nazi Crime Against the Jewish People* (New York: Duell, Slaon and Pearce, 1946).

Kandel, F., *Книга времён и событий: Истроия евреев Советского Союза (1945–1970)* [The Book of Times and Events: The History of the Jews of the Soviet Union (1945–1970)] (Москва: Мосты культуры, 2007).

Kaplan, E., *Из далекого детства* [From My Distant Childhood] [electronic version] (Association of Concentration Camps and Ghetto Survivors in Israel Website, 2008).

Kestenberg, J.S., 'Overview of the Effects of Psychological Research Interviews on Child Survivors', in J.S. Kestenberg and E. Fogelman (eds), *Children during Nazi Reign: Psychological Perspective on the Interview Process* (Westport, CT: Praeger, 1998), pp.3–33.

Krell, R., 'Children who survived the Holocaust: Reflections of a Child Survivor/Psychiatrist', *Echoes of the Holocaust*, 4 (June 1995).

Krell, R. (ed.), *Messages and Memories: Reflections on Child Survivors of the Holocaust* (Vancouver, BC: Memory Press, 1999).

Levin, A.M., 'Евреи и партизаны Белоруссии в годы нацистского геноцида [Jews and Byelorussian partisans during the years of the Nazi genocide]', in I. Altman (ed.), *Тень Холокоста: Материалы второго международного симпозиума 'Уроки Холокоста и современная Россия'* [Shadow of the Holocaust. Second National Symposium: Lessons of the Holocaust and Contemporary Russia] (Москва: Фонд Холокост, 1998), pp.89–92.

Markish, D., 'ЕАК: Время и место [JAC: Time and Place]', *Лехаим* [Lechaim], 4, 168 (2002), pp.28–32.

Tighe, E., Saxe, L., and Chertok, F., *Jewish Elderly Nazi Victims in the Former Soviet Union: Ongoing Needs and Comparison to Conditions in Europe, Israel and the United States* (Waltham, MA: Brandeis University Steinhardt Social Research Institute, 2008).

Veidlinger, J., *The Moscow State Yiddish Theatre: Jewish Culture on the Soviet Stage* (Bloomington, IN: Indiana University Press, 2002).

NOTES

1. V. Grossman, *Life and Fate*, trans. R. Chandler (New York: New York Review Books, 1980; original work published 1959), p.672.
2. E. Tighe, L. Saxe, and F. Chertok, *Jewish Elderly Nazi Victims in the Former Soviet Union: Ongoing Needs and Comparison to Conditions in Europe, Israel and the United States* (Waltham, MA: Brandeis University Steinhardt Social Research Institute, 2008; Claims Conference Website).
3. I. Altman, 'Мемориализация Холокоста в России: история, современность, перспективы [Memorializing the Holocaust in Russia: History, Modern Times, Perspectives]', *Неприкосновенный запас* [Emergency Ration], 2–3 (40–41) (2005), pp.2–3.
4. Z. Gitelman, 'Internationalism, Patriotism and Disillusion: Soviet Jewish Veterans Remember World War II and the Holocaust', in J.K. Roth and E. Maxwell (eds), *Remembering for the Future: The Holocaust in an Age of Genocide*, vol. 3, pp.296–308. (New York: Palgrave, 2001).
5. B.G. Glaser and A.L. Strauss, *The Discovery of Grounded Theory: Strategies for Qualitative Research* (Chicago, IL: Aldine, 1967).

6. J.L. Herman, *Trauma and Recovery* (New York: Basic Books, 1992); J.S. Kestenberg, 'Overview of the Effects of Psychological Research Interviews on Child Survivors', in J.S. Kestenberg and E. Fogelman (eds), *Children during Nazi Reign: Psychological Perspective on the Interview Process* (Westport, CT: Praeger, 1998), pp.3–33.
7. M. de Young, 'Collective trauma: Insights from a Research Errand', (1998) in The American Academy of Experts in Traumatic Stress: http://www.aaets.org/article55.htm.
8. Danieli analysed the effects of silencing the survivors in the United States, in the early years after their immigration, and found that silencing significantly inhibited their healing processes. Danieli called this impact 'second wound': Y. Danieli, 'Healing Components: The Right to Reparation for Victims of Gross Violations of Human Rights and Humanitarian Law', in D. Pollefeyt, G.J. Colijn and M.S. Littell (eds), *Hearing the Voices: Teaching the Holocaust to Future Generations* (Merion Station, PA: Merion Westfield Press International, 2000), pp.219–33.
9. E. Fogelman, 'Exploding Psychological Myths about Generations of the Holocaust in Israel and North America', in Roth and Maxwell (eds.), *Remembering for the Future*, vol. 3, pp.93–107.
10. R. Krell, 'Children who survived the Holocaust: Reflections of a Child Survivor/Psychiatrist', *Echoes of the Holocaust*, 4 (June 1995); R. Krell (ed.), *Messages and Memories: Reflections on Child Survivors of the Holocaust* (Vancouver, BC: Memory Press, 1999).
11. S.K. Cohen, *Child Survivors of the Holocaust in Israel: 'Finding their Voice': Social Dynamics and Post-War Experiences* (Portland, OR: Sussex Academic Press, 2005).
12. F. Kandel, *Книга времён и событий: Истроия евреев Советского Союза (1945–1970)* [The Book of Times and Events: The History of the Jews of the Soviet Union (1945–1970)] (Москва: Мосты культуры, 2007); Gitelman, 'Internationalism, Patriotism and Disillusion', p.296.
13. Kandel, *Книга времён и событий*; S. Dodik, *Судьба и жизнь мальчика из расстрелянного гетто* [Life and Fate of a Boy from the Executed Ghetto] (Москва: Калейдоскоп, 2004).
14. D. Bar-On, *The Indescribable and Undiscussable: Reconstructing Human Discourse after Trauma* (Budapest: Central European University Press, 1999).
15. Gitelman, 'Internationalism, Patriotism and Disillusion', p.299.
16. E. Kaplan, *Из далекого детства* [From My Distant Childhood] [electronic version] (Association of Concentration Camps and Ghetto Survivors in Israel Website, 2008); A.M. Levin, 'Евреи и партизаны Белоруссии в годы нацистского геноцида [Jews and Belorussian partisans during the years of the Nazi genocide]', in I. Altman (ed.), *Тень Холокоста: Материалы второго международного симпозиума 'Уроки Холокоста и современная Россия'* [Shadow of the Holocaust: Second National Symposium: Lessons of the Holocaust and Contemporary Russia] (Москва: Фонд Холокост, 1998), pp.89–92.
17. J. Veidlinger, *The Moscow State Yiddish Theatre: Jewish Culture on the Soviet Stage* (Bloomington, IN: Indiana University Press, 2002); D. Markish, 'ЕАК: Время и место [JAC: Time and Place]', *Лехаим* [Lechaim], 4, 168 (2002), pp.28–32.
18. Jewish Black Book Committee, *The Black Book: The Nazi Crime against the Jewish People* (New York: Duell, Slaon and Pearce, 1946); I. Ehrenburg and V. Grossman, *The Complete Black Book of Russian Jewry*, trans. D. Patterson (Piscataway, NJ: Transaction Publishers, 2003).
19. Altman, 'Мемориализация Холокоста'; Gitelman, 'Internationalism, Patriotism and Disillusion', p.298.
20. Herman, *Trauma and Recovery*, p.8.

12

'It Wasn't That Bad in the Ghetto, was it?' Living on in the USSR After the Nazi Genocide

ANIKA WALKE

When she inquired about financial compensation for survivors of the Nazi regime in 2000, a Jewish woman, 66 years old and living in St Petersburg, was told, in essence, that surviving a Nazi ghetto was not a particularly bad experience. The speaker, a Russian official, felt justified to deny her claim for monetary reimbursement shortly after the German government had approved the law that allocated financial compensation to former Nazi forced labourers.[1] Frida Pedko, who reported this experience to me one year later, was irritated by the fact that she was thus ineligible to apply for compensation. More than that, she was clearly upset about and hurt by the hostility of the bureaucrat's statement, seeing it as a devaluation of her wartime experiences that included her internment in a ghetto at the age of 8, the killing of her family, and her escape from the ghetto into a hideout in the Belorussian forest.

The bureaucrat's statement voiced in 2000 is and was meant to be an insult, and it seems to confirm widespread assumptions about the effects and tendencies of the official Soviet/Russian portrayal of the period that, in the (post-)Soviet context, is usually referred to as the 'Great Patriotic War'.[2] This official war portrayal favours the commemoration of heroic fighters, displayed in monuments, statues, parades on Victory Day (9 May), and decorative and monetary status awards given to accomplished war veterans. This portrayal is often described by critics as anti-Semitic or dismissive of the suffering of the Jewish population; as oblivious to the everyday life experiences of the civilian population and especially of victims; and as focused solely on remembering the victory and heroic defeat of fascism. The promotion of the collective victory happens at the expense of recognizing the disproportional suffering of the Soviet population due to the direction of all available resources to the military apparatus. It also neglects moments of loss and grief, and it denies instances of collaboration with the occupying forces. I could certainly leave it at that; numerous works describe the Soviet war memory in this manner, mine included. However, I believe that another reading of the bureaucrat's statement is possible; a reading that also takes into account the Soviet context where large proportions of the population suffered from the war. Everyone did not suffer equally in the USSR, and yet the war affected the whole Soviet population in ways that are clearly distinct from experiences in other European countries that were occupied by the Nazi regime.

I would like to explore in some more detail what the official's statement that 'life in the ghetto wasn't that bad' means in the context in which it was uttered. Looking at the historical circumstances the statement refers to, and at the conditions that make it possible, I analyse how the speaker justifies his remark. This dual approach helps to understand the emergence and persistence of a portrayal of the war that is harmful to people like Frida Pedko, and which not only shapes how institutions represent the past, but also affects how individuals perceive the war.

I hope to open up a space to reflect on the validity of a clear-cut dismissal of the official Soviet commemorative practice that is no doubt problematic because of its exclusion of the wartime experiences of millions of Soviet citizens. I argue that such dismissal also partially ignores the specificities of a historical experience: the war of annihilation against the Soviet population. We must scrutinize the Soviet commemorative discourse and how it affects material conditions of existence, with regards to marginalization and exclusions produced by a limited portrayal of the war.

The Russian official questioned Ms Pedko's claim to compensation for her wartime experiences, arguing that living in the ghetto meant 'simply [that] the Germans cordoned off a number of streets'. Thus, the man diminished Frida Pedko's and thousands of other people's suffering from starvation, forced labour, and pogroms in the ghettos established by the Nazi occupation regime. He equalled this suffering to the wartime experiences of non-Jewish Soviet citizens, whose lives were, according to his assessment, equally damaged during the war. However, his statement asserts that since non-Jewish survivors were not allocated special benefits, and since Jewish people like Frida Pedko suffered in the same way, Jewish survivors must not claim special benefits. Is this assessment justified? I will try to answer this question by analysing wartime and post-war experiences of Jewish and non-Jewish survivors of the German occupation. Looking at individuals' living conditions and at the state portrayal of the war, I trace the factors facilitating a statement that neglects diverse experiences of violence, war and their aftermath. A focus on the relations between Jewish and non-Jewish citizens will be especially enlightening, since it directly points to different experiences of the Nazi occupation.

My analysis is largely based on forty-one interviews with Jewish survivors that I conducted between 2001 and 2008 in St Petersburg and Minsk.[3] The women and men survived the Nazi genocide in occupied Soviet territories. Their personal recollections challenge a limited image of the past that focuses on the heroic victory over fascism and thus contribute to a critique of the dominant portrayal. This alternative portrayal of the past notes experiences of ghetto internment, forced labour, systematic massacres, and various responses to the Nazi genocide of the Jewish population, ranging from support for Jews to active collaboration with the German occupation regime. Thus, the portrayal given in the interviews opens up a critique of the state portrayal largely focusing on armed struggle and the collective efforts of the unified Soviet people. My discussion reflects on the aftermath of survival against violence, terror and genocide and the absence of an official recognition of these experiences. Eventually, it reflects upon the practice of reparation and compensation employed both by the Soviet state and by Germany as the state ultimately responsible for the damages inflicted on the country and the people.

'THEY WILL SHOOT AT ME?' – THE EXTERMINATION OF SOVIET JEWRY

In June 1941, German troops attacked the USSR, launching a four-year long occupation of Soviet territories. The whole population was affected by the war, but in different forms. Numerous civilians, Soviet prisoners of war and soldiers were killed; approximately 5,500,000 juveniles, women and men were deported to be forced labourers in the *Reichsgebiet* or other occupied areas; infrastructure was deliberately destroyed; and private property as well as agrarian and industrial products was looted and exported to

Germany. Belorussia, home to most of my interviewees, together with present-day Ukraine, were hit hardest under the German occupation, being occupied for nearly four years and continuously the scene of military clashes. Less than seven million Belorussians survived the war; every third or fourth of the formerly 9,200,000 residents died.[4] At the end of the war, 1,200,000 residential houses in the countryside lay in ruins; 90 per cent of urban houses and public buildings were uninhabitable. In Minsk, Gomel, and Mogilev, only 23 per cent of the pre-war living space was left for use.[5] Three million people were homeless or lived in makeshift dwellings dug into the soil.[6] From an economic perspective, the country's development was thrown back decades; 85 per cent of the industrial plants were damaged, the economy's capacity had decreased by 95 per cent, crop space was nearly halved, and 80 per cent of the cattle had been destroyed.[7] The property damage to civilians amounted to furniture, clothing and other things worth up to 23,600,000,000 roubles (1941 value).[8] Thus, the historian Zvi Gitelman argues, the 'general Soviet tendency to ignore or downplay the Holocaust'[9] was facilitated by the fact that 'no country in the west lost as many of its non-Jewish citizens in the war against Nazism as did the USSR, so that the fate of the Jews in France, Holland, Germany, or Belgium stands in sharper contrast to that of their co-nationalists or co-religionists than it does in the East'.[10]

During the occupation, up to 2,000,000 Soviet Jewish citizens were killed. Most of the Soviet Jews were not deported to concentration or extermination camps. Beginning with the invasion in June 1941, German troops began to assemble the male Jewish population, together with known functionaries of the Communist Party, and killed both groups on the spot, mostly at trenches at the outskirts of towns and villages. In August 1941, women were included in these massacres. In July of the same year, Jewish residents had to move into assigned places, the so-called 'Jewish residential areas': ghettos. During nightly pogroms or mass executions, thousands of girls, boys, women and men were rounded up, led to ditches and shot.[11] Many interviews say that surviving, or 'making it through', was all they wanted.

Frida Pedko remembers these months vividly. Shortly after German troops had entered her hometown, Slavnoe, near Vitebsk, members of the *Einsatzgruppen* searched for active communists. Frida's mother was the kolkhoz's party liaison, and because some residents tipped-off the Germans, she was immediately arrested and shot, in August 1941. On 16 March 1942, all inhabitants of the ghetto in Slavnoe were rounded up at the central square and led to a place at the outskirts of the town. Ms Pedko recalls that she was frightened and told her sister Elena: 'They will shoot at me? But that will hurt, it will make me bleed!' While hundreds of women and men, girls and boys were led to the place of the massacre, a local resident pulled the sisters from the crowd and hid them in the woods. For twenty-seven months, Frida and Elena lived on mushrooms, berries, herbs, and minimal food that a peasant woman offered infrequently. In the summer of 1944 the two children were too exhausted to imagine surviving another fall and winter:

> We decided to go to the local commander and ask him to kill us. We were so wasted, there was no real food ... It is strange, how calmly we spoke about this, that we would somehow make it through the summer, but that, if the country would not be liberated by the winter, we would surrender. We remember this often nowadays, it was so horrible.

The occupation of Soviet territories resulted in continuing hardship for local residents, beginning with the invasion in the summer of 1941 that levelled many residential areas. Hunger plagued the population, since the German troops charged high dues of scarce resources in grain, meat and other supplies. Due to the segregation of the ghetto, Jews had even less access to food, heating material or other necessary equipment. As Olga Semenovna, a non-Jewish woman living in Minsk, recalls, she and her sister were able to provide food to her friend Rosa Zelenko in the ghetto, because 'we were not in the ghetto, and my sister was very active and frequently went to the countryside to exchange clothes and other things for food. Back in Minsk, she would sell the produce; that was our income. One could get everything for money in Minsk ... It was easier for us, we had more freedom.' Many interviewees recall that the exchange of clothes for food through the ghetto fence was essential for their survival, as was the willingness of non-Jewish friends, neighbours or strangers to help.

Interviewees frequently point out that non-Jewish neighbours also posed a threat. The Germans relied on local residents to identify Jewish people, or active communists. Almost all of my twenty-five interviewees recall situations in which they faced the life-threatening consequences of collaboration and denunciation.

Drawing upon various sources, Bernard Chiari, in his impressive portrayal of everyday life in occupied Belorussia, demonstrated that Jews were those victims that occupants, collaborators, and non-Jewish population could agree upon.[12] He suggests that parts of the local population actively supported the anti-Jewish Nazi policy, which made survival for Jewish refugees outside of the ghetto highly unlikely. Thus, the Russian official's statement that life in the ghetto was not particularly bad neglects differences in experiences of hunger, arrest, and mass murder.

Several of my interviewees managed to escape from the ghetto, and most of them tried to join one of the numerous partisan units active in the forests. Being with a partisan unit proved essential to secure shelter, food, and care in case of illness or wounds. Also, partisan units provided protection against the ongoing raids by German troops and collaborators. However, several interviewees report that they had to face anti-Semitism among Soviet partisans when they were refused admission to a unit. Some were lucky enough to enter one of the few Jewish partisan units, created by people such as Michail Zorin, Tuvia Bielski and others, and specifically providing a safe haven for refugees from the ghettos. Others who were admitted to Soviet partisan units report that they were treated equally compared to their fellow partisans. For those who did not find these units at all, survival in the forest was under continuous threat, from the harsh climatic conditions, lack of food, and German troops.

LIVING ON IN THE USSR

After Soviet troops had liberated Belorussia, many surviving Jews returned to the places from which they had been forced during the war to evade the genocide. With very few exceptions, all interviewees lost their immediate family. At the end of the war, at ages ranging from 11 to 23, they had to start from scratch, as orphans, without a home, and in a destroyed country. Weakened by years of malnutrition, illness and military operations, surviving in hiding or in the partisan units, the young people had to organize food, housing and other essentials all by themselves. The country lay in ruins, all residents starved, and support from state institutions was hardly available. Strong efforts by the government to re-establish mighty military forces drew upon increased work norms for workers, who in turn were not sufficiently supplied with provisions. All

Soviet citizens faced continuing hardship during the first post-war years, as the Soviet regime continued to ask for sacrifices necessary to withstand a predicted attack by the allied forces.[13]

Soviet authorities proved to be unable – or unwilling – to acknowledge experiences of violence and extermination that had affected parts of the population more severely than others. Several interviewees recall how they struggled to make a living throughout the first post-war years, and how the repercussions of the anti-Semitic mobilization that began during the war and increased in the late 1940s affected their efforts to recreate a life in peacetime.[14]

Frida Pedko and her sister had lost all documents of identification when they were driven out of the ghetto. As was the case for many Jewish people, after the war it took her and her sister several days to prove that they were siblings and related to an aunt who offered to take care of the girls. Only at the end of this procedure was the aunt able to claim food ration cards for Frida and Elena Pedko. Rita Kazhdan had memorized her mother's sister's address in Moscow. It took several weeks until a letter she wrote in July 1944 arrived at her aunt's house and her uncle was able to pick up Rita and her brother Grisha in Minsk.

Lidia Dosovitskaia and many others shared a problem when they emerged from a partisan unit in July 1944 and returned to their hometowns. The home in Diatlovo, in which she had grown up and which her family had to leave when the occupation regime seized local houses, was completely empty. Local residents took what was left behind by the fleeing Jewish inhabitants or had not been destroyed during the final military operations and refused to return furniture and other things. In the aftermath of the so-called resettlement of the local Jewish population into ghettos, neighbours or strangers had occupied the relocated people's houses or apartments and were unwilling to leave the space after the war, often expressing anti-Semitic views that seem to entitle them to such repossession. Rita Kazhdan gives an example in narrating her return from the forest to Minsk as soon as the fighting was over in June 1944. She, her brother and two friends tried to find shelter in the friends' former apartment. A man whom Rita had encountered earlier opened the door. As she recalls:

> During the occupation, he had caught me in the Russian district of the city. That was when I carried some things I had received from Marusya, our former housemaid. She had

> given me some flour and oil. Gera [Rita's brother] was sick at that time. The guy grabbed me shortly before I reached the gate to the ghetto, and asked: 'You Jewish mug, what are you doing here?' He took all the things away from me and said: 'This is the last time I see you here in the Russian district!' And here we are [in liberated Minsk] and this Volodia opens the door. He said: 'Jewish mug, you are still alive?'

The young people were allowed to spend the night on the kitchen floor of their former home, but had to search for a new place to live the next day.

The memories attached to specific places certainly distinguished Jewish survivors' post-war perceptions and feelings from those of their non-Jewish compatriots and contemporaries. For Leonid Golbraikh, Rita Kazhdan, Boris Gal'perin, and Leonid Skoblo specific uses of space such as sites of killing, former ghetto territories or military facilities for Soviet projects after the war generated discontent. At the end of the war, Leonid Golbraikh's partisan unit was demobilized. Orphaned boys like the 14-year-old Leonid were sent to a military school where they were placed in barracks. Leonid remembers thinking, '"I am done with this. I don't need anymore barbed wire around me." So I left one night.' There is an unspoken understanding that it is the reminiscence of living in a ghetto, surrounded by barbed wire, that Leonid could not bear and which made him leave to find shelter somewhere else.

In late summer 1944, after she had met a friend of her mother in Minsk, Rita Kazhdan found herself housed in the area where the ghetto used to be. 'For him', she says, 'this didn't mean anything. But for me it was *ghetto.*' The man had worked as a military surgeon throughout the war and was busy rebuilding medical services in Minsk. He did not know that in the streets around his new home thousands of people had been humiliated, chased and killed. He did not know that Rita had last seen her mother walking along one of the ghetto streets before she was taken away and shot on the outskirts of Minsk.

Boris Gal'perin and Leonid Skoblo express their frustration about the unconsidered reuse of sites of imprisonment or extermination by Soviet institutions. In the 1960s, Boris Gal'perin found newly built dachas (country cottages) at the place in Ryzhkovichi where he had grown up and where his whole family was killed during the war. Leonid Skoblo once flew over Mineralnye Vody, where he and his cousin survived in hiding, only to see a military airport covering the area of several mass executions.

In light of common practices by the Soviet authorities to conceal places where numerous people had suffered or were killed, some of my interviewees developed their own, private ways to commemorate the dead, as exemplified by Nina Romanova. A long time after the Germans had killed her mother and her little sister in the small village of Gusino, she filled a bucket with soil that she collected at the mass grave where her mother and sister were buried, and brought it to Leningrad. She buried the soil next to her grandmother's grave in Leningrad, and set up a small gravestone: 'Now there is a place where one can go to, contemplate, and where I can light candles, lay down flowers.'

After the war, the Soviet Union worked to rebuild the damaged society, including the economic sphere and social infrastructure, and to train new professionals. Some of the interviewees had finished high school before the war, and all of them were asked to continue with whatever educational step would logically follow. Frida Pedko recalls how, after eventually arriving in Leningrad with her aunt, she was placed in a school that was largely attended by children of military personnel. Ms Pedko explains:

> I did not start school in September, but in October, because we made it to Leningrad so late. First of all, students kept looking at me, and only later they told me why. I was covered in lice at the end of the war, so they had shaved off all my hair. All the other girls had braids and such, but I did not. On the other hand, I had only such a coat made out of a goat's skin. And when I was called on in class, I did not speak. I did not know Russian. I only spoke Belorussian.

Frida faced additional hardship, since she had lost her entire family. As an orphaned child, she was eligible to state benefits, but her monthly stipend of five rubles only stretched so far: 'Red Beets cost five kopeks in the dining hall, so one had food for ten days. After that, I had bread, which we got for free in the dining hall ... Other than that, they gave us vouchers for a coat and the school uniform.'

Elena Drapkina remembers the difficulties involved in returning to the classroom and to sustained intellectual activity, saying:

> Beginning June 1941, there were absolutely no newspapers ... And in the ghetto, what did I read – announcements, decrees, but there were no papers ... There were no books either, our house had been burned, and where I stayed in the ghetto, there were no books. And when I was with the partisans – the only thing one could read there were leaflets ... Eventually, I did not read for three years.

Elena Drapkina and Frida Pedko were both lucky to find aunts who had survived the war and who were willing to foster them in Leningrad.

Lidia Dosovitskaia highlights the feeling of grief that, in addition to the economic hardship, overwhelmed and paralyzed her frequently:

> As a teenager, I often woke up in the morning, and immediately I saw my parents in front of me. No photo, I had nothing from them, I could not take anything with me. Somebody sent me a picture of my brother and my sister. I was so happy to receive that! But then again ... you get up in the morning and wonder, why it is that you can't stop thinking about it, after so many years. Why is that?

VICTORIOUS AND OTHER MEMORIES

Survivors' professional careers were often shaped by their wartime experiences. Official rewards and benefits function as an indicator of how survivors' experiences and actions were perceived and valued. They are closely tied to opportunities of participation in the social and political sphere, which were largely shaped by state-driven anti-Semitism that had increased in the late 1940s. Interviewees' narratives suggest two varieties of perception.

A first group of survivors includes people like Frida Pedko, who survived in hiding and lived on leftovers and other food substitutes that she and her sister found in the forest. Other members of this group participated in the so-called family units, which in the Soviet society were not considered to be 'proper' partisan units, despite their frequent involvement in military operations, and, first of all, the essential contribution these units made to the supply of fighting units with food, equipment, and medical aid.

After the war, the women and men in this group struggled to

finish high school, to learn a profession, or begin higher education. Several of the interviewees experienced restrictions in their choice: Lidia Dosovitskaia and Allevtina Kuprikhina had been unable to finish school before the war, could not afford to do so after the end of the war, and were thus highly limited in their professional career, finding only low-paid jobs. Leonid Golbraikh became a highly skilled mechanic, but was repeatedly excluded from promotions in the factory where he worked for more than thirty years. Rita Kazhdan and Frida Pedko were barred from access to degree courses and had similar difficulty finding jobs after finishing their education. Both emphasized the role of their Jewish nationality in the decisions made by the human resources departments of companies to which they had applied. Rita Kazhdan and Frida Pedko had to rely on personal friends who could convince human resources functionaries of their trustworthiness.

The second group of survivors includes men and women who participated in the military units of the partisan movement, which often refused to admit Jewish refugees from the ghettos. Compared to the first group, this group was able to acquire a rather high social status. Boris Gal'perin and Grigorii Erenburg were able to finish programmes in continuing education and became engineers. Both men recall that many of the senior professionals and unit managers in their factories had been partisans and were instrumental in hiring them. However, as Mr Erenburg says, he was excluded from business contacts or travel to foreign companies because he was a Jew. Elena Drapkina and Nina Romanova recalled that they had to endure anti-Semitic insults while working as physicians in the early 1950s. The period of state-sponsored campaigns against 'cosmopolitan' intellectuals and professions, the official disguise for a campaign directed mostly at Jewish citizens, affected their personal lives. Both remember that they were insecure about the future of their professional and social life during that period.

All these men and women of the second group were honoured as veterans of the war; they received medals and special benefits, such as monetary rewards, or travel grants for vacations. In contrast, members of the first group, which I introduced earlier, often had difficulties making a living. The two groups are united, however, by experiences of institutionalized anti-Semitism, which shaped the professional and social life of many Soviet citizens of Jewish nationality.[15]

POLITICS OF MEMORY AND COMPENSATION

Coming full circle, I would like to return to the quote I used to begin my discussion of Jewish post-war life in the USSR. The Russian official's claim that life in the ghetto was not worse than other Soviet people's wartime experiences provided the basis for my reflection on the war in the Soviet Union. Acknowledging the specificities of the historical experience of the Second World War in the Soviet Union, which affected large proportions of the population, I argue, as the interviews show, that Jewish children, women and men were singled out for extermination solely because of their ethnic or religious identity and thus suffered differently than their non-Jewish compatriots. Thus, the bureaucrat clearly neglects the particularities of Jewish suffering under the Nazi regime. However, reading his claim more generously and considering the effects of the war on the whole population, his statements might be an expression of frustration over general lack of recognition for civilians' war suffering in the USSR. To conclude this chapter, I would like to reflect briefly on the life of war survivors in the USSR on a more general level, thinking in particular about the practice of recognition as expressed both by the Soviet and the German states in the form of rewards and benefits. These practices assume, each in their distinct way, an equality of experience that is questioned by the portrayals given in the interviews.

The position that survivors of the genocide acquired after the war as 'eyewitnesses', 'subjects' or 'objects' of scholarly work on the war and in everyday life in the USSR is clearly distinct from those living in western countries. Catherine Merridale suggests that any survivors of violence and repression, not only survivors of the Nazi genocide, were pushed aside in all of these spheres in the Soviet Union; their experiences were not perceived as valuable contributions to historiography or worth attention.[16] Here, I see significant differences compared to the western Hemisphere – in the USA, the UK, France or Israel, for instance, a number of works on this genocide, often memoirs, were published. Only a few survivors managed to publish an account of their wartime experiences *as a Jew* in the Soviet Union. If possible at all, publications by individuals were subject to significant censorship. Most Soviet war memoirs, relating a personal perspective on the events, were the narratives of army officers or famous partisans.

In the societies named above, and also in Germany – albeit

belatedly – assistance was available for survivors to address health and mental damage resulting from arrest, deportation, and imprisonment in concentration camps. Academic research produced a number of publications in which challenges faced in the aftermath of the war that are closely linked to physical damages as well as to the loss of relatives and a social network were discussed under the umbrella term of 'trauma'. In contrast, Catherine Merridale found that trauma 'is not a problem that is recognized, to any significant extent, by Russians'. Partly this is the result of a social taboo to admit psychological illness. 'Far from receiving compensation', Merridale says, 'people who have been diagnosed as mentally ill (including sufferers from depression) risk losing some of their civil rights, and even their driving licenses, in Russia.'[17] Some of her interviewees would also say that they 'did not have time for that', for mourning or grief, pointing to the need to rebuild Soviet society after the war.[18] My interviewees articulated similarly that the required participation in rebuilding the country and the immediate return to education or work after the war were not always voluntary. And yet, the integration into social life aimed at reconstruction became reality; many survivors led future-oriented lives that were in line with the calls for building a socialist society. The aforementioned war memoirs by military personnel conformed to this active and dynamic self-image, highlighting heroes who were willing to make sacrifices in the name of a cause – the war victory, or the formation of a socialist reality. Voices of people who had 'only' survived and not participated in the military campaigns to overthrow fascism were not recognized within this discourse; their accounts of suffering, loss and death were marginalized to highlight the accomplishments of a unified Soviet people. Consequently, and as I have discussed earlier, benefits for war veterans were limited to those who participated in activities officially recognized as contributions to the military efforts.

In one of the interviews I understood how survivors' gender and ethnicity determined how their wartime experiences were perceived. Rita Kazhdan escaped the Minsk ghetto and was a member of the partisan unit that Mikhail Zorin had established. She told me that after the war she did not talk about being in a partisan unit. Asked for the reason to keep her activities secret, she responds: 'only fools like myself had kept it a secret ... because partisan women were considered to be fallen women. And for God's sake, nobody should think like this about me!' When she realized that the official recognition of her time as a partisan would grant her additional medical help such as, for example, to heal the frostbite she had suffered during the war, she applied. Sadly, she was denied recognition because she was a member of a so-called family unit, thus not part of a military unit.

This difference of perception is closely connected to the official Soviet war portrayal that focused commemoration and celebration on the heroic victory over fascism, thus neglecting the experiences of Jewish survivors. The interviews suggest that a concept of resistance that is limited to armed struggle is insufficient to grasp the experience of genocide and continuous warfare against the civilian population during the German occupation, since it discounts the only objective many people had: survival. And yet, public memory in and outside the (post-)Soviet context honours the participants of uprisings and armed rebellion more highly than those who secured their own and others' immediate survival.

I assume that constructions of ethnicity and gender are significant categories to understand these dynamics of survival and commemoration. The Nazi politics of mass extermination of the Jewish population, unscrupulously and publicly exercised in the occupied Soviet territories, provoked actions geared toward survival that in western and Soviet tradition are located in a feminine sphere of action. These acts included organizing and providing food, care, a place to stay and, in most cases, had to be hidden from public view. In contrast, official and collective war memory favours violent and militant struggle against the Nazi regime, celebrating heroic sacrifices and publicly displaying images of honourable fighters and military heroes. Furthermore, in the Soviet Union this hierarchy directly affected the living standard of survivors. Former partisans of recognized units, women and men, were awarded the status 'war veterans' and granted certain benefits such as higher pensions or extra bonuses. Women or men who had 'just survived', on the other hand, were often suspected to have been collaborators. Nina Romanova, for instance, relates how she was interrogated after returning to the USSR: 'How else could you survive the occupation [as a Jew]?'

The Soviet war portrayal largely ignored the high losses among the civilian population that resulted from terrorist warfare, deportation, forced labour or systematic mass murder. Thus, the Soviet politics of memory silenced moments of loss, grief and weakness as a consequence of occupation, mass murder and forced submission under an oppressive and exploitative regime, which fundamentally questioned the existence of the socialist state. The experience of the German occupation put central Soviet values, including internationalism, modernization and the historical necessity of communism's victory over capitalism, to the test.[19] Though the Soviet regime was victorious in the war, the fight against the Nazis also demonstrated the potential weakness in overall Soviet cohesion. This results in the absence of documentation or literary representations of what the majority of the Soviet population, and in particular the Jewish residents, experienced in the occupied territories. It is only in the last two decades that accounts of the genocide have become accessible to a broader audience, and that a number of books, booklets or anthologies that contain survivors' narratives have been issued in post-Soviet countries.[20] In addition, only a few books assembling documents or providing a comprehensive account of the genocide have been published.[21] Often, these writings address questions that had been precluded from the official Soviet war portrayal: indiscriminate massacres of the Jewish residents; the collaboration of non-Jewish citizens with the Nazi regime in these massacres; the inactivity of Soviet authorities, especially in the initial phase of the war, to evacuate the endangered population. These questions are, as Zvi Gitelman notes, not only of historical interest, but are 'serious questions about the relations between the indigenous or titular nationalities and the Jews and about responsibility for the atrocities of the war period and for the evils of the Soviet system'.[22] In the same vein, the suffering of the larger Soviet population needs to be acknowledged and documented.

Interviewees give a troubling account, pointing out differences in experience and memory, and confirming the official version of the past, or the portrayal of the past developed by those who do not want to acknowledge differences among the Soviet population. Memories of collaboration stand next to memories of solidarity and support; memories of German warfare that are shared by the Soviet population as a whole are complicated by memories of suffering and dying in the ghetto. Memories of forced labour that are shared by millions of deportees are complicated by memories of forced labour performed by workers who were under the constant danger of being identified as superfluous and thus 'killable'. Interviewees point out where they feel ignored or discriminated against in their efforts to rebuild a life after the war. But they are also very clear about moments in which they experienced such difficulties alongside their non-Jewish neighbours and friends, especially when it comes to the lack of material support given to those who suffer from the repercussions of the war until today:

> In any case, Jews did suffer a lot, but everything [i.e. help] should be distributed equally ... I understand that Jews suffered and that Germany is responsible for that, but those who suffer within their country, the Russians, they should be helped by their state. You see, when I take out the trash, then I see the old women digging through the trash piles. How can a state permit something like that?

CONCLUSION

For many decades, the Soviet politics of memory neglected experiences of the war that deviated from the official portrayal of the Great Patriotic War, denying support and recognition to civilians who suffered from the German attack against the Soviet Union, as survivors of warfare, occupation or forced labour. The Soviet regime neglected the experiences of Jewish survivors, who suffered from the German politics of extermination, from collaborationists among the Soviet population, and who often had to rebuild their lives after the war on their own. East Germany and West Germany as the successor states of the Nazi regime denied compensation and reparation for the damages endured by individuals for decades. The Soviet and East German regimes formed a close alliance in denying remembrance to victims not usually identified as victims of Nazi persecution targeting communists, socialists or anti-fascists. In the case of West Germany, anti-communist and Cold War politics foreclosed addressing the murder of the Jewish population in the USSR or the suffering of other eastern European victims of the war. Only after high political pressure in preparation for Germany's reunification were first payments made toward Jewish survivors in eastern Europe. It took fifty-five years after the end of the war for non-Jewish survivors of Nazi persecution [and] former forced labourers to be allocated financial aid for the first time. And while the Russian official has no right to question the severity of Ms Pedko's experience in the ghetto, he might be justified in his anger about the lack of recognition for non-Jewish survivors of the war. He chose the wrong target for his criticism – Ms Pedko, who is not responsible for this lack or differentiation of recognition. But he points to a tension within the politics of memory that shapes the politics of compensation, which cannot be denied and needs to be addressed.

REFERENCES

Interviews

Dosovitskaia, Lidia Gershovna: 7 May 2001, St Petersburg.

Drapkina, Elena Askar'evna: 10 September 2002, St Petersburg.

Erenburg, Grigorii Borisovich: 19 May 2005, St Petersburg.

Gal'perin, Boris Mikhailovich: 16 May 2001, St Petersburg, supplemented by materials Mr Gal'perin assembled to document the extermination of his hometown (copy in my possession).

Glasebnaya, Olga Dmitrovna and Zelenko, Roza Efimovna: 11 October 2002, Minsk.

Golbraikh, Leonid L'vovich: 3 September 2002, St Petersburg.

Kazhdan, Rita Abramovna: 24 May 2001, St Petersburg.

Ped'ko, Frida Iosifovna: 27 May 2001 and 13 May 2005, St Petersburg.

Romanova-Farber, Nina Gennadevna: 30 April 2001, St Petersburg.

Skoblo, Leonid Isaakovich: 16 April 2001, St Petersburg.

Published Sources

Aizenshtat, L.A. (ed.), *Kniga Zhivykh: Vospominania Evreev Frontovikov, Uznikov Getto i Kontslagerei, Boitsov Partizanskikh Otriadov, Zhitelei Blokadnogo Leningrada*, vols 1, 2 and 3 (St Petersburg: Akropol', 1995, 2004 and 2006).

Altman, Il'ia *et al.* (eds), *Kholokost – Soprotovlenie – Vozrozhdenie: Evreiskii Narod v Gody Vtoroi Mirovoi Voini i Poslevoennyi Period 1939–1948* (Moskva: Fond Kholokost, 2000).

Altman, Il'ia, *Zhertvy Nenavisti: Kholokost V SSSR 1941–1945gg.* (Moskva: Kovcheg, 2002).

Arad, Yitzhak, 'The Holocaust of Soviet Jewry in the Occupied Territory of the Soviet Union', in *Yad Vashem Studies*, XI (1991), pp.1–47.

Arad, Yitzhak, 'The Destruction of the Jews in German-Occupied Territories of the Soviet Union', in Joshua Rubenstein and Ilya Altman (eds), *The Unknown Black Book: The Holocaust in the German-Occupied Soviet Territories* (Bloomington, IN: Indiana University Press, 2008), pp.xiii–xvii.

Arkadyeva, O.M., *et al.* (eds), *... Na Perekrestkakh Sudeb: Iz Vospominanii Byvshikh Uznikov Getto i Pravednikov Mira* (Minsk: Chetyrie Chetverti, 2001).

Charnyi, S., 'Sovetskii godsudarstvennyi anti-Semitism v tsenzure nachala 60-kh godov (na primere sudby knigi B. Marka "Vosstanie v Varshavskom Getto")', in *Vestnik Evreiskogo Universiteta v Moskve* , no. 2, 15 (1997), pp.76–81.

Chernoglazova, Raisa (ed.), *Judenfrei! Svobodno ot Evreev! Istoria Minskogo Getto v Dokumentakh* (Minsk: Osobny Dakh, 1999).

Chiari, Bernhard, *Alltag hinter der Front: Besatzung, Kollaboration und Widerstand in Weißrußland 1941–1944* (Düsseldorf: Droste, 1998).

Ekshtut, Semen, *Predvestie svobody, ili 1000 dnei posle pobedy* (Moscow: Drofa-Plius, 2006).

Gerlach, Christian, *Kalkulierte Morde: Die deutsche Wirtschafts- und Vernichtungspolitik in Weißrussland 1941–1944* (Hamburg: Hamburger Edition, 1999).

Gitelman, Zvi, 'Politics and the Historiography of the Holocaust in the Soviet Union', in Zvi Gitelman (ed.), *Bitter Legacy: Confronting the Holocaust in the USSR* (Bloomington, IN: Indiana University Press, 1997), pp.14–42.

Federal Law on the Creation of a Foundation 'Remembrance, Responsibility and Future', *Federal Law Gazette* I 1263, Stiftung Erinnerung, Verantwortung, Zukunft <http://www.stiftung-evz.de/eng/about-us/foundation_law/>, 31 January 2010.

Litvin, Aleksei, 'K voprosu o kolichestve liudskikh poter' Belarusi v gody Velikoi Otechestvennoi Voiny (1941–1945gg.)', in V.I. Andreev (ed.), *Belarus V XX Stagoddzi* (Minsk: Vodolei, 2002), pp.127–38.

Lustiger, Arno, *Rotbuch: Stalin und die Juden: Die tragische Geschichte des Jüdischen Antifaschistischen Komitees und der sowjetischen Juden* (Berlin: Aufbau, 1998).

Merridale, Catherine, *Night of Stone: Death and Memory in Twentieth-Century Russia* (New York and London: Viking, 2000).

Redlikh, Sh., 'Evreiskii Antifashistskii Komitet v SSSR I antisemitskaia politika sovetskich vlastei v poslevoennye gody', in Il'ia Altman *et al.* (eds), *Kholokost – Soprotivlenie – Vozrozhdenie: Evreiskii Narod v Gody VOV i Poslevoennyi period 1939–1948* (Moskva: Fond Kholokost 2000), pp. 213–61.

Rol'nikaite, Maria, *I Vsio Eto Pravda* (St Petersburg: Zolotoi Vek 2002).

Smilovitski, Leonid, 'Bor'ba evreev Belorussii za vosvrat svoego imushchestvo i zhilishch' v pervoe poslevoennoe desiatiletie, 1944–1954gg.' in V.I. Andreev (ed.), *Belarus V XX Stagoddzi* (Minsk:Vodolei, 2002), pp.168–78.

Tumarkin, Nina, *The Living and the Dead: The Rise and Fall of the Cult of World War II in Russia* (New York: Basic Books, 1994).

Walke, Anika, *Jüdische Partisaninnen: Der verschwiegene Widerstand in der Sowjetunion* (Berlin: Dietz, 2007).

NOTES

1. In August 2000 the German Parliament adopted the Law on the Creation of a Foundation 'Remembrance, Responsibility and Future' that regulates the financial compensation to former Nazi forced labourers and 'to those affected by other injustices from the National Socialist period': Section 2, clause 1 of Federal Law on the Creation of a Foundation 'Remembrance, Responsibility and Future', *Federal Law Gazette* I 1263, Stiftung Erinnerung, Verantwortung, Zukunft <http://www.stiftung-evz.de/eng/about-us/ foundation_law/>, 31 January 2010.
2. The term was first used on June 23, 1941 in an article in Pravda, the major Soviet newspaper, to call on the Soviet people to defend the country against the 'fascist invasion'. See N. Tumarkin, *The Living and the Dead: The Rise and Fall of the Cult of World War II in Russia* (New York: Basis Books, 1994), p.61.
3. For more information on the interviews, see A. Walke, *Jüdische Partisaninnen: Der verschwiegene Widerstand in der Sowjetunion* (Berlin: Dietz, 2007).
4. A. Litvin, 'K voprosu o kolichestve liudskikh poter' Belarusi v gody Velikoi Otechestvennoi Voiny (1941–1945gg.)', in V.I. Andreev (ed.), *Belarus V XX Stagoddzi* (Minsk: Vodolei, 2002), pp.127–38.
5. L. Smilovitski, 'Bor'ba evreev Belorussii za vosvrat svoego imushchestvo i zhilishch' v pervoe poslevoennoe desiatiletie, 1944–1954gg.', in Andreev (ed.), *Belarus V XX Stagoddzi*, pp.167f.
6. C. Gerlach, *Kalkulierte Morde: Die deutsche Wirtschafts- und Vernichtungspolitik in Weißrussland 1941–1944* (Hamburg: Hamburger Edition, 1999), p.11.
7. Ibid.
8. See Smilovitski, 'Bor'ba evreev', p.169. It has proved difficult to convert this amount into a currency and rate that makes it possible to perceive the dimensions according to present standards. Part of the problem is that the Soviet rouble was not convertible in other currencies or not usable for international financial transactions.
9. Z. Gitelman, 'Politics and the Historiography of the Holocaust in the Soviet Union', in Zvi Gitelman (ed.), *Bitter Legacy: Confronting the Holocaust in the USSR* (Bloomington, IN: Indiana University Press, 1997), p.14.
10. Ibid., p.18.
11. For the most recent and summarizing account of the Nazi genocide in the Soviet territories, see Y. Arad, 'The Destruction of the Jews in German-Occupied Territories of the Soviet Union', in Joshua Rubenstein and Ilya Altman (eds), *The Unknown Black Book: The Holocaust in the German-Occupied Soviet Territories* (Bloomington, IN: Indiana University Press, 2008), pp.xiii–xvii. An earlier and more detailed account by the same author: Y. Arad, 'The Holocaust of Soviet Jewry in the Occupied Territory of the Soviet Union', in *Yad Vashem Studies*, XI (1991): pp.1–47.
12. See B. Chiari, 'Die Ermordung der weißrussischen Juden', in B. Chiari, *Alltag hinter der Front: Besatzung, Kollaboration und Widerstand in Weißrußland 1941–1944* (Düsseldorf: Droste, 1998), p.231–69.
13. See S. Ekshtut's vivid account of the discontent generated by these sacrifices: Semen Ekshtut, *Predvestie svobody, ili 1000 dnei posle pobedy* (Moscow: Drofa-Plius, 2006).

14. See also the letters Jewish survivors sent to the Jewish Anti-Fascist Committee, describing anti-Semitic assaults by civilians and lack of support from state authorities, quoted in Smilovitski, 'Bor'ba evreev', p.170.
15. See, for instance, A. Lustiger, *Rotbuch: Stalin und die Juden: Die tragische Geschichte des Jüdischen Antifaschistischen Komitees und der sowjetischen Juden* (Berlin: Aufbau, 1998); Sh. Redlikh, 'Evreiskii Antifashistskii Komitet v SSSR I antisemitskaia politika sovetskich vlastei v poslevoennye gody', in I. Altman *et al.* (eds), *Kholokost – Soprotivlenie – Vozrozhdenie: Evreiskii Narod v Gody Vtoroi Mirovoi Voiny i Poslevoennyi Period 1939–1948* (Moscow: Fond Kholokost, 2000), pp.213–61.
16. C. Merridale, 'Listening for the Dead', in C. Merridale, *Night of Stone: Death and Memory in Twentieth-Century Russia* (New York and London: Viking, 2000).
17. Ibid., p.331.
18. Ibid., p.328.
19. According to the state portrayal, fascism and, thus, the Nazi regime was the 'open terroristic dictatorship of the most reactionary, most chauvinistic, most imperialistic elements of finance capital', a definition that Georgi Dimitrov had introduced in 1935.
20. For instance: L.A. Aizenshtat (ed.), *Kniga Zhivykh: Vospominania Evreev Frontovikov, Uznikov Getto i Kontslagerei, Boitsov Partizanskikh Otriadov, Zhitelei Blokadnogo Leningrada*, vols 1, 2 and 3 (St Petersburg: Akropol', 1995, 2004, 2006); O.M. Arkadyeva *et al.* (eds), *... Na Perekrestkakh Sudeb: Iz Vospominanii Byvshikh Uznikov Getto i Pravednikov Mira* (Minsk: Chetyrie Chetverti, 2001); M. Rol'nikaite, *I Vsio Eto Pravda* (St Petersburg: Zolotoi Vek, 2002).
21. For instance: R. Chernoglazova, *Judenfrei! Svobodno ot Evreev! Istoria Minskogo Getto v Dokumentakh* (Minsk: Osobny Dakh, 1999); I. Altman *et al.* (eds), *Kholokost – Soprotivlenie – Vozrozhdenie: Evreiskii Narod v Gody Vtoroi Mirovoi Voiny i Poslevoennyi Period 1939–1948* (Moscow: Fond Kholokost, 2000); I. Altman, *Zhertvy Nenavisti: Kholokost v SSSR 1941–1945gg* (Moscow: Kovcheg, 2002).
22. Gitelman, 'Politics and the Historiography', p.15.